CW01024253

This is number one hundred and four in
the second numbered series of the
Miegunyah Volumes
made possible by the
Miegunyah Fund
established by bequests
under the wills of
Sir Russell and Lady Grimwade.

'Miegunyah' was the home of
Mab and Russell Grimwade
from 1911 to 1955.

BLOOD & TINSEL

A MEMOIR

JIM SHARMAN

THE
MIEGUNYAH
PRESS

THE MIEGUNYAH PRESS

An imprint of Melbourne University Publishing Limited
187 Grattan Street, Carlton, Victoria 3053, Australia
mup-info@unimelb.edu.au
www.mup.com.au

First published 2008

Designed and typeset by Stephen Banham, Niels Oeltjen and
Tim Mang at Letterbox and Megan Ellis
Printed in China through Publishing Solutions

National Library of Australia Cataloguing-in-Publication entry:

Sharman, Jim, 1945–

   Blood and tinsel: a memoir / author, Jim Sharman
   Carlton, Vic.: Melbourne University Publishing, 2008

   978-0-522-85377-3 (hbk.)

   Sharman, Jim, 1945–
   Theatrical producers and directors—Australia—Biography

792.023092

Dedicated to those who come after.

*What is this unseen flame of darkness
whose sparks are the stars?*

TAGORE

1

Ringside

2

Dancing

3

Sarsaparilla

1

Ringside

RINGSIDE IN THE RIVERINA

My grandfather was good with his fists. The repercussions from a punch he threw in 1911 still resonate today; the echo has ricocheted across time.

The fight took place at the Olympic skating rink hall in the Riverina town of Wagga Wagga. Jimmy Sharman was a 24-year-old lightweight with a knockout punch. He was squaring up to his opponent in an improvised ring, surrounded by a crowd of local boxing fans and hungry punters.

The fight was going my grandfather's way but, at his urging, his seconds cautioned the referee to stop it. Jack Carter, his opponent, was in bad shape, and to allow the boxing to continue for another round was asking for a bloodbath.

Fight on! was the ref's stern reply.

In the fight game, rules are rules. The fight resumed. My grandfather threw a southpaw punch that he hoped would finish things quickly. It sent Jack Carter reeling to the canvas. He was clutching his face and eyes.

Grandad won, but Jack Carter was blinded.

Jimmy Sharman was haunted by his hollow victory. He'd won seventy-seven of the seventy-eight bouts he'd fought in the Riverina and was in line for the Australian lightweight crown, but he and Carter were best mates.

My grandfather would never get over it. He continued his interest in boxing but never fought professionally again. The following year he married his local sweetheart, Violet Byrne, and she gave birth to their only child, my father.

After a brief stint as a fight promoter at the Star Theatre in Temora, my grandfather set up and managed a travelling boxing troupe that was destined to become a legendary part of Australian folk history: *Jimmy Sharman's Boxing Troupe*.

Riverina champ: Jimmy Sharman

Jimmy Sharman Boxing Troupe, Sydney Royal Easter Show, 1937

IN 1912 ...

The *Titanic* sank and 1500 passengers drowned at sea. A touring Italian opera company performed Wagner's *Ring Cycle* for the first time in Australia. In Paris, artist Marcel Duchamp, inspired by stop-motion photography, created a painting that would scandalise and revolutionise the art world: *Nude Descending a Staircase No 2*. In the United States, pulp western writer Zane Grey published *Riders of the Purple Sage*, and in Vienna, composer Gustav Mahler's prophetic Ninth Symphony was posthumously premiered. Thomas Mann wrote the novella *Death in Venice* and Europe headed towards a cataclysmic war.

In 1912, my father was born in the leafy Riverina town of Narrandera, and the future Australian Nobel laureate, Patrick White, was born in London.

INITIATION

The apparition loomed large in the glow of footlights, like a stevedore in drag. He, she, whatever, slowly, teasingly, turned to face the eager crowd. The under-lit greasepaint made the pantomime dame look delightfully macabre.

Now, kiddies ... pause for effect ... *Who wants one of these?*

The leering figure brandished a handful of chocolate-coated caramel toffees called Fantales. They were wrapped in lurid, acid yellow wax paper and boasted collectable movie-star biographies. I loved them, even collected them—but not today.

Please God, I'll be good ... not today.

My reticence was not shared by the audience at this Saturday matinee. The children around me screamed in alarming un-animous assent:

Meeeeee!

A sole dissenter, I shrank back into my portable seat. My eyes rolled upwards and I found myself inspecting, in unnecessary detail, the touring tent of *Sorlie's Travelling Variety Show*. It billowed and glowed hot and amber from the tropical sunlight blazing down on those of us huddled under its canvas sky.

With a twirl and pitch that would have done a baseball player proud, the grotesque spectre hurled the confection in my direction. Outside, local kids would be playing marbles, cricket, football. Why couldn't I be one of them?

Like any kid, I was tempted by the prospect of free Fantales, but I was alarmed to find myself the sudden focus of everyone's attention and I missed.

That's why I wasn't playing cricket outside. I was meant to be here, inside, on a hot Saturday, witnessing a hyperactive audience of children and a sinister ghost in greasepaint inciting them to pandemonium; it was my fate.

A second Fantale came my way. Embarrassed by this determined and, I felt, *No, I KNEW*, unnecessary attention, I retreated further into my seat: *Why me?*

The third Fantale was unleashed with perfect aim.

The kids around me screamed in delight.

Third time lucky—I couldn't help but catch it.

The spectre beamed and smiled—possibly in relief.

The old transvestite devil had snared his baby Faust.

I guess that was where it started.

I was five years old.

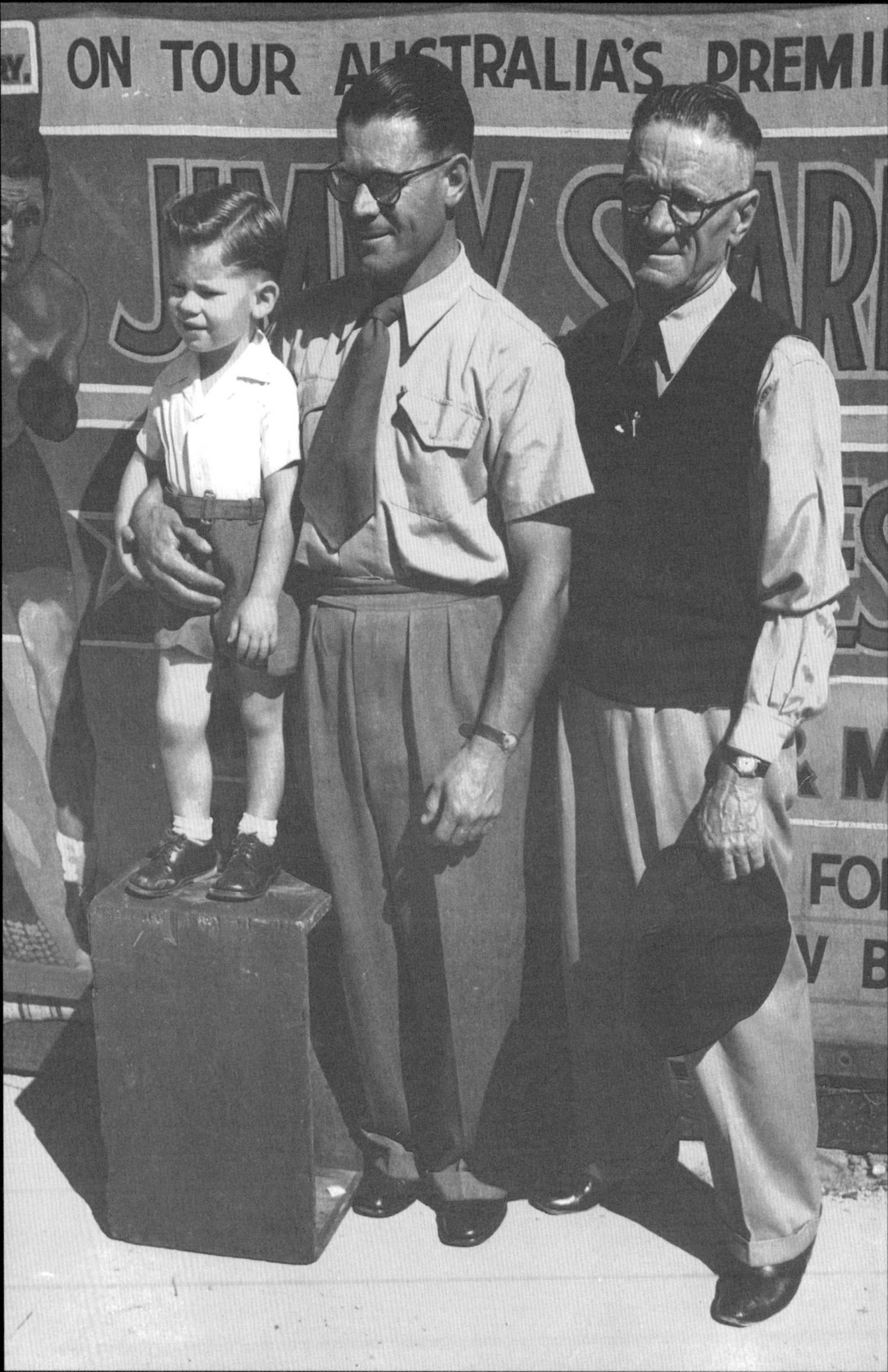
ON TOUR AUSTRALIA'S PREMI

SIDESHOW ALLEY

Once the spruiker had finished urging, and the brass bell had ceased its jangling, and the bu-boom bu boom of the bass drum had been silenced, and the crowd had settled into the tent to cheer or boo their local favourites, my father could finally relax.

It was the last show of the day, and the late afternoon was softening into twilight. This was his favourite time, before the hard yakka of packing tents under kerosene lamps, loading trucks and coupling up caravans and driving, often through the night and on unsealed red-dirt roads, to the next town, and the next, and the next.

He would exchange a glance with his ticket-seller and troupe manager, Rud Kee. Old Rud was a fixture on the showgrounds, though only Dad knew his real name was Cheong Lee. He'd been with the outfit since my grandfather started it in 1911, through two wars and the Depression. Rud's gaze was steady and reliable, like the man himself; and it would silently communicate the state of ticket sales. They were favourable in this remote tropical town. In an era before television, there wasn't much competition in what showmen called the entertainment stakes.

James Michael Sharman would perch his still-handsome ex-sportsman's frame on the orange metal ladder, like a magpie on the branch of a jacaranda from his native Riverina. The ladder leant against the gaudy red and yellow banners that proclaimed *Jimmy Sharman's Boxing Troupe* was in town.

Dad would scan the now diminishing crowd at the bar facing his tent and the passing parade of wide-eyed show-goers exploring sideshow alley, either out of curiosity or following entreaties from their excited offspring clutching show bags.

He'd inhale a whiff of showground air; a not unpleasing mix of afternoon breeze sweetened by burnt sugar from toffee apples and fairy floss, oil from battered hot dogs, musky sawdust, mouldy canvas, and the earthier aromas from distant pavilions housing livestock, chooks and pets crowing and barking and miaowing, some boasting red, blue or gold championship ribbons and proud owners.

Three generations of Sharmans

He was sitting on the precise rung of the ladder where his own father had sat for decades before him. My father had often asked his old man why he took time out for crowd-watching from this particular vantage point. The familiar enigmatic smile had always implied: *You'll find out.*

As in some Zen archery exercise, like scoring bullseyes without ever looking at the target, my father did, by perseverance and experience, finally discover the secret. Through daily observance from his orange perch, my father began to slowly intuit the nature of passing crowds. Like his father before him, he gradually became an expert judge of character and inherited the mantle of showground philosopher. An instinct for character was crucial in this game, where a man had to match his own fighters with challengers from the crowd, and put together boxing and wrestling bouts that would keep the entertainment flowing and not exhaust the fighters. It was invaluable in his daily dealings with everyone—showies, pugs and thugs, cops, locals—everyone from the mugs to the dignitaries and more than a few characters who might mask criminal intent behind a likable grin, or the simple desire to *do you like a dinner*, in the here today, gone tomorrow world of travelling sideshows.

Dad liked to boast about an ambitious young copper who met his match when trying to put one over him. The troupe's long history and good reputation had earned it kudos. This meant it commanded the best positions on the showground. For a show that pandered to blokes and families with a sporting instinct, the best *possie* was opposite the bar. The proximity of a bar guaranteed a captive audience who got things rolling when the signature whistle sounded, the weather-beaten brass bell was rung, and Dad launched into his familiar *Roll Up! Roll Up!* routine. This built the crowd numbers for his *Who'll take a glove?* pitch.

As he started to spruik, he observed the young copper taking back-handers from spielers, or pickpockets, waiting at the bar. Spielers were regarded as vermin by the showies and were banned from the tents—a ban the police enforced in return for a few discreet freebies.

Dad was spruiking but observing the action as more spielers gathered around the cop at the bar, like cockroaches on heat. They were obviously preparing to unleash themselves on the unsuspecting crowd inside the boxing tent. The cop was pocketing cash faster than a popular priest at a church raffle. Then, bold as brass, the same young copper fronted to collect his free tickets and Dad took him on.

The copper merely smirked and slyly implied the problem could be resolved by an unmarked envelope stuffed with *the right coloured notes*. Dad refused him admission to the tent, called him everything under the sun and unceremoniously booted him out.

Thinking he was in deep shit, Dad was surprised to be congratulated by the embarrassed head of local area police. No more spielers were seen near the tent, though the young cop, whose name was Terry Lewis, quickly rose through the ranks to become Deputy then Commissioner of Queensland Police. Some years later, he was dismissed and sentenced to a long prison term by a Royal Commission of Inquiry into police corruption in Queensland.

Sideshow alley had its own codes, rules and meritocracy. My grandfather had established the boxing troupe as quality family entertainment warranting respect, and my father intended to keep it that way. There was fair dealing, no racial barriers and the fighters were contracted and looked after. The show lived up to expectations and often exceeded them. Given the rip-off and riff-raff merchants that permeated the fringes of showground life, this was important to Dad. Despite being a proudly knockabout bloke—and one who claimed to have broken most of the commandments the nuns had belted into him through his long, solitary boarding-school childhood—his fall-back advice was always: *Do unto others …*

As my father surveyed the crowd, the soundtrack for his reverie was the calliope from a nearby merry-go-round playing *La Vie en Rose*, the *Trish Trash Polka*, themes from popular films of the day such as *La Ronde* or the zither refrain from *The Third Man*. Romantic accordions competed with the echoes of spruikers, the shuffle of crowds, distant loudspeaker announcements of winners in ring events, and noisier, more recent American interventions: like the crash-thump-wallop of dodgem cars and high-energy motorbike displays like *The Wall of Death*. World War II was five years past, and rock-and-roll six years away. The attention seekers made do with the amplified clang of Hawaiian guitars playing *The Tennessee Waltz* or *Ghost Riders in the Sky*.

Dad would leave his perch and, satisfied that all was well inside the tent—and the whoop and roar of the crowd guaranteed that—he'd stroll the grounds and pop his head inside his own caravan before returning to referee the final bout of the day. While the country locals circled sideshow alley with a kind of glazed amazement at the other-worldliness of it all, for my father it was a breezy afternoon stroll around a friendly neighbourhood.

Appearances mattered on the showground, and Dad cut a familiar figure in his snap-brim hat, crisp white short-sleeved cotton shirt, neat tie with a clip, Fletcher Jones strides and well-shined shoes. *Put a shine on your shoes and a melody in your heart …* was a favourite tune of this inveterate whistler, along with the popular jazz riffs of Fats Waller, Louis Armstrong and Ella Fitzgerald. A whiff of Californian Poppy floated from his shiny hair, above his rectangular black-rimmed glasses. It mixed well with the dash of Eau de Portugal patted onto his genial, close-shaved face.

What are you old rogues up to? Affectionate abrasion was the preferred form of conversational banter on the showgrounds. Dad might have been addressing a cabal of elder showies, including his own father, now semi-retired, but still travelling and dabbling, or the businesslike and debonair duo Greenhalgh and Jackson, or the impish Dave Meekin, who, between them, imported shows featuring everything from Chinese acrobats to a tribe of African Pygmies. The Pygmies were led by Princess Ubangi, a great mate of my grandmother, Violet *Pud* Sharman. Inside this circle of elders were the influential Vince *Pedro* Labb and Stan Durkin, who had *The Big Wheel*.

As a second-generation showie, my father would have sought out his own younger mates, including the American-born silhouette artist Johnny Ross and his wife Phyllis. Despite their friendship, Dad never tired of pointing out that Johnny *wasn't short of a quid*. Or his good mate Bill Howard, who sold Dagwood dogs from shiny silver caravans with flip-down counters, and operated the laughing clowns and a few Knock-em-down stalls. Here success was rewarded by an array of tiny pink-tuille-clad dolls-on-sticks. These prizes would later inspire the title of Ray Lawler's popular Australian play *The Summer of the Seventeenth Doll*.

Bill Howard's caravan was an exception on the showground; it boasted a modest library. Showies only had time for popular radio quiz and variety shows with Jack Davey or Bob and Dolly Dyer, the BBC world service news, sports broadcasts and little else. My father's reading habits never progressed beyond Zane Grey westerns and Mickey Spillane thrillers from local newsagencies, and a few news and football magazines. As an ex–sports journalist, he contributed to the *Sporting Globe* a regular column of touring tales and sports gossip: *Around Australia with Jimmy Sharman*.

We're speaking of 1950, the year that Prime Minister Robert Menzies introduced the Communist Party Dissolution Bill and myxomatosis to combat the rabbit plague. These events were often confused in my young mind, so I assumed the government was trying to get rid of a plague of communist rabbits. In 1950, Bill Howard, *a red-hot commo* according to his mate, my father, would have been reading Frank Hardy's controversial left-wing exposé *Power Without Glory*. As a staunch supporter of conservative PM Menzies, my father would have frowned at this. He'd also whinge about copies of the *Tribune*, the communist weekly, littered around Bill's caravan. Whether it was the politics or the litter that was the concern was never apparent; my father encouraged contradictions. He could be a tyro or a neat and considerate man. Dad swept the canvas boxing mat in his own tent like a meticulous housewife. He was also part of that now-extinct race who collected other people's discarded rubbish in the streets and disposed of it in a tidy-bin.

Despite their postwar conservative bent, Australians voted against outlawing communism and, in a similar spirit, my father never allowed politics to stand in the way of friendship. Bill was a good bloke, and that was that. There were other colourful characters: Stumpy, a midget Lebanese SP bookie, whose real name remained forever a mystery to me, and, in later years, Rainbow, an ex–legal clerk turned cab driver. Colourful characters were a requisite for friendship, and Bill and the scissor-wielding silhouette artist Johnny Ross were Dad's mates and allies on the showgrounds. I was grateful to both. Johnny Ross allowed me a naïve entry to the world of art through the shadow-play of silhouettes, and I was grateful to the red-hot commo for encouraging my interest in books and instilling in me the need to question things; other people's assumptions.

I relished visits to Bill's caravan and the mysterious world of literature, a world of books I could touch and smell but barely understand. I knew one day I would. It was as magical to a kid as visiting King Solomon's mines.

Of course there were enemies. Aggressive and Irish-tempered on this score, adversaries brought out the Jimmy Cagney movie gangster in Dad: *Fuck 'em!* he'd say. No doubt they felt the same way about him. Despite the camaraderie of the showies, there was also a take-no-prisoners attitude that provoked its share of enmity and feuds. Still, the idea of colourful characters with strong convictions stayed with me. I was always intrigued, seduced even, when I encountered such figures in later life.

Dad's caravan was a tiny oval contraption, later replaced by a sleeker long rectangular arrangement, with a separate shower and sleeping area. This flasher, more modern caravan sadly met a watery fate in outback Queensland. It sank while being towed across a flooded Burdekin River.

Vehicles loomed large in the showies' pantheon of enthusiasms. They were both necessary and their only status symbol. My father drove a sedate grey Vauxhall Velox. He later graduated, via a pale green Ford V8 Truck, which operated as a temporary work-horse, to his pride and joy, a silver Mercedes. Grandad preferred two tone Chevrolets and giant Pontiacs with extra-terrestrial fins.

Unlike my father, who was happy to rough it on the showgrounds with the troupe, Grandad stayed in hotels. He loved the old-style pubs with their wide verandas and dining rooms set with shiny silver cutlery and starched linen tablecloths; his favourite pub was the Golden Fleece in Melbourne's Russell Street—his home away from home.

On the showground, well-equipped caravans and big, petrol-guzzling American cars were the fashion—and size did matter. The arrival of the showies in any country town would be heralded by a cavalcade of brightly coloured Buicks, Packards, Oldsmobiles and sometimes even a Caddie, or Cadillac.

Little of this showground ostentation impressed my mother. From Scottish Presbyterian stock, Christina Macandleish Sharman, née Mitchell, would sit in the family's tiny-but-tidy caravan, an elegant brunette, dressed in a box-pleated skirt and fine pale silk blouse adorned by a single strand of pearls, flipping the pages of Vicki Baume's *Grand Hotel*. On the table would be her recently completed work—the neatly accounted takings for the day. There was no chenille dressing-gown, shandy-in-the-hand or ciggie-out-the-corner-of-the-mouth laid-back attitude about her, and no nonsense either.

My father would pop his head around the caravan door and she would rattle off the total day's take. There it was, neatly counted and sculpted in brown-paper-wrapped columns, with tiny port-holes to instantly identify the contents: two-bobs, deeners and zacs. Behind this colonnade of coins were calico bags in different colours for the tenners, fivers, quids and ten-bob notes, all crisply snap-bound in colour-coordinated rubber bands.

Christina, or more familiarly Chris Sharman, had something of the natural glamour and professional style of the career women movie stars she admired: Greta Garbo, Marlene Dietrich, the young Lauren Bacall, Bette Davis, and her favourite, Katherine Hepburn.

Her husband would be pleased about the takings and equally pleased at the sight of his cool, smart wife. The Irish–Scottish, country–city, earthy–aspiring mix was volatile, but that's the way they both seemed to like it. Their marriage was another contradiction. In the argot of the day, he'd scored *a classy dame*. Just as his Vauxhall car was modest and elegant compared to the broad-finned American models, he was pleased to have married a woman of style and aspiration. Though sometimes, especially when he was on the road, he might have been tempted by the earthier shandy-and-chenille women who thrived on the showground life, toughing it out on a diet of Ford Pills for slimming and Bex or Vincent's Powders to placate headaches and diminished ambitions.

In truth, my mother never felt at home on the showgrounds. Her natural reserve, her citified dress sense and sometime severity were seen as out of place, snobbish even. Once I was of school age, I provided my mother with the perfect excuse to base herself in Sydney. Through this decisive action, I was spared the discarded-at-boarding-school fate that had befallen my father. I became the first Sharman to have a regular and secular public school education in the city. In this decision, my mother was not alone. Johnny Ross's equally urbane young wife, Phyllis, one of my mother's few showground friends, also swapped the adventure of travelling rough alongside her husband for city supervision of growing sons. Chris Sharman and Phyllis Ross would work and support their husbands at the capital city shows—Brisbane, Sydney, Melbourne—but rarely ventured on the country show circuit. Macho boxing troupe life, in my father's repeated words, was no place for a woman.

It was, however briefly, a great place for a kid. The showies themselves often resembled big kids. They demonstrated an enthusiasm for adventure, escape and romance that helped them overlook the grittier realities. As a child, this suited me down to the ground, but my mother had other ideas. Her maternal concern for my welfare and whereabouts often took on a determined, obsessive quality. In my father's more easygoing view, solo adventures were to be encouraged. In this divided notion of child-rearing, often expressed in heated words through the open door of a caravan, the seeds were sown of an emotional tug-of-war that my father, for all his strength, was destined to lose.

On one occasion, he came up with a winner. To keep me amused on a busy show day, he bundled me off to a Saturday matinee at *Sorlie's*. A pantomime. Perfect for a kid. It would give Chris a rest and their son an outing. My mother was initially resistant, but consoled by my being in the care of a babysitter, *Sorlie's* gifted teenage soubrette, Gloria Dawn; though my mother would grumble:

That girl sings sweetly, but she can be a grubby little thing.

My father assured her that his great mate, Bobby Le Brun, the pantomime dame, would look after me. Dad had even shouted Bobby a beer, just to make sure he'd toss the kid a Fantale or two.

I returned from the panto, dropped off by a decidedly respect-ful and respectable Gloria Dawn, my five-year-old face buried behind a whirl of pink fairy floss. While my relieved mother settled into making a cup of tea for Gloria, I followed Dad back to the boxing tent with tales of panto dames and Fantales, and other afternoon exploits in which he feigned interest. I enquired where we were heading, and received the enigmatic family shrug.

We slipped under the canvas into the tiny area beneath the line-up board, where the boxers changed and waited for their bouts. Here, there was more activity than usual. Troupe boxers, whatever their nationality, and almost all nationalities were represented at some time or another, tended to save their bravado for the crowd; left to their own devices, they were surprisingly quiet. However, this was the last show of the day and anticipation was in the air. They bantered, posed, played cards, yarned and puffed on roll-your-owns like sportsmen, army recruits or rock-and-rollers on tour.

In this intimate space, there was always an undercurrent of change-room sexuality. It was fuelled by linseed oil, sweat, sawdust, towels, jockstraps, humidity and flesh. Sinewy young bodies and satin shorts made tent boxers a magnet for local groupies, of which there was no shortage. On the rare occasion when the groupies failed to come across, well, they always had each other. Sexuality was far from my five-year-old mind, but I'm sure I took in a whiff of the eroticism that floated in the linseed-scented air. The younger fighters knew that if they made good time in packing up themselves, the troupe, the tent, the big red Reo truck, they might find time for the tent-show trifecta: a feed, a fight and a fuck.

My father escorted the fighters to ringside. I followed at a respectful distance, relieved I didn't have to pass the sentry, Rud Kee. I loved old Rud, but he wouldn't let anyone in without a ticket, not even the boss's son.

The boxing ring, or the mat as it was called, was flanked by two king poles swathed in coloured bunting. At each pole was a stool where the warriors psyched up for their contest, their seconds fanning them with towels and urging bottles of water to keep dehydration at bay. The crowd were eager. They huddled expectantly around the square canvas mat, which was stretched tight as a drum. It was stained in sweat and blood and circled by sawdust. I crouched among the other kids, close to ringside.

My father would give the fighters quiet instructions on the way to the ring. Earlier, there would probably have been a grudge match between two townies, or locals. Often, when a brawl erupted in a pub over a girl or whatever, the police would separate the two opponents and tell them to cool off and settle it in Jimmy Sharman's tent. When this happened, my father couldn't have been happier. It saved wear and tear on his own fighters; it guaranteed a full house, because the whole town would want to see the outcome; and it made his show part of the ritual pattern of life in country Australia.

These amateur combatants had passion in their gloves, something to prove, and a whole town watching them try to prove it. The referee's job was to keep it lively, yet make sure the locals didn't get too damaged. To this end, as with many fights in the tent, there was surprising flexibility in the timing of rounds.

Bells would ring to avoid anything referees thought best avoided. Crowd outrage, often and vocal, at these controversially abbreviated or extended rounds, only raised the temperature for the next fight and made for even livelier entertainment.

There were many great fights in the Jimmy Sharman tent. Over sixty years, it nurtured an impressive array of champion boxers and became an Australian sporting and showground legend. However, there was also the day-to-day entertainment to consider, and so the final bout of the day would be more an exhibition match between two troupe fighters.

In this case, it was an Aboriginal boxer, Carl, standing on the line-up board, and a skinny redhead with freckles who challenged from the crowd. My father instantly nicknamed him Carrot Top. He said he was a jackeroo who'd just blown in to town. My father matched him with a troupe boxer who equalled him in weight and skill—in this case, Carl. The boxers were mates, and, in another hour, they'd be packing tents together, sharing camp-fire food and maybe a girl or two by the river or, less romantically, in the back of a truck.

The outcome of these exhibition bouts was often decided by the make-up of the crowd. If, for instance, my father spotted a large group of Aboriginal women, he'd ensure Carl won, maybe after losing a round or two to up the ante. Aboriginal country women, especially those in possession of umbrellas, could be a deadly force. Like country women at a footy game, they'd make Terry Lewis and his band of spielers look like cream puffs.

Dad would whistle for attention as he stepped into the centre of the ring. With one hand over an ear, and the other cupped to his mouth, he'd start spruiking:

Now this local bloke ... Carrot Top! Carrot Top!—Laughter—*Well, he's a bit of a Ginger Meggs, isn't he? ... He claims he's good with his fists and he reckons he can handle himself ... He's challenged Carl here, one of our fighters. Well, he looks like he's got a big fighter's heart and we like to give these young blokes a go, so ... it's a round or two, for a pound or two. How's that?*—Head nods—*OK! Good luck, old son! There'll be three ... three minute rounds ... May the best man win ... Come out fighting!*

Bells. Fists.

Sawdust flies as the fighters swerve on and off the mat.

Nuggety Carl and thin Carrot Top crash into the packed crowd—screams!

A cloud of sweat from the fighters sprays the spectators.

Naked black and white flesh collides with well-ironed RM Williams attire and floral frocks.

More squeals.

Bells.

Water swilled and savagely spat on the mat.

Grunts. Groans. Curses. More bells.

The fighters dance on the spot as more water is tipped over them.

A shock second-round reversal: Carl goes down.

A fleck of blood from a cut lip.

An outraged chorus of black umbrellas lashes out at Carrot Top.

Chaos! Bells! Bells!! Bells!!!

The referee warns the crowd that they must calm down or *all bets are off*.

Expectant hush.

Bell!

The last round.

Nuggety Carl suddenly turns on the fireworks.

A series of spectacular jabs, followed by a king hit.

It's a KO.

Bells.

Carl's hands are raised to heaven in triumph as he does a little victory dance.

Carrot Top staggers out, half-carried by his second, but he's still able to manage a see-you-later wink to a passing groupie.

Screams. Applause.

Outside, the big bass drum resumes its beat—*ba-boom* … *ba-boom* …

The tent starts coming down even as the crowd exits.

An eager country pug, wide-eyed and ambitious, begs my father for tips.

He's solemnly offered the tent boxer's mantra:
Stay hungry!

I revelled in my role as anonymous spectator. My father wondered excitedly, but in vain, if the experience had triggered any sporting instincts. I smiled, in the enigmatic family way. In truth, I found sport of little interest, boxing even less so, but the three-round drama, the theatrical excitement and the understanding of how such an experience was shaped, defined and brought to a climax ... well, the lessons of that afternoon would linger.

For the locals, it was the end of a long, action-packed day— a once-a-year festivity that celebrated their lives, the land and its produce and, along sideshow alley, offered them a chance to embrace the illusion of danger: boxers risking life, limb and dignity, silk-clad acrobats jumping through hoops of fire, big wheels whizzing kids through the air, motorbikes rattling around giant, rickety wooden drums while terrified punters beheld them in terror and awe.

Where the fear is—there lurks the interest. Along sideshow alley, that was the name of the game. The stakes had to be high for the drama to engage. It was an understanding I would store and put to later use.

After all the action came the nocturnal departure. Sitting huddled by the camp fire with Rud Kee, like a sentry keeping vigil, I'd watch as my father calmly and methodically supervised the load-up of the big red Reo truck. Through a sliver of light from an open caravan door, I'd glimpse the silhouette of my mother quietly packing inside. I'd observe the illusion give way, the impermanence confirmed. By daybreak the ground that had hosted this extravagant spectacle would be just another empty paddock.

The locals would all be safely home and tucked up in their beds. Not so the showies. They'd be busy by camp fire and under kero lamps, coupling caravans in the beam of car headlights,

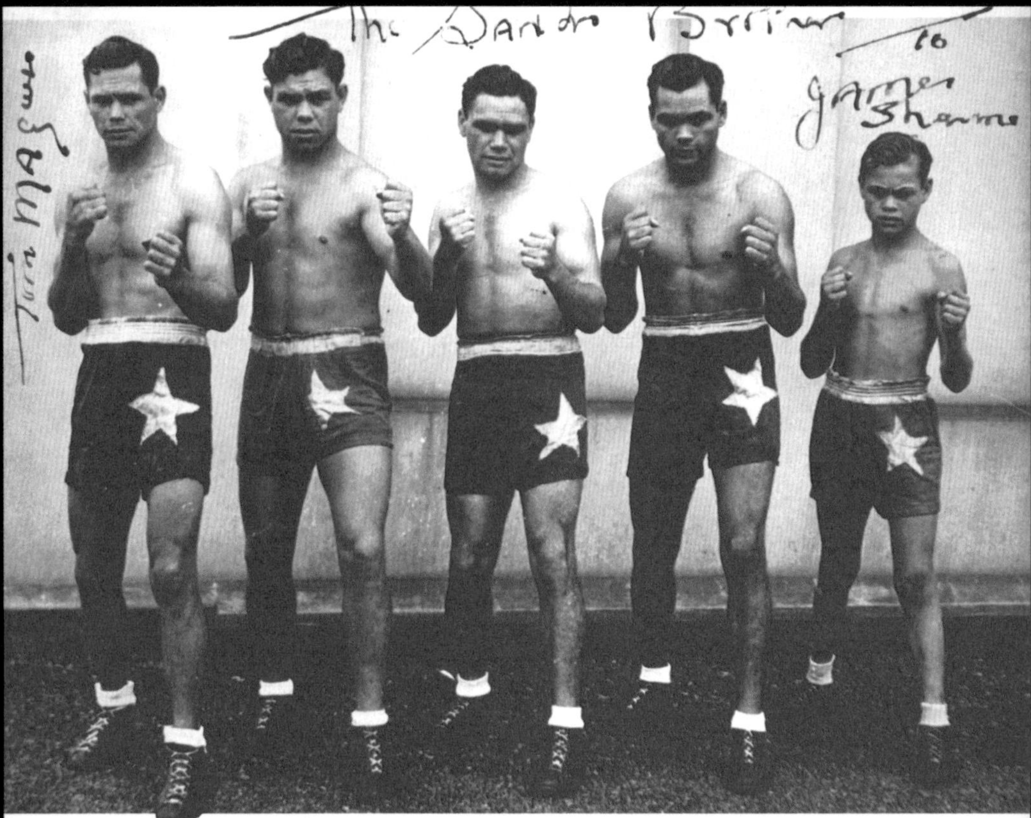
JIMMY
SHARMANS
TROUPE
JIMMY
SHARMANS
TROUPE
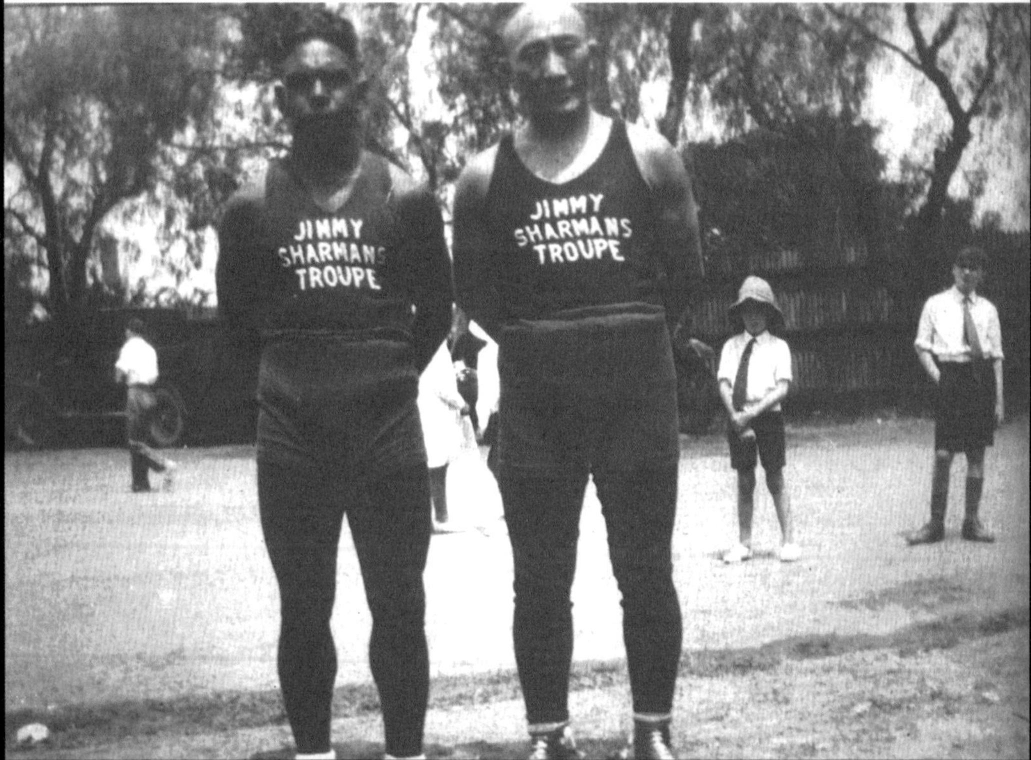

and then driving, driving, on unsealed roads, through cane fires and flash floods. Maybe Carl or Carrot Top might manage their feed, fight and fuck—their tent-show trifecta. Then it would be on, and on, on and on—to the next town and the next and the next.

Ba-boom ... ba-boom ... ba-boom ...

TOP: The Sands Brothers, legends of Australian boxing
BOTTOM: Doug Nichols (later Sir Douglas Nichols, Governor of South Australia) and Rud Kee

IN 1945 ...

Tokyo was firebombed by the US Airforce, and 100000 Japanese died. The German Führer, Adolf Hitler, suicided, and Germany surrendered, bringing European hostilities to an end. The Italian dictator Benito Mussolini was executed by partisans and strung from a telegraph pole.

Anticipating the Russian occupation of Japan, the United States dropped the atomic bombs Fat Man and Little Boy on Hiroshima and Nagasaki. Japan surrendered to US forces, ending the Pacific War. The occupation of Japan secured the United States a stronghold in Asia. Through the invention of the hydrogen and atom bombs, the world had learnt how to incinerate itself and a nuclear cloud hung over the future.

Europe was partitioned between East and West. In the United States, ballpoint pens, or biros as they became known, were marketed. In London, Benjamin Britten's opera *Peter Grimes* was premiered.

After an extended and painful eight-day labour, during which it was thought neither mother nor child would survive, I was delivered to Christina and James Sharman at Crown Street Women's Hospital, by caesarean section. My father had called a priest. Last rites were administered. It was touch and go. Then, my birth and baptism. My mother and I must have been two very determined people; almost dead and then alive, within moments. I emerged shortly after midnight on 12 March in the Chinese Year of the Rooster, under the sign of Pisces, represented by two fish swimming in opposite directions.

TOP: Home on wheels
BOTTOM: My parents in Cairns

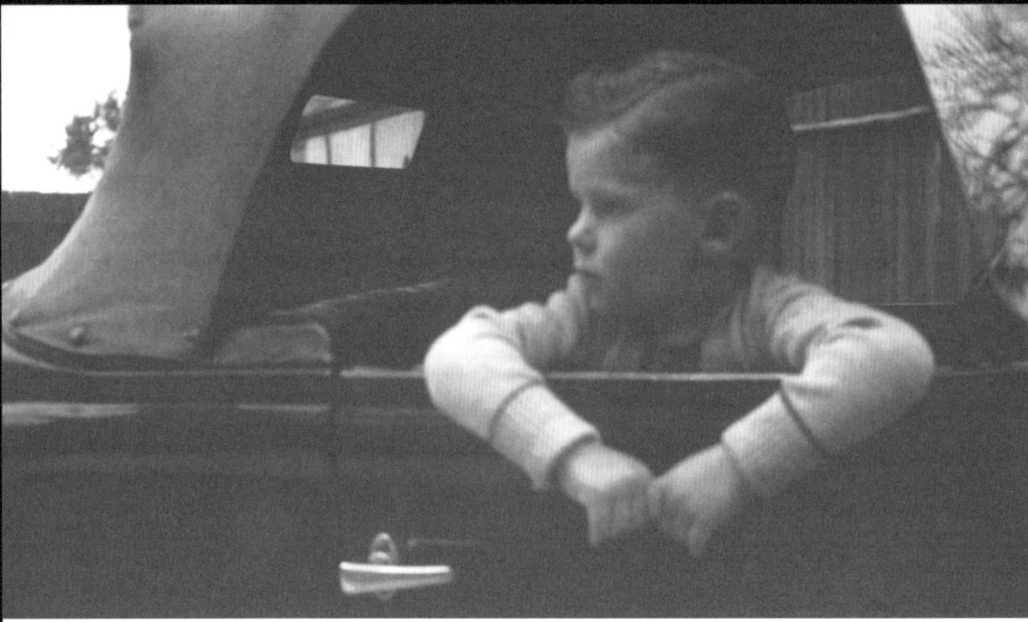

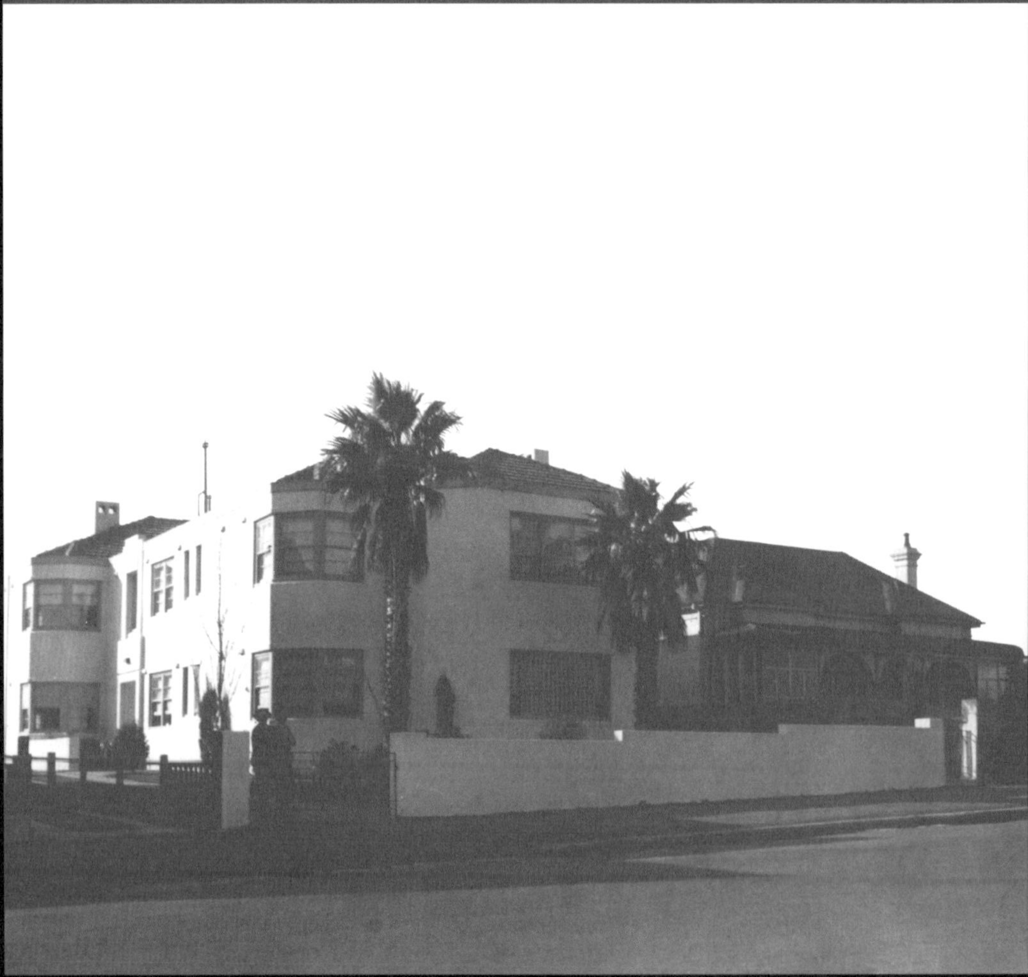

TRAVELLERS AND SETTLERS

I was inside, looking out. The palm fronds brushed against the window of the carriage in the rickety little steam train as we snaked our way up the Queensland coast and deeper into the tropics. The soundtrack was a rhythmic *thwack thwack thwack* of mysterious vegetation on glass. My child's face was pressed tight against the cool surface of the train window as I gazed at this blurred vista of luscious green.

My parents were with each other and with me. After sunset, the compartment beds would flip down as the train clattered into the sweaty indigo night. It was a time when you could still see the stars winking down at you. Hot chocolate would be passed around by my mother from the lid of an anodised silver thermos, and I would sip and stare and observe.

As I glanced from face to face, I realised my parents were an attractive couple. A sense of tropical romance was palpable, inside and outside the train carriage. It's a comforting memory, idyllic and slightly voyeuristic; a fleeting moment that couldn't and wouldn't last. Yet it remains as an insistent recollection.

Nearly five, I was not yet old enough for school so I travelled with my parents on the long journey from Brisbane to Cairns with the travelling shows.

They would board what was known as the Show Train at Brisbane, with trucks and caravans and canvas tents stored. It was a carnival in motion, an eclectic mixture of races: émigrés and locals thrown together, some by choice, many by economics; others by the vagaries of time and circumstance. The complex collection of characters on that train offered a preview glimpse of a different and more culturally sophisticated Australia, one that was waiting in the wings. The mostly young itinerant side-show workers would smoke and play card games and sleep in the trucks. The management and featured performers would do more or less the same, but in train carriages. A hand of euchre or gin rummy passed the time. The train would pull into country stations bedecked with tropical flowers. Here, the convoy of trucks would be off-loaded. The pleasant escape of travel would give way to the grit of familiar activity.

TOP: The passenger
BOTTOM: Randwick

Once the physical labour was completed, circus performers would don costumes and create an impromptu street procession, with trumpets and drums and clowns and animals and leaflets, announcing show time.

The tents would be trucked to the showground, unpacked and unfurled; the carriages discreetly shunted into a siding. The show would last a day and a night or two, then the showies would reload the train, and the carnival would move on. Cairns, in the tropical north, would be the final destination. After the Queensland coastal tour, some showies and workers would return with the train, though most drove home by truck and caravan or by car.

The long and exhausting drive back down the coast contrasted with the flickering sensuousness of the view from the train window and my dreamy recall of carnival life. Dreams were already important in my young life, crowded, as they were, with graceful acrobats, sweat-soaked boxers, and magicians like the Great Levante, waving wands and sawing ladies in two. All these were left behind, along with the scent of sawdust and the after-taste of Dagwood dogs and fairy floss, the faces of laughing and crying children clutching show bags and the procession of *mugs*, as the punters were cynically known.

My father drove. He was happiest behind the wheel, in control of his own destiny and navigating his personal illusion of freedom. His was the enduring frontier fantasy: the kid on a pony, the cowboy on a horse, the driver on the open road.

My mother sat in the passenger seat, fanning herself and giving a few too many driving instructions. I was either squashed between them in the front or, like most kids, shoved in the back seat where, too short to see the vista ahead, I would often succumb to motion sickness.

Dad navigated with ease the seemingly endless terrain of plains and mountains, skies and rolling clouds, the monotony only broken by the occasional spark or flash of fire and flood. I have nightmarish recollections of driving through heat haze and smoke from burning cane fields and bushfires; of slow crossings over flooded rivers; of ominous, apocalyptic images of biblical landscapes. Plagues of locusts would descend and obliterate the windscreen; kangaroos might unexpectedly materialise, caught in a sudden blaze of headlights, and end up as road kill; damp handkerchiefs were held over mouths and noses to avoid the clouds of ochre dust from unsealed roads.

The beauty, variety and subtlety of the native Australian landscape take time to appreciate. Through a child's impatient eyes, it seemed boring, a trial to be endured—an endless tedium of unending motion and a seeming infinity of trees. First came the palms, then the ghost gums and the scrub and, at last, a town. With it came a pub with a shaded veranda; a rest, a shower and a meal. Life on the road was in turn romantic, dramatic and tedious.

Our return to Sydney and a neat spacious apartment in suburban Randwick offered a stark contrast. My mother was instantly happier and more relaxed. Christina Sharman enjoyed her domestic empire. *Civilisation!* she would sigh, and feel very house proud. The rigours of cramped caravan life were consigned to a distant memory, though that tiny van was kept spotless and shiny—a refuge from what she saw as the chaos of the anarchic showground world. My mother was a suburban beauty and she aspired to an elegant life. The irony lay in the fact that her aspirations were paid for by the sweat, blood and vulgarity of showground life.

My father enjoyed a break from his punishing routine of life on the road, but, ever a cowboy at heart, he was soon restless and arguments would flare. Through my young eyes, marriage seemed like endless verbal stoushes involving intricate psychological games. At these, my mother appeared an especially enthusiastic player. I would retreat to the solitude of my room and wait out these rows, or I would step into the ring as an apprentice referee and practise my conciliatory diplomatic skills. I came to recognise the eruption of domestic spats as the signal that my father was frustrated by too much domesticity and was eager to get back on the road… separation suited this marriage.

I would see little of him over the next decade, as I was only allowed to travel on occasional school holidays. I missed him terribly; in my mind, my father was defined by his absence. He often arrived by postcard or a letter typed on his Remington portable. Dad was an endearing letter writer, with a born raconteur's delight in a good yarn. His column for the *Sporting Globe* had the same folksy charm, peppered with the country gossip and love of Australian slang that littered his letters and conversation. My father's missives would be eagerly awaited and read many times over. I savoured the images on his postcards, especially the colour photographs that flipped down, like a strip of film, revealing multiple vistas of towns, highways, tropical gardens and expanses of ocean beach.

The Menzies era in Australia was prosperous, conservative, comfortable, secure and provincial: work; mow the lawns; shop; listen to the radio and watch television. For many, life was relaxed and comfortable, but I'd been spoilt for suburban living with its certainties and mortgages and neat houses and tidy lawns, domestic rituals and conversations about real estate and concern over insurance policies. I'd been initiated into adventure, imagination and travel. I was being encouraged to become a settler but I knew, at heart, that I was a traveller and a seeker with a restless curiosity and an ambitious imagination.

On the road, I had instinctively understood that real life didn't come with an insurance policy. The sideshow world had given me a taste of risk and danger: acrobats juggling fire and motorbike riders circling each other inside steel cages or around trembling wooden drums in a flirtatious dance with death. I'd experienced a transitory, illusory, extraordinary world, and some subversive seeds had been planted. They would take time to blossom into rebellious entertainment and mature into an art that would ruffle a few feathers.

In a child's bedroom, late at night, a half-understood idea was gnawing away. It was the growing realisation that what appeared true to most people was merely an illusion and that what was seen as transient and illusory was true.

STREET SCENE

1960: I was an awkward, introverted fifteen year old waiting outside a hotel in Exhibition Street, Melbourne. It had been months since I'd seen my father. I'd travelled to Melbourne and arranged to meet him in front of his city hotel. I was tightly, anxiously, clutching a parcel; shifting from one foot to another.

A tramp stopped and observed my concentration on the object I was holding, hugging ever so tightly.

That must be important, he observed.

It's a present. The tramp nodded.

It's for my father. Pause. *It's his birthday.*

The tramp smiled at this tense display of filial devotion and walked on.

THE FOUNTAIN

Walking, no, gliding, flying almost, across the Sydney Domain
and into Macquarie Street. The whole world seemed transformed. I emerged from the Art Gallery of New South Wales
in thrall to a minor epiphany. It was a Sunday in 1968 and I was
in my early twenties. I'd drifted into the gallery, that secular
church, in search of artistic stimulus.

The year before, I'd seen *Two Decades of American Painting*,
an exhibition from the Museum of Modern Art in New York.
It was my introduction to Pop Art and the first sighting of
the work of Robert Rauschenberg, and Roy Lichtenstein, plus
Andy Warhol, who inspired me with his depictions of everyday objects, people and events transformed into searing icons
of popular worship.

I passed through the familiar collection of colonial paintings.
My pace increased as I passed the Australian abstracts; they
seemed to belong to the fashion and enthusiasm of a previous
generation. The real revelation waited below, in what was then
the basement, in a large touring exhibition of more than seventy
works by the French artist Marcel Duchamp.

My knowledge of art history was slender, my imagination
formative, but as I came face-to-face with *Nude Descending the
Stairs No 2* and the large glass entitled *The Bride Stripped Bare
by Her Bachelors Even*, I was stunned. A wall of Duchamp's early
and more conventional paintings followed, no doubt included
to calm conservative nerves. These led to a collection of his
found objects or *ready-mades*. Chief among this intriguing array
of spades, bicycle wheels and other everyday bric-a-brac was a
ceramic urinal on a tripod, with R MUTT scrawled on its side
in charcoal, labelled *Fountain*.

A urinal in a public art gallery.

If I'd known more about art history, I might have enjoyed the
joke. I did laugh—there should be more laughter in galleries
—but I was also amazed, as I had been the previous year by
Warhol's everyday icons and would soon be again by Christo
wrapping Sydney's Little Bay coastline in billowing fabric to
better reveal that landscape's form and sculptural power.

The rest of the art gallery seemed to dissolve, and the procession of precious colonial and old master paintings evaporated; they were relics of another time. The future was in front of me, in ceramic. Suddenly everything was art, or could be seen as art, or held the possibility of art within it. Everything changed for me from the moment my eye caught that urinal on a pedestal in the gallery: mounted, named, spotlit. *Fountain*.

Then came the riddles. Was it art simply because it had been chosen by an artist and exhibited in a public gallery? This was one provocative question posed by Marcel Duchamp's enigmatic work. If this was art, anything, seen in a certain way, was art. That was the logical conclusion. My first glimpse of that urinal struck hard, like a punch. My reaction to this transformation of the everyday into the extraordinary wasn't stimulated by drugs, though the effect was similar.

Out on the street, everything seemed heightened. The world was a familiar, yet a strange new place. There was a rush of genuine wonder as everyday sights took on a deeper, more poetic dimension. I became aware of the intricate weave of telegraph wires, the abstractions of pedestrian crossings, the hidden beauty of tiny gestures from passers-by and the secret language of clouds.

After Duchamp, everything would be different. I now understood that there was another dimension to everyday experience; a new world revealed by art. And lurking somewhere in the entrails of that idea was the true purpose and value of art.

There was more: alchemy was involved. A little magic was required to transform everyday dross into art. This clarified insights I had already gleaned from a background that mingled everyday urbanity with carnival and tawdry yet miraculous sideshows.

Without understanding it, I felt liberated by this experience, and I knew it would somehow inform everything from that moment on. I was determined to share this revelation; to put it to some good use.

An artist could be an alchemist, a transformer, a magician. Marcel Duchamp had opened my eyes.

ELECTRONIC ALTARS

The grandfather I never met was David Mitchell, my mother's father. He had concert pianist aspirations, but these were put on hold as he transported his family from Aberdeen in Scotland via New Zealand to Australia. He died early, in his forties, of cancer, before I was born. His daughter Christina, who adored him, had also played the piano, but her early musical enthusiasm was sacrificed to the demands and practicalities of marriage.

Nonetheless, our home boasted a collection of recordings of piano music from the popular classical to the merely popular; from Chopin polonaises to *Winifred Atwell at Her Other Piano*: a medley of jazz, ragtime and sentimental favourites performed by an Anglo-Jamaican who flashed expensive rings and a dazzling smile. I was taken to see her at the Tivoli, Sydney's vaudeville theatre, on one of her many Australian visits. *Winnie*, as she was affectionately known, was so popular here that she finally immigrated to Australia, ending up in Surfers Paradise, playing occasional dates at the local RSL.

Before her marriage, my mother had worked at Hiram-Smiths, a store that specialised in cameras, film, recordings, record-players and billiard tables. By some quirk, possibly hereditary, I developed a fascination for all these—certainly cameras and even, briefly, snooker and billiards. My mother's experience in this audiovisual emporium meant that pride of place in our living room was reserved for the latest entertainment device, be it a console radio, a radiogram or an AWA mahogany all-in-one-radio-and-record-player, later usurped by an Admiral rosewood 17-inch black-and-white television with swivel stand.

These electronic altars, disguised as furniture, stood in the place that once would have been reserved for the piano. My favourite of these intriguing, ever-changing devices was the mahogany all-in-one, though I later learnt never to buy an all-in-one anything; when one element fades you're robbed of the rest while waiting for repair or replacement.

Music became my religion. I would sit hunched on the floor, entranced by whatever magically emerged from the booming 12-inch speaker, be it symphony orchestra, ragtime piano or talking book. The last was a children's learning device with a large picture book and a recorded narrator who would interrupt the story with a friendly reminder to turn the page.

Oscar Wilde's *The Happy Prince*, a beautiful tale of charity, sacrifice and redemption, was my favourite talking book. It was a thoughtful gift from my mother, which established the idea that books could be my friend. I loved the cadence of the opening:

High above the city, on a tall column, stood the statue of the Happy Prince ... and the refrain: *Swallow, swallow, little swallow* ...

On instruction I would dutifully turn the page and, bingo, a new chapter would begin. Each was accompanied by a lavish illustration. Later in life, at moments when things weren't going well, the memory of this friendly reminder would return to haunt me. I sensed that I'd forgotten to turn the page. This often turned out to be true and, when I did act to transform my situation, things magically improved. Of course, many people go through life quite happily without ever turning the page or, for that matter, opening the book.

I played the family record collection endlessly, though my mother drew the line at a racy little ditty she'd collected to entertain a few girlfriends over sherry: Rosemary Clooney and Marlene Dietrich singing *He's Too Old to Cut the Mustard Anymore.*

When I was school-age and had my own room, the best present I ever received was a powder blue Pye portable stereo with grey speakers. I would squirrel myself away and play DJ with cardboard records—a cheap novelty of the day, affordable on pocket money—using headphones to line up the latest single from Ricky Nelson or LaVern Baker or The Platters or Roy Orbison and intersperse them with improvised DJ banter.

Popular music took over my imagination until a chance discovery in an alcove of the Randwick Presbyterian Church Hall during a brief flirtation with church fellowship. I came across a pile of serious-looking 12-inch 78-rpm recordings, and on top of the pile was Beethoven's Symphony No 3, the

Eroica, conducted by Otto Klemperer. Carefully skirting a Bible study class, I made my way to the sound booth, secluded myself, and listened to it, record by shellac record.

After this experience, popular music, which I continued to enjoy, sounded a bit thin. Klemperer's *Eroica* was the genesis of an enthusiasm for great music interpreted by great conductors. First impressions are important, and I had been fortunate to happen upon one of the finest conductors of the day. I progressed to Klemperer's other recordings, including Mozart's *Magic Flute*, Beethoven's *Fidelio* and Mahler's *Resurrection* Symphony.

Much later in life I would become equally enthused by conductors like Carlos Kleiber and, especially, Pierre Boulez, with his revelatory readings of Stravinsky, Bartok, Debussy and Ravel, and his modernist Mahler. I was interested to read that young Pierre's musical education included attending many Otto Klemperer concerts.

Audio altar worship finally gave way to the visual variety when the Admiral television entered the living room in 1956. Many nights were then spent in pyjamas and dressing gown as a supplicant on the pale green Axminster, in thrall to *I Love Lucy, The Patti Page Show*—*How Much is That Doggy in the Window? Ruff! Ruff!*, *The Mickey Mouse Club*—*Who's the Leader of the Band That's Made for You and Me?* or Della Street—so like my mother—helping Perry Mason solve a tricky criminal case. Or I'd be finger-popping along to the theme of *77 Sunset Strip*— *click-click*—or slyly admiring Troy Donahue in *Surfside Six*.

American television captured my young imagination but music had already captured my heart and soul. I often wonder what would have happened if there had been a piano in pride of place in the living room, instead of an audio-electronic altar.

Maybe the grandfather I never met would have come out to play?

THE ODYSSEY

1968: I was drifting down George Street on one of those Sydney summer days when you bask in the sun's charitable rays—a thongs-shorts-and-tropical-shirt kind of day. I enjoy drifting. I did then and still do. You're open to things: thoughts, new ideas, flights of imagination. I often enjoy airports for the same reason. I'm in transit, the locale of impatience, impermanence or dreams; a vacuum, waiting to be filled.

I strolled towards the Plaza Cinema, a vast, Arabian styled picture palace that has long since been transformed into computer game alleys and fast food outlets. It was around 11 a.m. and I noticed workmen installing a sign on the marquee in electric light bulbs: *2001:A SPACE ODYSSEY—A Stanley Kubrick Film*. I knew nothing about it but was sufficiently intrigued to become the sole audience at the first session.

I sat up front and alone in the stalls, enveloped by the giant Cinerama screen and, turning around, I stared back at the cavernous rows of empty cushioned seats and up to the plaster skyline and fake minarets of this old dream palace, ready for … I knew not what.

The pay attention chords of Strauss' *Thus Spake Zarathustra* thundered and I was drawn into another world, a timeless one. Prehistoric bones were thrown into the air by apes and transformed, by the magic of inspired editing, into spacecraft floating in syncopation to Viennese waltzes. Astronauts battled through the void of time and space, and objects floated through this world without end to melancholy strains of Khachaturian and Ligeti.

The sense of solitude in the infinite cinematic landscape seemed to echo that of the only customer at this early morning session. The emotional chords in the film were struck by the astonishing death throes of an IBM computer called HAL. Hal was slowly murdered—*I wouldn't do that, if I were you, Dave!*—to the eerie accompaniment of a child's nursery rhyme.

After a procession of intensely coloured abstract images, Dave, the astronaut turned time-traveller, emerged as the sole occupant of an intergalactic hotel room. He grew ghostly as he aged and finally died, only to be reincarnated and returned to earth as a haloed embryo.

Put like this, it sounds like the retelling of an old legend: a simple fable of life, death and rebirth; and possibly it was. If so, this wasn't immediately apparent. Echoing my experiences on first encountering Duchamp and Warhol, I emerged inspired and, in some unknown way, changed by Kubrick's aural and visual poem.

2001: A Space Odyssey created a critical storm; it was hailed as visionary or dismissed as hollow, incomprehensible and pretentious. For me, it was a reminder of the unexplored possibilities of cinema. To my eyes, most other films suddenly seemed like old-fashioned theatrical soap operas.

Like many of my generation, I was hungry for new ways of looking at the world, and the complexities of Kubrick's extraordinary film touched me deeply. It presented a challenging labyrinth that I was determined to explore, and my enthusiasm was heightened by the fact that I'd stumbled upon it on my own and by mere chance.

Outside the cinema, I stood dazed by the suddenly too bright Sydney sunshine. I spun around and straightaway bought a ticket for the next session.

The Astronaut

INFLUENTIAL ELDERS

Nana Johns and Uncle Harry

In the absence of the grandfather I never knew, my mother's side of the family was represented by my grandmother. The Scottish-born Mary Mitchell was a delightful and generous soul who happily, from my child's point of view, had no qualms about spoiling her grandchildren. She was a great baker of scones and delicious cakes and was a generous dispenser of ice-cream.

Mary Mitchell had remarried and become Mary Johns, or Nana Johns. For a replacement husband, my widowed grandmother had chosen a seemingly unremarkable man: a real estate agent, with the equally unremarkable name of Harry Johns. He proved remarkable only in death. When Harry Johns' Last Will and Testament was read and various mysterious female beneficiaries had been contacted, it was discovered that unassuming old Uncle Harry, as I called him, had enjoyed a previous life as a travelling salesman in Tasmania. He had a string of aliases and was a multiple bigamist.

Most of the family were shocked and retreated into a dignified silence over this unpalatable revelation. Nana Johns, supported by my mother and her sister, Annabella, shared collective Scottish outrage at having been thus deceived and betrayed; but to me, this made the old philanderer a lot more interesting than I'd previously thought. And it taught me never to underestimate appearances. Once I'd looked up the word in the dictionary, a bigamist seemed merely dodgy, but a *multiple* bigamist suggested more extravagance, virility and criminal imagination than I would ever have suspected of Uncle Harry.

Harry Johns died after a long respiratory illness, having been nursed by Nana Johns and my parents through his last days in one of our family's Randwick apartments.

The patient was set up in bed on a mountain of pillows, with a respirator and an oxygen tent, and a mask over his face through which he breathed fitfully. This set-up made me curious, and I exhibited a sense of philosophical enquiry, scientific interest or sheer morbidity, depending on your point of view. Each day of his illness, I would enthusiastically ask my parents if I could go next door and watch Uncle Harry die.

Don't say that! was the firm and not unreasonable reply.

Once I had rephrased the request to suit the manners of the day, I would be duly granted permission to do my homework in the patient's room as it meant someone was in attendance and my parents, my grandmother and other grieving relatives gained a brief respite from duties of care.

I would tiptoe into the otherwise deserted apartment and sit quietly in a corner of the room, listening intently to the heartbeat rhythm of his breathing and watching the balloon-like bag of air filling and emptying. It felt like a kind of meditation— until one day it faltered.

I went calmly next door to my parents, who were in the kitchen preparing dinner and, after politely waiting for them to finish their conversation, I gravely announced:

I think Uncle Harry's a goner!

A great deal subsequently happened from which, as a child, I was naturally excluded. However, my response to the departure of Uncle Harry was not one of grief or trauma, but curiosity: a simple puzzlement over where Uncle Harry—who was still there, but no longer with us—had gone. Thus the question of where do you go when you die was firmly planted in my mind.

This line of enquiry encouraged a subsequent and precocious teenage interest in plays like *Hamlet*, which opens with the question *Who's there?* and then proceeds, for several hours, not to answer it. My adolescent interest in Shakespeare's popular play was often accompanied by earnest stares into suburban bathroom mirrors, as I intoned *To be or not to be*, with various inflections, as if the right emphasis might solve the riddle.

I credit Uncle Harry's demise for an ensuing and fashionable later flirtation with existentialism and a less fashionable yet continuing interest in comparative religion.

Where do you go when you die?

Even if the answer is nowhere, it remains an intriguing question.

ABOVE: My grandparents' friend: Grace Sorlie of *Sorlie's Travelling Variety Show*
OPPOSITE: Grandmothers, mother and son

Grandad

The travelling boxing troupe pioneer Jimmy Sharman Sr was renowned for many things, public and private. One of his lesser known eccentricities was his enthusiasm for ridding restaurants of chipped cups. He would simply smash them.

Born in 1887, in a plague-infected century, my grandfather couldn't abide germs and he considered chipped crockery to be unhygienic. He'd sit down, observe the chip in a cup or plate with displeasure and ... *crash!*

Just like that.

They won't bloody well serve that up to anyone else again!

At a time when tiled floors were popular in cafés and restaurants, these percussive displays would appall, embarrass or delight his fellow diners. His young grandson was especially impressed by this delightful quirk.

Grandad's actions weren't as eccentric as they sound, and there was method to his seeming madness. He had his reasons, though he rarely chose to explain them. His mixture of Depression-era country practicality and aggressive public behaviour defined a man whose often good intentions could result in socially awkward outcomes. He'd justify himself with the dubious maxim: *I'm only being cruel to be kind.*

To me, Grandad Sharman was a distant yet intriguing figure, and I enjoyed the rare visits to his headquarters at Narellan, on the edge of Sydney. His reputation as an ex-champion pug and Irish-Australian farmer's son—he would often boast that his own father could only sign his name with an X—had proved useful in establishing an intimidating reputation in a tough game.

Grandad was renowned for his firmness and resolve. Everyone approached him with caution. He was also well known for his intolerance of drink among his touring boxers; they would be sacked on the spot at the first sign of it. He was a teetotaller for most of his life, yet he succumbed to drink himself in his later years.

This hastened his death in 1965 at the age of seventy-eight, which was quite young in Sharman-time. His farming predecessors, literate or not, had clocked in at over a hundred and my father lived for ninety-four years.

Despite Grandad's reputation for coldness and severity, we got on well. A young grandson probably brought out the playful, sentimental side of his Irish nature. He called me *Little Joe* and had a boomerang specially carved and painted with the name by an Aboriginal artist friend, as a special gift for me. I still have it.

Grandad separated from his wife and childhood sweetheart, Violet, after falling for his secretary. He never considered divorce, as this was against his Roman Catholic faith. Like all the Sharmans, Grandad wasn't short on contradictions. He set up my grandmother in a modest, pleasant apartment in middle-class Woollahra, while he lived with his secretary and accountant Florence Carroll, whom I knew as Auntie Flo, in his secluded weatherboard shack at Narellan. It was far from our suburban Randwick home and his wife's leafy Woollahra address, but it was close to the old family farm at nearby Camden, where he had been raised.

As an adolescent, Grandad had not exactly run away with the circus, but he had turned his back on his family's dairy farming tradition and had left behind his parents, his two young brothers and seven sisters, and his inevitable fate as another proud-but-honest dirt-poor Irish Catholic farm labourer. A few successful local boxing bouts had earned him pocket money and the wrath of his parents. This was accompanied by a thrashing with a belt. He packed his swag and jumped the rattler, heading for Riverina country to make his fame and fortune as a professional boxer.

After being returned by amused police from a few such adventures—and being greeted on each return with a thrashing—he finally made it as a successful fighter and was able to sustain himself on his earnings. He worked as a billy boy, or tea carrier, on a construction site and engaged in amateur boxing, from which he quickly progressed to professional status. After a few victories in the ring, Grandad saved enough cash to resettle, under the watchful eyes of distant relatives, in Narrandera, near Wagga Wagga, in the heart of the Riverina.

In those days, the only way such a boy could escape a farm-hand fate was through sport or entertainment. Grandad started with one and ended up with the other, the rewards of which he passed on to his son.

Grandad hoped that the social progression he had initiated would continue down the family line. In his desire to have a doctor or lawyer in the family, he sent my father to a private Roman Catholic boarding school: initially, St Patrick's in Goulburn and, later, to St Joseph's College at Hunter's Hill in Sydney.

My grandfather was a true Australian in his aspirations. After all, egalitarianism meant that anyone could make something of themselves, and if Grandad could go from an illiterate farming background and become a prosperous boxing entrepreneur, then his son could really hit the heights. But my father's considerable achievements were on the football field rather than in the classroom, and he harboured the peculiarly Australian attitude that combined a contradictory respect and contempt for anyone of any academic achievement. It was an attitude I often sensed he applied to me.

Excelling at sport rather than academia, my father flourished under the tutelage of Brother Henry, a legend among school football coaches. The item of honour in my father's room, even in old age, was a large school photo of the St Joseph's College rugby team, with himself as captain and Brother Henry beaming proudly from the row behind. Perhaps Brother Henry gave him the praise, attention and support that his own father withheld. This was another family trait. Certainly, it was a matter of pride that a showman was able to send his son to a private school, but maybe pride in the achievement was greater than pride in the son.

My father would never fulfil his own father's ambitions. Instead, after an interview with Rugby League boss Harold Mathews, my father became a professional footballer and, ultimately, captain of Western Suburbs Rugby League team—his proudest sporting achievement. The subject of the rugby interview was residency requirements, still applicable in that era. To play for Wests you had to be resident in the area. Dad wasn't, but he wanted to play for the club. They wanted him, so ...

Question: *State your full name.*
Answer: *James Michael Sharman.*
Question: *Where do you live?*
Answer: *I don't know.*
Question: *Where does your father live?*
Answer: *He doesn't live anywhere.*
Question: *And your mother?*
Answer: *She lives with my father.*

As Dad's parents lived in a caravan, his answers were both accurate and amusing. He was accepted into the team. To support himself, he worked as a part-time sports journalist and at Anthony Hordern's, a city department store. The handsome young footballer in country orders soon fell for the cool glamour girl behind the perfume counter.

My parents must have been an attractive couple as they foxtrotted at the Trocadero or dressed up for a dinner dance at Romano's on a special occasion. They married in 1937, and, soon after World War II ended, Dad started touring and managing the boxing troupe. He took over its fulltime operation in the 1950s.

In the progressive barn dance of fathers and sons in our family, I would come closer to fulfilling my grandfather's expectations. My own father had harboured sporting ambitions for his only son. I became the child he could admire but not comprehend. For that, we would both have to wait until later in our lives.

Having an oft-absent father and being surrounded by my mother, doting grandmothers, aunts and the like, made the distinctly male environment of visits to my grandfather's shack uncomfortable for me. Apart from Auntie Flo, who would quickly retire to the kitchen with my mother, there were only men present: mates, relatives and stray boxers from the nearby shed that housed the troupe's tent and the big red Reo truck in off-season.

On one such visit to Narellan, on a hot and stagnant day, Grandad asked me to fetch some beer from the icebox to quench the thirst of a roomful of blokes. Only one bottle of beer was left and, as a dutiful eleven year old, I returned with the solitary bottle balanced on a tray stacked with glasses. As I stepped into the room, silence fell. Everyone eyed the precious amber bottle. The tray unbalanced. I tripped and fell. The bottle smashed. Just like that. Its contents spilled across grey linoleum.

My eyes briefly met my grandfather's and I encountered a savage glare. I experienced what his opponents in the ring must have faced; it was not a look you'd forget in a hurry. I still wince at the sound of breaking glass.

Deep inside Grandad's glare was the angry echo of an irate parent reaching for a strap to punish a delinquent runaway son. Then, just as suddenly as he had glared, he laughed, as if he'd had a sudden insight into my dilemma. The realisation that I was not cut out for all this—for beer and mates and the like. The sense of a kindred spirit who might one day abandon his family and carve out his own future. Despite Grandad's flaws and eccentricities, and the vast distance that separated us, I sensed in that frozen moment, and from inside his dark laughter, the old pioneer had understood more about me than anyone else would for some time to come.

TOP: The Sharmans
BOTTOM: Grandad and the billy-goat cart

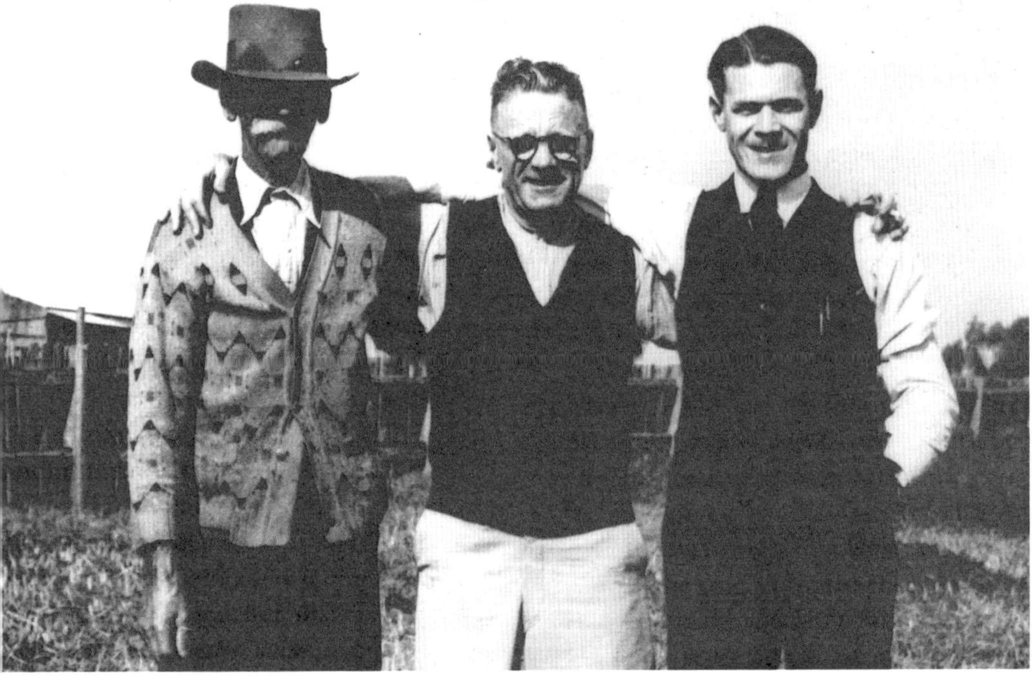

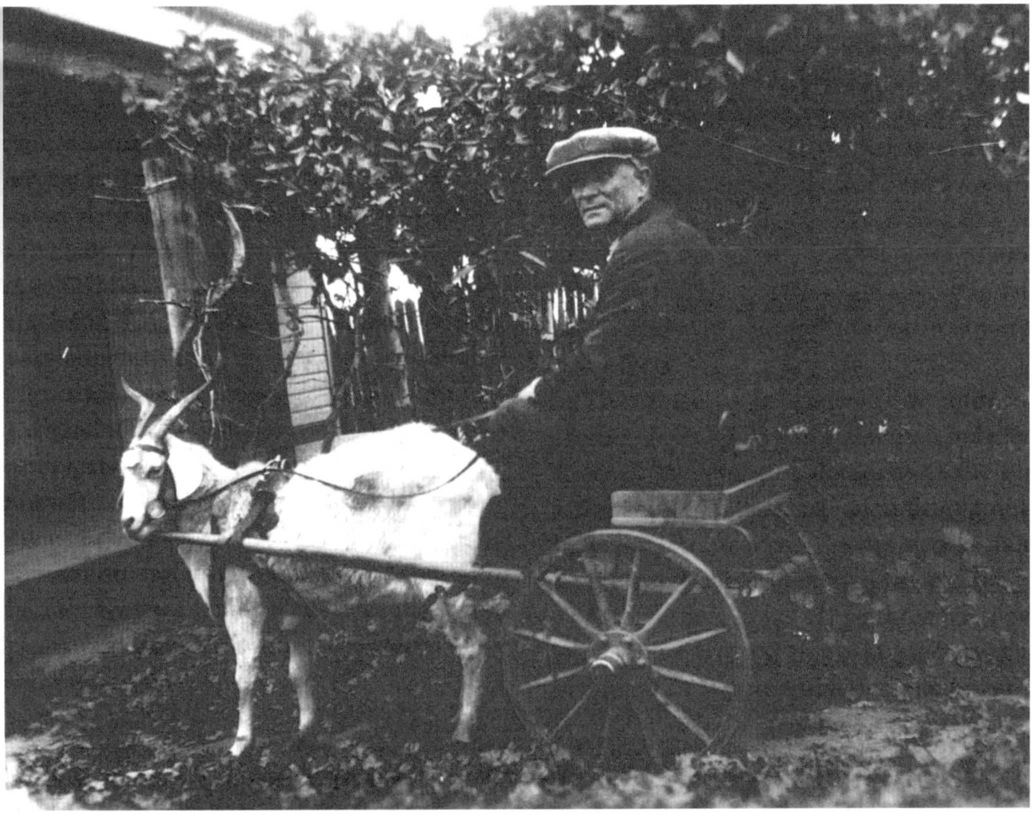

Nana Pud

A tall, dark brick block of brooding apartments in Edgecliff Road, Woollahra, was home to my paternal grandmother, Violet. Another Sharman living alone. The building, called *Lyndhurst*, had a long, garden-lined entrance way tiled in crazy paving and, inside, a labyrinth of serious-looking wood-panelled halls and carpeted stairways. It still stands today, and on the rare occasions I find myself on that tree-lined road I'm tempted to step back inside, as if my dear old grandmother might still be there, splashing on some last-minute eau de cologne and preparing to receive her guests. The lavender scent I always associated with her lingers in some subterranean cavern of my senses.

Christmas lunch at *Lyndhurst* was both an annual ritual and an event. Nana Pud lived up to her nickname, appearing fleshy and perfumed and as plump and cheery as a Christmas pudding. Nana by name and Nana by nature.

Something of the vivacity of her vaudeville mates had rubbed off on the old girl, and there was a flamboyance and theatricality added to her generous country demeanour: the Riverina girl from the Byrne clan who, through marriage, had become both Catholic and citified.

The Christmas guest list was small: my father, mother and me, and the local priest—chunky, middle-aged and slightly balding Father Bongiorno. The still handsome Italian-born priest would say grace devoutly, yet swap sly little winks with my grandmother. These intimacies confirmed that Father Bon's relationship with dear old Nana had strayed well beyond spiritual guidance and into more earthly areas of experience.

Seated at the head of the table, on this occasion, in a baby's high chair clumsily adapted into a domestic throne, was a very short, dark and imperious figure. This was our Christmas Day guest of honour, the Pygmy Princess Ubangi. In an era when specialty attractions, commonly known as freak shows, were still permitted on Australian showgrounds, Grandad's mate Dave Meekin had travelled to Africa and imported a group of Pygmies to Australia, led by Princess Ubangi.

Their show was simple. The Pygmies danced and gave examples of their polyphonic rhythmic chants, while their princess—presumably a tribal elder whose title had been translated into Anglo-Saxon hierarchy—looked on impassively from an African throne. Some cultural commentary was offered as background to dignify the chance for the paying public to stare at the Pygmies. Royalty-starved Aussie crowds were always up for a gawk at a visiting princess, so the show was a crowd pleaser. Ubangi's novelty act was turning chanteuse and singing *Lili Marleen* in Afrikaans.

Beryl Meekin, Dave's daughter and an ex–Tivoli singer, was a close friend of my grandmother, and through this connection, Nana Pud developed a friendship with Ubangi. On her frequent stays in Sydney, Ubangi was my grandmother's guest at her Woollahra home. This current visit coincided with Christmas and so Ubangi, seated princess-style, at her insistence, presided over our family lunch. *The smallest woman in the world*, as she was billed, sat at the head of the table facing Nana Pud, the ubiquitous Father Bon, my parents and me; I was only slightly taller than the visiting royalty.

Nana Pud always had special treats for Ubangi, who seemed to enjoy both the attention and the festivities. It was whispered that her greatest pleasure, when she finally retired to Australia in her seventies, was playing the poker machines on the Gold Coast. I like to imagine Ubangi perched on a high chair at the pokies while Winifred Atwell belted out *The Black and White Rag* at the Surfers Paradise RSL. It may well have happened.

Christmas luncheon with Pygmy princess blow-ins and Italian priests with a roving eye seemed natural to me. I just assumed that was what everyone did, and I was surprised when I slowly discovered this was not the case. What seemed much stranger was that we would all have to sweat our way through courses of roast this and baked that and delve for threepences in heavy-weight Christmas puddings smothered in custard in some strange imitation of European tradition that ignored the fact that we were all—princess, priest and mere commoners—sweltering in a subtropical Christmas heatwave.

TOP LEFT: Nana Pud and Grace Sorlie   TOP RIGHT: Young Violet
BOTTOM LEFT: Princess Ubangi   BOTTOM RIGHT: Beryl Meekin and Princess Ubangi

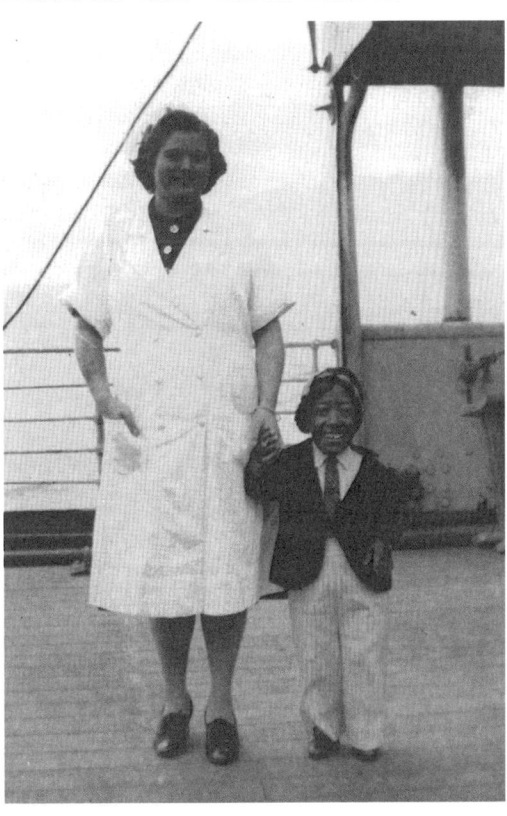

These European hangovers would spread to after-lunch events involving Christmas trees sprayed with *Santa Snow* and cards with silver glitter and other wintry reminders of a northern climate. They didn't, however, prevent a child's pleasure in bon-bons, party hats, gift-wrapped presents and the like.

To my chagrin, all the best presents went to Ubangi. I didn't mind having to wait until Ubangi ate first at table and other princess-like affectations, but I wasn't so keen to share Santa's much-awaited Christmas stash with *The smallest woman in the world*.

Princess Ubangi, or Maria Peters as she was known after immigration, remained a loyal and faithful friend to my grandmother and later became a regular visitor to the Gold Coast nursing home where Violet Sharman spent her last days.

Nana Pud had relished the old-world traditions and was happy to share them. When she finally decided to travel abroad, it therefore came as a surprise that she overlooked Europe, the United States and Africa, home of Princess Ubangi, and decided to visit Hong Kong and Japan on the cruise ship *Mariposa*. Maybe there was some link here with wise old Rud Kee, from the boxing troupe, but the idea of travelling to *The Orient*, as it was then known, seemed very exotic.

We went to the wharf to see off Nana Pud. The ship was a fine sight heading out of Sydney Harbour under a splendid sun and swathed in colourful farewell streamers. Nana Pud was accompanied by departing waves from fluttering handkerchiefs, and welcoming ones a few weeks later, on her return. She emerged from customs looking oddly triumphant, flushed with the excitement of arrival. We exchanged a volley of welcomes and kisses, and Dad drove us all to *Lyndhurst*.

There was much intriguing chatter detailing the wonders of the East and some *ohs* and *ahs* that accompanied the distribution of gifts—polished and carved rosewood chests with gilt corners and an overnight-tailor-made suit from Hong Kong for my father.

Nana Pud appeared momentarily uncomfortable; she excused herself and retired to her bedroom.

After a few silent moments I followed, nosey and uninvited, and discovered her peeling off her corset to reveal, attached by copious amounts of sticky tape to her ample if sagging breasts, an array of silver Marquisette and rhinestone watches— probably copies of some fashionable French design. We were mutually embarrassed by loosened corsets, powdered breasts and contraband. I broke the ice by pointing to the tiniest watch, secreted between her breasts.

Pud smiled: *For Ubangi.*

Nana Pud's Hong Kong trip, the cruise ship, the streamers and the contraband all created an Asian fascination for me, igniting my interest in international travel. It would be over a decade before I could act on it and even longer before I developed a deeper understanding of Asia, as I read and nodded in silent agreement with the popular sentiment of the day:

The east will wake and the west will quake.

IN 1956 ...

Soviet President Khrushchev denounced the dictatorship of his predecessor, Joseph Stalin. Russian tanks invaded Budapest, violently crushing the reformist Hungarian Revolution. The Olympic Games in Melbourne were opened by HRH the Duke of Edinburgh. Conflict broke out in a water polo match between Russia and Hungary, and the pool turned red with Slavic blood. The British-led invasion of the Suez Canal proved a disaster and hastened the process of decolonisation and the end of Empire. There were reports of UFO sightings in the United States. Elvis Presley appeared on *The Ed Sullivan Show* and rock-and-roll became an official craze. Elvis was only shown from the waist up, for fear of popularising what were described as his suggestive *nigger-type* hip movements.

These events provided background for a low-budget B-movie-style underground feature I would direct in 1972, about a sub-urbanite driven mad by conformity: *Shirley Thompson Versus the Aliens*.

DISCOVERY

I stepped out of the house with my satchel which contained an exercise book, a pencil, a freshly cut sandwich and an apple for lunch. For any child, the first day of school represents their separation from the comfort of home and family and their entrance into the wider world. Most kids greet it with a display of tears and tantrums. My reaction was different; I could hardly wait.

After an enthusiastic *bye bye* wave to my mother, who stood poised with her Kodak Box Brownie camera to capture the moment, I marched into this adventure with a determined stride and didn't look back.

To my surprise, I spent my first day at school comforting tearful tots who didn't share my enthusiasm for the future. They obviously felt they'd been thrown in the deep end of the pool, and if they weren't exactly drowning, they were certainly waving.

PREVIOUS PAGES: Nagasaki
OPPOSITE: To school

As I'd grown up surrounded by adults, rather than other children, I slipped into a mentoring role, reassuring my fellow five year olds that everything would be just fine. Maybe they knew something I didn't, but more likely they were scaredy-cats. My Pollyanna-like mixture of empathy, optimism and amateur philosophy seemed to work. It would come in handy later, given my chosen profession and the legendary insecurity of performing artists.

School turned out to be neither the escape route from the humdrummery of domesticity nor the bed of roses I had imagined. I soon proved to be a sickly, bronchial, allergy-prone and asthmatic child.

Medically, the life and death struggle of my birth had been followed by a small drama at the age of one, when I greedily swallowed the contents of a bottle of glycerine—an incident that resulted in parental anxiety, a late-night dash to the hospital, and some stomach pumping. My early childhood was accompanied by illness: measles, chickenpox and persistent and often life-threatening bronchial asthma attacks.

I learnt to bounce back quickly, emerging from one of the most extreme of these gasping and wheezing episodes to confront the anxious faces of my mother and the family doctor with the cool enquiry: *What's for dinner?* The doctor chuckled, and suggested to my mother that I might have the makings of a philosopher.

And so, my twelve years of schooling were mostly spent in the quiet domesticity of one or another of the family's Randwick apartments. The white, Art Deco block was set well back from the street, like a discreet fortress, with a garden as its moat. The apartments had wonderful, old-style, spacious rooms with high ceilings.

Spending lots of my waking hours with my mother seemed to suit us both. We kept each other company and I relieved the tedium of my recurring illness by developing my imagination. My mother sensed my interests and actively encouraged them, perhaps hoping that some of her own frustrated artistic ambitions might come to fruition through me.

There's a tradition of equating art with illness, and my own experience has encouraged me to subscribe to it. Illness creates vulnerability, and surprising sensitivities emerge, even in the most committed pragmatists. My sick days were many and formative, filled with books, drawing, writing, music.

I enjoyed building miniature sculptures with a Meccano set and constructing model houses with a beloved Bakyo building set; my only prize-winning skill as a schoolkid. This colourful and constructive toy fostered an early interest in design and architecture; the shape of things. My earliest career ambitions were to become an international architect, or to pursue a career in diplomacy. Travel was part of this equation. If I'd known of the French Foreign Legion, I probably would have enlisted.

My parents alternated between being indulgent and strict. Self-reliance and stoicism were encouraged from the cot up. Infant tears and tantrums were studiously ignored, at the insistence of my father. My mother initially protested, then followed suit. In retrospect, I'm grateful for this early education in dealing with life's adversities with minimum fuss, though I would later discover that stoicism has its limits.

I sensed my breadwinner father felt guilty about being so often away, and he attempted to compensate for any perceived neglect by being attentive during his brief home stays. This didn't quite work. In his absence, my mother and I became used to looking after each other, and the affection a wife might normally have offered her husband came my way. My father's arrivals were so infrequent they seemed like an intrusion into our established routine.

Over time, my mother became an increasingly lonely and isolated woman. I once observed her in silence in her bedroom staring at a photo of an old flame: a handsome air force pilot ...

Who's that?

My mother sighed and held back a tear:

The man I might have married.

Her sensitive and gentle nature developed a nervous and anxious aspect and, like a virus, some of that anxiety was transmitted to me. After a volley of absences from school, my mother explained to the headmaster that I was *highly strung*. The unimpressed headmaster replied that if I missed any more valuable schooling then, one day, I probably would be.

My frailty and propensity to illness, and my impressive array of fourteen allergies, all disappeared with the onset of puberty. After the surprising discovery that a bit of stroking produced a gummy liquid from my penis—and that this game could be even more fun if aided by visual stimulation from pictures of androgenous pop stars and svelte young swimmers from cheap fanzines—things started to look up.

A little investigation revealed that masturbation was generally frowned on and was meant to be bad for you. Like politics, death and religion—all areas I would later explore as a theatre director—sex was never discussed in our home. It was deemed unhealthy. This was not my experience. Once I discovered how to jerk off, I started to shed allergies, bronchial problems and asthma, and I became stronger, healthier and happier.

I even started some adventurous investigations of a biological nature with a fellow twelve year old: a South American friend from the public housing estate up the road. His family were recent arrivals—the word *immigrants* was only whispered in suburbia.

Playing in my backyard one day, our game took us into the sweaty confines of the tiny adjacent laundry. Cloistered in the heat, steam and the pungent scent of lavender that emanated from the boiling copper tubs, we became stimulated and aroused and started to strip off, innocently eager to explore each other's hidden bits.

One thing was about to lead to another when my mother decided to check on the progress of her washing. On discovering there was more on the boil than her sheets and towels, she swiftly banished my Latin American friend and exiled me to my room. The public housing estate was declared forever off limits.

After my interrupted attempt at laundry diplomacy, it was back to schoolwork and an occasional wank in the bathroom. It would be decades before Latinos or svelte swimmer types re-entered my life.

Shortly after this incident, which was never discussed and, I suspect, was kept from my father, my mother took me to see *The Man with the Green Carnation*, starring Peter Finch as Oscar Wilde. I enjoyed it and was moved by Wilde's *The Ballad of Reading Gaol*, which I read soon after, although I was never sure if my mother's choice of film was meant as a cautionary tale or career advice.

Over-protection became the new household regime, and visits by friends were no longer encouraged. Indeed, any outside contact appeared unwelcome—even pets—apart from a begrudgingly admitted budgerigar, Blinky Bill, which died. The family home became even more of a fortress. My mother's favourite flowers were orchids. I often felt I was being raised like a rare orchid, one that should be sheltered from the light. Although I enjoyed, even basked in, the intimacy and the care, over time I came to resent this over-protection; it sowed deep seeds of future rebellion.

My adolescent response to the rare-orchid treatment was to retreat into my room, the traditional site of teenage sulking and chaos, concerns about acne, and a cauldron for over-heated imaginations. Here I listened to music on my beloved Pye portable stereo and embraced the new sounds of popular culture.

In the mid 1950s, the term *teenager* was invented to describe those in the thirteen to nineteen demographic. This was later revealed to be an American advertising ploy. If so, it worked. It made us feel special. Being a teenager was fun, but hard work. Being a gay teenager was harder. In 1950s Australia, homosexuality was classified as a crime and a psychological disease. Sexuality was a taboo subject in the home, so I suffered in silence: a troubled teenager, alone in my room.

All the images surrounding me were *straight*, so I assumed I was the exception and sublimated. Of course, this perception was far from the truth. The popular movies of the day were romantic sitcoms starring that sexually ambivalent duo Rock Hudson and Doris Day. Anthony Perkins starred as a transvestite killer in Alfred Hitchcock's *Psycho*, and the bestselling record of the day was *Cry*, by the arrested-for-cruising Johnny Ray.

A side effect of repression is that it encourages delusions of uniqueness. This sense of otherness, or alienation, can be crippling for an individual with conventional aspirations. In a nascent artistic personality it can tap a deep well of emotion and inspiration. Sublimation has produced some of the greatest art; so has its opposite. As an adolescent, my homosexuality was a source of private discomfort, but outwardly I exhibited a relatively curious and cheerful, if somewhat introverted, disposition.

My relationships with school friends were strictly asexual. Beyond early attempts at laundry diplomacy, my erotic adventures were confined to momentary enthusiasms during school swimming carnivals at the Coogee Aquarium. I've been miffed to read of the proclivity of incidents involving the molestation of minors that stemmed from this time. Why didn't anyone want to molest me? Maybe they did and I was too naïve to notice.

I was left with the bathroom mirror and *to be or not to be*. From the waist down, pop stars and swimmers might have held their sway, but, from the waist up, my existential hero was definitely Hamlet.

When I recall the stories that had engaged me since childhood—Enid Blyton's *Famous Five* and stories from the Bible, moving on to *Sherlock Holmes* and, later, Raymond Chandler's detective novels; *The Kon-Tiki Expedition*; Patrick White's *Voss*; favourite operas like *The Magic Flute*; movies such as Stanley Kubrick's *2001: A Space Odyssey*—they all involved quests and explorers and detectives and mysteries. *Who's there?* echoed through them all.

As a teenager, the answer was less likely to be found in literary sources and more likely to emerge from a set of headphones or vinyl-covered speakers, often via trashy popular music. These sounds brought with them a sense of outsider identification, musical exhilaration, release and escape from suffocating conformity. Lou Reed spoke for legions of repressed suburban teenagers when he sang *My life was saved by rock-and-roll*.

My musical tastes would later turn classical, but as a teenager my vinyl collection was predominately white boy rock-and-roll, which, from Elvis onwards, represented the first call to arms of the sexual revolution. Elvis, with his southern blues-inspired rock and swivelling hips, was the Dionysus du Jour. Through popular song and dance, he smuggled African-American sexual energy into white middle-class homes.

My enthusiasm for real African-American music would come later. I'd love to suggest my early influences were Mississippi Delta blues and jazz pioneers like L'il Brother Montgomery, but these would only emerge with time. What held sway on Aussie teenage turntables were vanilla pop chart cover versions of real black music: Elvis' *Heartbreak Hotel*, Johnny O'Keefe's *Shout* and Bill Haley's *Rock Around the Clock*.

Showtunes and musicals formed a more acceptable and equally important part of my adolescence. Most Saturdays, a well-turned-out mother and son would head into the city for a matinee, preceded by a mixed grill at Cahill's, located across from the Prince Edward Cinema, a grand picture palace featuring *Noreen Hennessy at Her Organ*. Cahill's adjoined our matinee destination: JC Williamson's Theatre Royal, which boasted a decorated Victorian foyer, plush red velvet seats, a gilt proscenium and dodgy reproductions of imported shows.

It was a step up from *Sorlie's* pantomimes and tent show variety, if not quite as raw and exciting. I was haunted by the ghost of Grace Sorlie in her extravagant, high-necked black gowns, garlanded with a choker of pearls, sitting grandly at the little fold-up card table that doubled as a ticket desk outside *Sorlie's* tent. On one occasion, Grace interrupted a polite chat with my parents to reveal her deadly weapon: a giant metal torch. Grace thumped a drunk over the head with it and kicked him out, then sweetly offered us complimentary tickets:

Here we are! E 16 to 18. Enjoy the show!

My mother preferred plays to musicals. Googie Withers in *Woman in a Dressing Gown* was her favourite, though, more surprisingly, *Auntie Mame*, with its ribald wit and extravagantly bohemian heroine, also took her fancy.

I loved musicals, but from the outset it was less the mainstream Broadway school than the more challenging variety.

The Piaf-tinged cabaret world of *Irma La Douce* in Peter Brook's staging of a musical about *The girl who helped all Paris relax*, with its Montmartre demimonde and spinning windmills, caught my young eye, as did *West Side Story*. For weeks I was singing *When you're a Jet, you're a Jet all the way* and doing finger clicks in clumsy imitation of Jerome Robbins' dance moves. A few years later it was replaced in my affections by the *Food, Glorious Food!* chorus from Lionel Bart's *Oliver!*, brilliantly designed by Sean Kenny with a revolving Dickensian stage.

Dad's variety contacts guaranteed us frequent visits to the Tivoli, with its vaudeville shows featuring comedians like George Wallace, Buster Fiddess, and Roy Rene as *Mo McCackey*, and glamorous showgirls imitating the dancers at the *Moulin Rouge* or *Casino de Paris*. Nudity was only permitted on Australian stages if the showgirls were static—it was always showgirls, never boys—so variety shows featured erotic tableaux in the spirit of Delacroix. They were solemnly announced as being *Direct from le Louvre*. These tableaux offered titillation disguised as culture and were hugely popular with the Australian public.

Dad also managed to get ringside seats at Sydney Stadium for concerts by imported American entertainers like Johnny Ray, Roy Orbison, Frank Sinatra—who wore Sinatra Red suits—and Guy Mitchell, who wore Mitchell Blue. I was intrigued by Spike Jones and his City Slickers, a surreal comedy act with a dwarf who scampered out of a drum kit. Dad's favourite was Louis *Satchmo* Armstrong.

I have my parents to thank for a generous introduction to the showbiz end of theatre and performance, yet it was another relative who opened the door to a world that combined music and theatre: opera.

My cousin Shirley was an eager recipient of Dad's annual free tickets to the Easter Show, and she relished her visits to sideshow alley. Maybe they triggered a few romantic showbiz inclinations, as Shirley went on to marry an operatic baritone: John Germain. Shirley traded in her job as a hairdresser and became wig mistress with the opera company. To reciprocate my father's Easter Show generosity, she arranged for me to attend opera matinees at the Elizabethan Theatre at Newtown.

The Barber of Seville, with Cousin John as a fine matinee Figaro, was thought suitable for a teenager, and so it proved to be. My first attempts at shaving were accompanied by loud renditions of the barber's catchy anthem: *Figaro, Figaro, Figaro!* I also recall an exciting outing to Bizet's *Carmen*, where the curtain had to be held between acts. The lead tenor was rushed to hospital after a sword-fight mishap, but he returned triumphantly and finished the show with many bows and to great applause. I'd developed a taste for tinsel at Saturday matinees, but I liked being reminded that a bit of blood, sweat and tears from boxing troupes past were still part of the equation.

As an excited thirteen year old, I accompanied my parents to the opening night of the first Australian musical on the Elizabethan Theatre stage, also courtesy of the generous Germains. Cousin John had scored a featured role in this show. *Lola Montez* was set in Ballarat during the gold rush. An opening chorus celebrated southerly busters and introduced the refreshing idea that musicals could encompass the Australian vernacular. I remember standing through much of the performance, partly from excitement and partly because I wasn't much higher than the rail of the theatre box from which we viewed the show.

The story concerned the goldfields tour of the Irish-born *Spanish* femme fatale Lola Montez, and featured her set-piece, the provocative *Spider Dance*, accompanied by the reactions of the Ballarat locals. The highlight was Lola horsewhipping the editor of the local rag in the main street after a less than generous review of her dubious stage act.

Buried in the tuneful score and lively if conventional staging were a few sharp observations on culture, local and imported. *Lola Montez* proved a deserved success with audiences and pioneered the notion that a large-scale, sophisticated Australian musical was possible.

As short pants gave way to long, I was allowed to attend the theatre by myself, and I continued the Saturday matinee ritual well into my late teens. On one such outing, I had a minor epiphany that anticipated future encounters with the work of Duchamp, Warhol and Kubrick and was just as influential. My revelation occurred in the dress circle of the old Theatre Royal, the venue where I had been a spectator to so many imported plays and musicals. This was my first taste of a play that captured my own experience of life in the suburbs and presented it in an imaginative, poetic style that succeeded in mythologising the everyday.

Patrick White's *The Season at Sarsaparilla* spoke in a voice I recognised. It was simultaneously familiar and imaginatively strange. Set around three households in the mythical suburb of Sarsaparilla—the Boyles, the Pogsons and the Knotts—it unfolded like a mediaeval mystery play, with each suburban kitchen representing a vision of heaven, earth and hell; though which was which remained an open question. It certainly didn't pull any punches about the spiritual damage inflicted by the mind-numbing conformity of suburbia.

The satire was hilarious and certainly struck a sympathetic chord with me, but it was the mysteries of heaven, earth and hell wrapped in a theatrical razzle-dazzle of familiarity, the delight in rich vernacular language and the stark dramatic confrontations in suburban homes that truly engaged my imagination. I was also intrigued by the play's suggestion that in the battle between desire, represented by the baying dogs of Sarsaparilla, and repressive suburban conformity, the life force was the ultimate victor.

Until *Sarsaparilla*, most Australian theatre had implied that life was something that happened elsewhere—usually London, Paris or New York. White's play changed all that for me. It was what I had been unknowingly seeking through my youthful theatre-going, and John Tasker's inventive production gave resonant voice to White's brilliant charade of suburbia. Australian playwriting was beginning to make its presence felt around the country, but *Sarsaparilla* was an inspiration, and it was to *Sarsaparilla* that I was destined, one day, to return.

Another theatrical epiphany had preceded *Sarsaparilla* some years earlier, when I was about fourteen. After returning home from an especially enjoyable variety performance at the Tiv, the family settled in for a cup of tea and a post-mortem on what we'd all just seen. I became particularly thoughtful before quietly announcing to my surprised parents:

I would like to do something like that.

My father looked very alarmed. I'm sure he was picturing his offspring weathering a lifetime of unemployment, penury and dodgy company.

He replied slowly and sceptically:

You want to be a performer?

No.

Pause.

There must have been someone who ... imagined it up.

Long pause.

That's what I want to be.

WALKABOUT

Walking, walking. For many years I lugged a Globite school case stuffed with essays, heavy text books and my daily rations of cheese and tomato sandwiches along the one-mile stretch down Avoca Street to Randwick Boys' High School. Before the current, more enlightened, fashion of colourful back-packs for kids, these lumpy brown Globites introduced generations of Australian schoolchildren to lopsided posture, hunched shoulders and a downcast, bitumen-focused gaze. The march of the Globites inevitably led to school. In my case, the drudgery was only alleviated by the encouragement of an inspiring English and music teacher, and the chance to play percussion and dabble backstage on school productions of *Trial by Jury*, *South Pacific* and, every schoolboy's adventure fantasy, *The Pirates of Penzance*. Fortunately, our headmaster, Mr Johnstone, harboured Broadway impresario aspirations. Each year my increasingly mediocre grades, especially in science and maths, were balanced by my zealous commitment to Mr J's high school spectaculars.

Randwick Boys' High was a lively, if rough-and-ready, school. A rugged environment for a sensitive, would-be thespian. We weren't cosseted, and we quickly learnt strategies for dealing with the harsher realities of life in a wider world. That my school indulged in extra-curricular theatre was a bonus, as the showbiz bug had bitten early and the itch would help sustain me through my otherwise uneventful school years.

My theatrical involvement had its provenance at the Randwick Municipal Library. Here, aged eight, after some hasty lessons from the Great Levante, I made a precocious Saturday matinee debut as an amateur magician. It was a brief performance to a boisterous audience of fellow tots, comprising cloaks and wands and disappearing eggs. The climax, borrowed from Les Levante, involved sawing my assistant in half in a make-shift cardboard box. My assistant was only seven and very plump; but she was beautiful to my eyes.

PREVIOUS PAGES: Clovelly

Walking, walking. And sweating in the stinking heat along with thousands of other forcibly assembled schoolkids. All of us were in Centennial Park, gripping tiny Union Jacks to wave at a swiftly passing Land Rover containing the recently crowned Queen Elizabeth II and her cardboard cut-out of a uniformed husband. In the quacking duck pond of a park that had once celebrated the birth of Australian Federation, my republican sentiments were born. It was the intolerable heat, the forced assembly, the speeding Land Rover, the brevity of this foreign monarch's wave, the general absurdity of the whole situation. This ludicrous experience was crowned when I opened my sunstruck Globite and was hit by a right royal stench. Any lingering monarchist sentiments vanished as I stared into a putrid pile of melted cheese and tomato sandwiches.

Walking, walking. Running, fielding, bowling, batting, and then, thankfully, reading—usually after I'd been bowled out for a duck at the cricket pitch on school sports days.

Many of my schoolmates were from immigrant families, which meant their strengths were either sport or debating. I was the only Celt on our school debating team; there was one Anglo type and the remaining members were Greek or Russian or from Jewish families who had immigrated to Australia via Shanghai after the war. The parents ended up playing the pokies at the Hakoah Club at Bondi, while their kids jostled with bleached blond stompie-wompie surfer boys on what became known as the Jerusalem Steps at Bondi Beach.

The smartest of these kids went on to become doctors and lawyers, while the rest became tradesmen or went into real estate and development. The realtors, sad to say, helped transform the lovely old houses of the area into rows of ugly, box-like home units—a Sydney tradition that persists today.

Since the arrival of the First Fleet, immigration and cultural integration have been central to Australian life and the driving force behind the country's development. Wars and revolutions are often the catalyst for immigration, and the settlement rituals remain essentially the same. I first saw them enacted in the concrete amphitheatre of the Randwick Boys' High School playground. New arrivals were always greeted with suspicion. Their parents, disconcerted and often language-challenged, had brought up their children in the ways of their old culture, be it European, Mediterranean or Asian. They would cling to familiar traditions while their kids desperately wanted to belong. Things were sorted out in the rough and tumble of the schoolyard.

Kids hate being called names: Chinks, Wogs, Dagos, Tin Lids, Blacks, Lebs, Slopes, Skips, Cats, Towel-heads or Mussies. Later, they might become more sophisticated and wear these labels as a badge of honour, but initially they either retreat or become more Aussie than the Aussies. The next generation usually balances their parents' cultural past and their Australian future, and then another wave arrives and the whole cycle begins again.

I recently returned to my old school and was relieved to discover that the POW Nissen huts shipped from Darwin after the war to serve as classrooms had mercifully vanished, and that grass and garden areas had humanised the bleak cement playing areas. However, playground assimilation rituals remained in full swing; though these days it's between Chinese, Japanese, Thais, Indians and Pacific Islanders. Diversity has been with me from showground to schoolyard. I grew up in an era fearful of immigration, and wherever possible I have opened up opportunities to those who could bring a different perspective to Australian culture. Our society was built on immigration, yet each new generation seems to find new ways to resist the idea. It remains fodder for politicians, who play on either the fear or the promise brought by new blood, energy and ideas. The cycle seems endless: visionaries promote hope; reactionaries promote fear. In my experience, it's in the school playground, far from the citadels of political power, where the realpolitik of tomorrow's cultural landscape is determined.

Walking, walking. Saturday was entertainment day in the city, but I was left to my own devices on Sundays. In that six-o'clock-pub-closing, standing up for *God Save the Queen* and church-going era, the seventh day was God's Day; so there was nothing to do. Shops, pubs and restaurants were closed, apart from corner stores dispensing bread and milk. It was around this time that I realised heaven, to which we were all meant to aspire, might be a very boring place. To fill the Sunday void, there had been short lived attempts at church fellowship and boy scouts; but I was a loner, not a joiner. So I walked.

My weekend pleasure involved a long and wonderful solitary hike from Coogee to Bondi along a miraculous stretch of Pacific coastline: all craggy rocks scented with salt-sea air and forever vistas of sea and sky, with a *to be or not to be* cliff-top cemetery thrown in for good measure.

I'd set out early on Sundays, past village-like shops, and churches with their neatly attired congregations, then downhill past beach-side homes, fish and chipperies, squash and tennis courts where I often played, on to Coogee Beach, with its rowdy milk bars and elegantly tiled and cabined swimming aquarium, and its snug white curve of sand marked out with little yellow and red flags and a lookout tower for lifesavers.

From here, the real walk began. I'd stride around the untouched cliffs and headlands, passing moored dinghies, weekend anglers and the fish scaling granite slabs of Gordon's Bay; then the black-rubber-clad snorkellers and divers at surf-free and Mediterranean-style Clovelly Beach … walking up and down the escarpments and beyond the graveyards past the family barbecues on Bronte Beach, and Tamarama, later known as Glamarama, with treacherous surf and cliff-top views of sunbakers … walking, circling around to my destination … the boomerang-shaped beach and wide curling waves of Bondi and a welcome ice-cream soda.

The walk took three hours. Then, I'd catch the bus home. I did this religiously, most Sundays of my teenage years. I could take that walk in my sleep; often do. Coastal walks are in my blood. If I have a songline, it's that stretch of coast.

Walking, walking. I walked out of Randwick Boys' High into an uncertain future. My schooling had concluded with indifferent exam results and I failed to qualify for university. This was a severe blow, as an arts degree offered the best possible way to pursue my artistic aspirations. My parents were very understanding and, while my mother realised it was a setback for my ambitions, my father felt that by joining the work-force I might get some experience of what he called *real life*. After all, the Sharmans were not known for their academic prowess; their skills lay elsewhere. I wanted to pursue my directing dream, so I looked for something vaguely arts related and found a job with an advertising agency. Here I was meant to work my way up from the ground floor as a humble messenger boy, and I might eventually acquire skills in television production.

The job was really a compromise worked out with my parents, who remained dubious about my theatrical ambitions. Having flunked university entrance, there were few educational outlets available to me as an aspiring thespian. *Go to England* was the advice. Advertising seemed a pragmatic alternative, at least until something better presented itself.

Being the messenger boy meant more walking as I crisscrossed the city, delivering my parcels. I was a quick walker, which gave me time to stop off at a few book and record stores, such as Rowe Street Records, tucked discreetly behind the iconic—at least to me—Theatre Royal. Edels Record Store in King Street became the scene of a later and fateful meeting with the author and playwright Patrick White.

I would browse in these shops and keep up with the latest, occasionally parting with my modest earnings on a new book or recording. There were only a few such havens in Sydney at this time, and the proprietors and sales assistants, such as George Cooke at Rowe Street and Peter Sainthill at Edels, saw themselves as cultural emissaries. In an era before anony-mous check-outs, they would strike up conversations; enjoy my youthful interest; encourage me to listen to this or to read that. I became the appreciative audience for their en-thusiasms and sought out anything that was new or interesting.

I'd missed out on a tertiary education, so I would make up for it on the hoof.

The local branch of the American-based advertising agency where I worked, Hansen-Rubensohn-McCann-Erickson, was located in a modern building that, in 1963, passed for a skyscraper. Caltex House, all eight storeys of it, was on the Sydney Harbour Bridge approach. The agency turned out to be a magnet for many would-be artists earning a steady wage while waiting for their dreams to be fulfilled; and many were. They were a smart lot. The staff included author-to-be Bryce Courtenay, who managed the Coca-Cola and Mortein fly spray accounts, and copywriters and directors like film-maker Bruce Beresford, future screenwriter and political speechwriter Bob Ellis, and Sandy Harbutt, an Ensemble Theatre actor and the director of Australia's first ever biker movie, *Stone*.

The agency staff were friendly, and as many were frustrated artists, we were in the same boat; though, as well-paid graduates, they were travelling first class, while, unqualified and a teenage courier, I was in steerage. I recall great conversations with and good advice from Bruce Beresford, who allowed me to observe filming and to help out on the documentary he was making at weekends about sculptor Clement Meadmore. Bruce's generosity offered me a first glimpse into the mystery of film-making.

The writer Bob Ellis intrigued me by arriving late every day, dishevelled and eating yoghurt, which seemed very bohemian and impressive. Bob would apprehend me on my office rounds to engage in entertaining chitchat about theatre, books and politics. His opinions would be interspersed with gossipy tales of his exaggerated love-life: stormy episodes involving daughters of media moguls and late-night car chases. Bob's capacity for self-dramatisation was highly enjoyable and a sure indicator that his screenwriting ambitions would be fulfilled. I recall his description of Clem Meadmore's sculptures as *giant leaden butterflies*, and around this time I began to see the connection between writers and directors, how writing prompted a visual response and vice versa.

Bob was the first in a long procession of writers I would meet and, had he been Shakespeare, I couldn't have had a livelier introduction to the ways of this brave new world. Through our innocent corridor conversations I was unconsciously rehearsing a pattern of connection that would augur well in future writer –director collaborations.

Walking, walking. Aged eighteen, I walked away from advertising and into public broadcasting, but I was still a courier. My exit from advertising had been prompted by a test aimed at assessing the imaginative potential of the staff. Given my history with school exams, I approached the test with caution. I needn't have worried. School exams, especially in that learning-by-rote era, were about regurgitating facts, but a test involving imagination produced a very different outcome. I scored 100 per cent.

What would you like to do? enquired a surprised executive.

Well ... I considered ... If I'm that imaginative ... leave.

And I did. Just like that.

My new job at the Australian Broadcasting Commission was of a similar shit-kicker variety, but it held the promise of bringing me closer to my goal. I would work hard and climb the ladder towards the holy grail of becoming a television director. This simplistic theory didn't take into account the fact that the ABC was part of the public service and, as in most bureaucracies, it moved slowly and valued plodders and time servers ahead of those with more talent and less patience. There would be no imagination tests at the ABC. After the zoom and zip of advertising, the city crossings with record store stopovers, it was a shock to find myself stuck in a kombivan driving from building to scattered building, from department to department, in the company of an entertaining, if foul-mouthed, driver. Like Fagin from the musical *Oliver!*, our slightly crazy man-at-the-wheel, whose delightfully eccentric sister played harp in the ABC Orchestra, spent cabin time between stops recounting lascivious tales of his sexual conquests and instructing his young charges in how best to rort the system.

It wasn't all bad. Delivering mail meant we touched base with every department, and I soon gained first-hand experience of how a large arts organisation was run. And in an echo of my corridor chats at the ad agency, I met colourful characters.

The most stimulating and enduring of these encounters was with composer Richard Meale, at the time head of music programming for the ABC. Richard recognised something in me and took me under his wing, continuing from where the record store emissaries had left off. Through him, my knowledge of music was widened, and I was introduced to the pleasures of Stravinsky and Bartok and heard influential obscurities like the Virgil Thomson and Gertrude Stein modernist miracle *Four Saints in Three Acts*—one of the liveliest, if least known, twentieth-century operas. I attended concerts by the Sydney Symphony Orchestra under their African-American conductor Dean Dixon. Richard introduced me to a world of musical sophistication, and I was an eager and attentive student. He also introduced me to literature, and it was through him that I first encountered Patrick White's *Voss*, which I found to be both extraordinary and difficult to read, and Genet's *Our Lady of the Flowers*, the first book I read that dealt with homosexuality in an era of secrecy, illegality, censorship and blackmail.

Richard himself was *a confirmed bachelor*, as gay people were known at the time, though he didn't dwell on the topic, especially with an impressionable teenager. I gained insights from reading the subversive Genet novel, with its lovingly detailed criminal exploits of Darling and Divine in their Montmartre attic overlooking the cemetery—even though it was a million miles from my own experience, or lack there of.

It was a lively time for contemporary music in Sydney. There seemed to be premieres of orchestral or chamber compositions almost every month. I heard early performances of Richard's *Homage to Garcia Lorca*, *Clouds Now and Then* and *Very High Kings*, and new works by Peter Sculthorpe and Nigel Butterly, all composers in their creative prime.

This compensated for the tedium of my job. I had made the innocent error of being proficient at my work and was soon virtually running the department, which meant the public servant in charge could take longer liquid lunches. Consequently, he wasn't keen to recommend my promotion. Months of mail-shovelling passed as incompetents were moved up the ladder while my diligence was rewarded by shrugs and shaking heads.

To compensate for the frustration of my working days, I enrolled in a technical college night course to study television production. I also involved myself in amateur theatricals, and at the behest of a friendly, rotund solicitor and his soprano companion, I was soon in productions of the topsy-turvy operas by those great purveyors of Empire, anarchy and tuneful satirical songs, Gilbert and Sullivan.

In collaboration with old schoolfriend Ian Cookesley, I established the Young Savoyards, under whose banner we presented a startling version of the G&S obscurity *Princess Ida*, at the Sydney Conservatorium. This amateur production was my first theatrical outing as a director. Its modest success encouraged my directorial ambitions, and the production had some surprising consequences. Among the cast was a tenor named Ian Campbell who would one day become an opera impresario and invite me to direct Benjamin Britten's *Death in Venice*. But that was years away; for the moment, Ian Campbell was an amateur teenage tenor playing an improbable mediaeval knight disguised as a transvestite nun in order to gain access to his beloved Princess Ida, who was locked behind convent walls. Still living at home at Randwick, and at eighteen still relatively sexually innocent, I no doubt had some sympathy with her plight.

Being a production student by night and a diligent courier by day was an exhausting combination, but my ABC promotion did eventuate. The next step up the ladder was becoming a stagehand for ABC Television. As a rookie, I was rostered on to the dawn shift at the aptly named Gore Hill. By night, I was studying or rehearsing, then waking at 4 a.m. to catch a bus to the ABC studios on the other side of the harbour. Once I signed on, I would lay endless checkerboard tiles for television variety shows.

My limited manual skills and physical frailty did not recommend me for this job. In a climactic scene worthy of a silent movie comedy, I was blown down a hill while carrying a tall canvas flat in a strong gale, ending with my head poking clownishly through the torn fabric. I was sacked, but as no one is dismissed in the public service, I was merely bundled back to the mail department. The drunken department head was smug and triumphant. He resumed his long lunches and I shovelled mail in despair.

Shortly after this demise, I was also thrown out of the television production course. My departure followed an incident where I declined to change a camera-operating student's cathode-ray tube while I was meant to be directing a program. My arrogant, if accurate, defence was that there were many students who knew how to replace equipment but only one who knew how to direct. This was thought unteam-like, unegalitarian, almost unAustralian. Again, I was out on my ear. Decades later, the tutor who had dismissed me apologised when he found himself sound assistant on one of my feature films. It was an awkward scene of guilt and regret that we both managed with some grace.

At this bleak moment in 1963, I was desperately in need of someone to throw a Fantale my way.

My cousin Shirley Germain miraculously came to the rescue, and the page-turning took care of itself. Shirley understood my situation better than most, having married a baritone and thrown in her job security to join the ranks of the recently formed, but by no means established, Elizabethan Trust Opera. My mother and Shirley were close, and the latter was aware of my thwarted desire to enter the theatre, having seen my amateur G&S production. Through her opera contacts, Shirley was also aware of the recently opened National Institute of Dramatic Art—NIDA.

It was a sign of the changing times that there was suddenly a place in the cultural landscape for a training institute for the serious study of theatre in all its forms. It would be another two decades before the Australian Film, Television and Radio

School—AFTRS—was established for the training of future film-makers. Once I became aware of NIDA, I became determined to study there, though I would need some economic support to see me through the two-year production course. I'd saved some money from my modest advertising and ABC wages but I needed supplementary income from my parents.

My father was happy enough to see me involved in amateur theatricals. He had even driven our G&S band around on nocturnal poster-pasting adventures, but he could not conceive of theatre as a career. In his mind, it was all unemployed hoofers, artsy types, poofters—he obviously hadn't been informed about the laundry incident—and pie eaters, so named because cheap pies were all theatrical types could afford to eat.

He didn't have the numbers. John Germain's experienced entreaties, backed up by Shirley and my mother, along with my own determination, were a formidable force. This was the battle my father was destined to lose. After a few days of nail-biting anxiety on my part, during which I privately determined it was time to leave the family home, my father emerged from his deliberations.

Well. If that's what my son really wants, who am I to stand in his way?

A decade later, and after a string of theatrical successes and a necessary, if very awkward, conversation about my sexuality —the fact of my homosexuality being something my father acknowledged but subsequently ignored—this was recalled as:

I was with him every step of the way!

I was nineteen. It was 1964. And the gods entering Valhalla couldn't have been happier than I was as I stepped excitedly out the front door and strode down to High Street, Kensington, and through the gates of NIDA, into an uncertain but self-determined future.

Walking, walking. My Sunday coastal walks became a thing of the past. They were replaced by a daily stride from Randwick to the University of New South Wales and a cluster of shacks and charming old Racecourse Totalisator Buildings that housed NIDA. The welcome sight of an ancient, brooding and magnificent Moreton Bay fig that presided over the leafy courtyard more than compensated for any loss of coastal vistas. It was a very different landscape from the vast bustling empire that NIDA has since become. In those early days of NIDA's evolution the modesty of the venues seemed to suit the times.

I was at a point in my life when, in order to mature, I sensed the need to be tested by an idea bigger than myself. Given my background, the curious mix of carnival and conformity, of solitude, sublimation and illness spiralling back to my *to be or not to be* birth, I wanted to explore life's complexities; theatre was a way of achieving this aim and sharing whatever insights I gleaned along the way with a wider audience. From the outset, I saw theatre as a vocation and a place of revelation.

For many fellow students, NIDA meant career preparation. Some had romantic and, it must be said, short-lived fantasies of stardom; a few sought entry into a glamorous world of sex, celebrity and parties. But to me it felt like I had finally found my calling. I was up for the challenge, to be tested and found worthy or wanting.

Eager for knowledge, I set out to extract every possible scrap of theatrical insight available. Young students who had arrived virtually straight from school and hadn't experienced what my father called *real life* often appeared to be waiting to be instructed, to be told or taught something; I'd had a taste of life and was hungry to learn. I was grateful for the opportunity to pursue my vocation and determined to make the most of it.

Which was just as well, for, in those early years, not a lot was taught at NIDA, though a great deal could be learnt. The subject of directing, for instance, was often dismissed as *something you'll pick up along the way*. The emphasis was practical: making scenery, costumes, rigging lights; and this I enjoyed.

As production students, we were also unpaid labour, amateur technicians for the on-campus professional theatre, the Old Tote. This meant long hours, studying by day and working shows by night. Others regarded this as exploitation, and, as a training system, it was banished decades ago; but I seized the rare opportunity for practical experience. That I neither saw daylight nor had any social life was all grist to the mill.

The NIDA staff of the day included some of the great warrior-pioneers of postwar Australian theatre: the enigmatic theatre politician Robert Quentin, the genial and practical Tom Brown and the Australian drama advocate Robin Lovejoy. I eagerly knocked on their doors and sought out their knowledge and advice. Through their mentoring, especially that of Robin Lovejoy, who seemed tuned to my needs, I learnt a great deal.

The fashion of the day was Theatre of the Absurd, and I experienced early productions of works by Harold Pinter, Max Frisch, Joe Orton and Edward Albee. These were mostly directed by a recent arrival from Tasmania, John Clark, who was to become director of NIDA and who oversaw its expansion into the current and impressive collection of theatres and village-like training studios on Anzac Parade.

John was the only modernist theatre director at NIDA, and his excellent production of Albee's confronting *Who's Afraid of Virginia Woolf?* revealed how controversy could shift the boundaries and perception of theatre from cottage industry to headline-grabbing, hit-the-nerve box-office bonanza. I worked on many productions over my two years, but it's the memory of spending night after night trying to study Stanislavsky or Brecht while simultaneously operating creaky lighting equipment as my ears were pummelled by Albee's rhythmic, gut-wrenching dialogue that has stayed with me from this time.

The acting students spent their days hurling their bodies around in leotards to *O Fortuna*, from Carl Orff's *Carmina Burana*, in Margaret Barr's legendary movement classes, or pacing under the courtyard fig tree, earnestly learning lines and gossiping about who got what part while biting their nails, flirting or showing off. Nail and knuckle biting were common in the often hothouse atmosphere of NIDA, and I was a prime offender. The only negative inheritance from my student days was the taking up of cigarettes—replacing one bad habit with another—after a fellow student stared in horror at my hands and announced to anyone who could hear:

Your fingers are bleeding!

While the actors were a world apart from the production students, I became close friends with a few: Helen Morse, Ross Thompson and Helmut Bakaitis, the future screenwriter of my first film, *Shirley Thompson Versus the Aliens*. Helmut, who had European heritage, introduced me to German language theatre through a recording of Kurt Weill's *The Threepenny Opera* (*Die Dreigroschenoper*) featuring Lotte Lenya. I was entranced, and through Lotte's husky voice, my romance with German cabaret and Weimar theatre began. It would filter through much of my work, including *Rocky Horror*, and its influence is still present today. Both Helmut and Lotte have a lot to answer for.

Other discoveries included Strindberg's *Dreamplay*, for which I developed a fascination that would be explored later, and, on a Broadway note, the Leonard Bernstein musical *Candide*. Tom Brown, NIDA's director at the time, had assisted Tyrone Guthrie on the original Broadway production. This musical satire, a pilgrim's progress of a young naïf through the glories and disasters of the eighteenth-century Enlightenment, was based on Voltaire, with a score by Bernstein and book by Lillian Hellman, and abrasive lyrics by other New York literati including Richard Wilbur and Dorothy Parker (*Poets have said love is undying, my love / Don't be misled / They were all lying, my love*). Its chaotic structure and subversive satire gave it cult status, but having had more than a few *Candide*-like experiences myself in my apprentice days, it became part of the soundtrack to my NIDA years, and was often a subject of enjoyable discussion between Tom Brown and myself.

At the end of our course, and facing an uncertain future, I put together a modest production of Shelagh Delaney's *A Taste of Honey* at the Cell Block Theatre. I cast both Helmut and an incandescent Helen Morse. Many of the tender sensitivities of our young student lives were translated into that production. It was a great success and helped us to establish our various professional credentials.

Years later, and after dozens of productions, I asked my mother to nominate her favourite and she recalled this initial one.

Why? I asked.

Because it was the last time you allowed a human emotion to cross a stage.

In truth, my parents only occasionally saw my productions, though they would later enjoy the musicals. There were no Mrs or Mr Worthingtons in my home—no pushy stage parents.

In my second year, when I had finally cut the link with home and moved into a student share-house, the family reactions were the opposite of what I expected. My mother was upset, possibly seeing her life diminished in those solitary months stretching ahead when her husband was away, while my father, either through relief or economic gratitude, was enthusiastic. In truth, he was the more realistic and aware that the time had come for me to make my own way in the world. Whatever private doubts he harboured about my chosen profession and my companions, he ultimately endorsed my independence. Leaving home, after all, was something of a Sharman tradition.

There were no sentimental farewells; I packed and converted daily contact into weekend phone calls. Just like that.

My workload meant that I saw as little of the pleasant enough Coogee Beach student share-house as I had the family home. However, there were a few candlelit student dinners, after which guitars appeared. Helen Morse, who was a fine throaty singer, Helmut and others would offer renditions of songs by Piaf, Brecht and Weill. Euro-cabaret chimed with my showground background and became an enthusiasm that developed into an obsession.

It was in stark contrast to the Stanislavsky-style norm we were taught at NIDA. Brecht and cabaret valued action over motive, fact over fiction, and they directly addressed the audience, carnival style. It was considered vulgar at the time to overly consider the audience, yet this made little sense to me, as the presence of an audience was the central ingredient in making it theatre. These ideas were in chrysalis stage, but those late-night sing-a-longs and the casual introduction to Brechtian-style theatrical ideas were crucial to my rejection of the fashionable naturalism of the day; they were the genesis of what would later emerge as an untypical and highly personal approach to theatre.

Everything that happened, on- or off-campus, in those two years at NIDA contributed to my growth and experience; but an incidental event that occured almost by chance left the most telling impression and conveyed a deeper insight into my chosen profession.

I had expressed concern that there was no training available in directing opera. The response was to invite Stefan Beinl, an elderly Viennese director who had worked at the Wiener Staatsoper, to take some classes. Stefan was now resident with our opera company, but his ways were those of an earlier era and his classes were quietly derided by my colleagues. Herr B's approach was puppet-style:

You put him … here! She holds him … there!

All this was delivered in a thick Austrian accent, as Stefan flung sniggering students around the rehearsal space. Rebellion was in the air. I could tell my fellow students would not take much more Teutonic puppet-mastery. Yet, this man had lived through astounding times and experienced great periods of European theatre history, including the work of Max Reinhardt, Bertold Brecht and Walter Felsenstein. If we could get beyond the traffic cop shoving and shouting, I felt sure there was something to learn.

I was pondering all this in Ashwoods, a popular second-hand record shop, when I chanced on a recording of highlights from a 1933 version of Strauss' *Der Rosenkavalier*, conducted by Wilhelm Furtwängler. The opera was schmaltzy, at least to my taste, yet it exemplified Viennese romanticism and I sensed it might strike a chord with Herr B. I bought it.

My colleagues' complaints had been heard. Our next opera lesson with Herr B was to be the last. Aware of the mood, Stefan arrived looking a little melancholy as he prepared to launch into our final session of push and shove. I enquired if he would listen to something with us and, perhaps, explain it.

Intrigued, he agreed. I put on the recording. Slowly, as the crackling sounds of a prewar era emerged from the speakers, this tall, rigid man became very agitated. The ageing character of the Marschallin launched into her great aria, and Herr B reached for a handkerchief. It was the voice of legendary German soprano Lotte Lehmann, singing of passing time, ageing, loss and regret.

Herr B burst into tears and seemed almost to dissolve in front of his embarrassed, awed and suddenly very attentive students:

They … they are all dead … the war … the war … and Lotte … Furtwängler … Where? … And I am … here … in Australia …

Herr B's words trailed off. The class didn't resume. We sat together and listened to the recording. In the silence that accompanied our meditation, I intuited a little about opera and a great deal more about time and history and the hidden power of art.

Walking, walking. No, running. Running up the stairs of a nondescript office block in Hunter Street, Sydney. I was eager to meet the Wizards of Oz. The frosted-glass panel in the door leading to *Oz* magazine reminded me of the 1940s private detective–type offices from Dashiell Hammett thrillers. I calmed myself and entered. Instead of Hammett's hard-bitten protagonist Sam Spade, I was confronted by the very attractive and always serenely businesslike Marsha Rowe. Marsha was aware of my interest in creating a stage revue from the popular and controversial satirical magazine and pointed me in the direction of the Wizards. I set off down the yellow brick road to meet all three; I had a plan.

My NIDA years had ended well: a merry-go-round design for Kurt Weill's *The Threepenny Opera*, followed by a graduation production of Tennessee Williams' portrait of over-sensitive youth, *The Glass Menagerie*. On leaving NIDA, I had formed the Group Theatre—*A Taste of Honey* was our first production.

Things were off to a good start, but I was looking for something less conventional for the next Group Theatre production. It was around this time that I chanced on *Oz*, which embodied the street-smart iconoclastic humour of the day and seemed ripe for adaptation to a very Australian satirical revue.

The three Wizards were writers Richard Walsh and Richard Neville and cartoonist Martin Sharp. There were other contributors to *Oz*, like Peter Draffen and the excellent, if oddly named, Richard Raper, but the initial trio were the origina tors, editors and driving force behind the magazine. My meetings with them were as curious as they were revealing.

As well as editing *Oz*, Richard Walsh was studying medicine and had a night-shift job as a lift operator. He was a fabulous workaholic, and it was not surprising that he ended up running one of Australia's largest publishing empires. I enjoyed my many nocturnal conversations with him as we went up and down between floors in a dingy old-fashioned elevator, with Richard occasionally referring to a medical textbook balanced precariously on his knees.

Richard Neville worked in advertising at Jackson Wain, and I met him at the North Sydney pool, where he reclined in a banana chair while dictating advertising copy for menthol cigarettes to a glamorous secretary in a bikini. I assumed he was a playboy. Richard went on to establish *Oz* in London and became embroiled in a famous obscenity trial that ultimately helped to repeal British press censorship laws. The exponent of free love then returned to Australia, married and became a social commentator.

I first met Martin Sharp in his family home, *Wirian*, where he still resides, though now in a different wing. His mother padded about in slacks, looking like Judy Garland, with an ever-present glass of whisky in her hand, while Martin sat, with brush and pen, and worked at turning a white page black.

He had a beautiful blonde girlfriend, Anou Kiisler, who seemed to know exactly when the drawing or cartoon was finished and would snatch the paper away. Martin would continue, unperturbed, on the next page. He developed a unique form of narrative cartoon and, from this satirical base, developed into one of Australia's most original, eccentric and inventive artists.

After a brilliant period in London, Martin returned to Australia, where time and events finally tempered his output and he appeared to retreat into *Wirian*. Apart from the composer Richard Meale, Martin was the first person I'd met whom I regarded as a serious artist. To me and many others, he was the real Wizard of Oz.

All three agreed to the revue and all contributed great material. As cartoonist and satirist, Martin ended up contributing most to the success of what became known as *On Stage Oz*. It played for months at makeshift venues, capturing the imagination of an increasingly large audience and helping to revitalise revue in Sydney.

While it was the kind of satirical revue that, today, would feature on television or in a comedy festival, it was my first experience of an original work that spoke directly to its audience. The success of the revue gave me the confidence to continue pursuing productions with a distinctly Australian voice.

My contact with the slightly older Wizards also led me out of suburban Coogee and into the newly renovated and briefly bohemian Paddington. I moved into a converted terrace house near the Windsor Castle Hotel, a small rowdy pub that was once, inexplicably, the hub for Sydney's youth-quake generation.

Overnight, I entered the world of fashion, Pop Art, sex and drugs that swirled around the Wizards in the mid 1960s. As I was younger, shyer, more suburban and probably more puritanical, something held my enthusiasm for these temptations in check, though drugs certainly kicked in: my intense production schedule encouraged an enthusiasm for Dexedrine and tiny amphetamine tablets called Purple Hearts. It was a short-lived enthusiasm I was destined to regret.

I was rehearsing different plays in the morning, afternoon and night. Some were short works for a city lunch-time theatre, others were oddities like a kids' commedia dell'arte version of

Punch and Judy performed in shopping malls. This production was obviously intended to amuse children while their parents emptied their pockets in the neighbouring shops; however, it proved far too visceral and startling for its infant audience and several crying tots had to be taken away and comforted in the mini-mall.

There was a brief attempt at combining theatre and disco in the tiny, backstreet Wayside Chapel Theatre in Kings Cross. In the hope of opening theatre to a young audience, dance sets were interspersed with bursts of short plays, culminating in a midnight performance of Genet's *The Maids*. Richard Meale recorded a soundtrack, improvised on the chapel's organ, and the murderous maids were played by two handsome young actors straight from a brief stint in jail for shoplifting.

Against a setting of black-and-white hothouse flowers designed by my extrovert artist-to-be housemate Michael Ramsden, the actors emerged in sweaty plastic French maids' outfits to confront a masked Madame, played by my other housemate, Pat Bishop. This kinetic midnight mass production created a sense of delirium in the audience, and I often had to help revive fainting patrons.

All this was heady stuff. A busy social life sent me reeling from drag shows at the Purple Onion—where the wickedly inspired David Williams, as drag diva Beatrice, reigned supreme in transvestite entertainments like *A Streetcar Named Beatrice*—to dancing *In the Midnight Hour*, an anthem of the day, at Rhubarbs, an underground club in the Spanish ghetto of Liverpool Street, and to the gritty sounds of rhythm and blues band Python Lee Jackson. I sustained myself with a steady diet of amphetamines that started as casual pill popping to get me though my often eighteen-hour days and became more compulsive as my schedule increased.

All good things must end. There are signs that flash and warn you it's time to turn the page. One night I left Rhubarbs and walked into a scene of violence and chaos as police broke up a gang of drunken suburban kids beating inner-city clubbers with tyre bars over the hood of that classic Aussie icon an

FJ Holden. Ambulance sirens competed with snaking guitar riffs from the club as blood trickled along the gutter and police from a paddy wagon cleared the area. I felt queasy and disoriented as I continued to my nocturnal destination— a Paddington party.

After what I'd just witnessed, the revelry in Paddington took on a garish, carnival air. I weaved numbly past dancing or coupling friends, through a kitchen-full of political debate and out into the relative calm of a back garden. There, a friend joined me and casually, yet very deliberately, remarked that many of my contemporaries were jealous of my early output and achievements. They were comforted, however, by the fact that I would soon destroy myself with drugs. Having already seen gutters run with blood that night, this news added to my unease. It had the desired effect and rang the right alarm bells. I wasn't eager for an Icarus-like blaze and demise. I stopped taking amphetamines the next day.

Withdrawal produced a few weeks of depression, which startled me and which would fitfully recur. I was already prone to extreme highs and lows, and the amphetamines had exacerbated these. This early lesson made me cautious about drugs, especially addictive stimulants. Childhood illnesses had taught me the art of bounce back, and a return to my Sunday walking track, always a lifesaver, helped me out of a brief and exhilarating but ultimately too dark and nocturnal period.

Walking, walking. Like sleeping and dreaming and other solitary activities, walking was an important part of my creative education. It helped give shape to the confetti of random notions that bombard a young imagination. As a boxer, my grandfather had walked away from the security of his family and into his own destiny. He established a tradition of solitude and endeavour that would transform itself and be passed down the line, via his gregarious but also solitary son, to me.

During my long Sunday walks, I would process the complexities of the preceding week, months, years even: the shadows of boxers and vaudevillians reflected on canvas skies; the upside-down images of family life captured in the viewfinder of Box Brownie cameras, the ill health, exams and playground tensions of school; the uncertainty, ambition and bravura of early theatrical efforts; all the hard and good things about being young and finding yourself alone and alive and in the world.

Step by sandshoed step, I marked out my future in the rhythmic patter of feet on wave-swept rock, on the shifting sands and sometimes treacherous ebb and flow of surf. Bit by bit, I pieced together the jigsaw of my own emerging personality and the fate that awaited me as surely as it had once awaited my grandfather in a Riverina boxing ring.

IN 1966 ...

Inter-generational conflict broke out. The war in Vietnam escalated, and Buddhist priests immolated themselves in protest. Anti-war marches began, and student riots broke out on US university campuses. Black Power emerged; the revolutionary Black Panther Party was formed and riots followed. Folk singer Bob Dylan went electric and was called *Judas* at an Albert Hall concert; he replied by turning his back on the audience and playing even louder. Animator Walt Disney and satirist Lenny Bruce died. Truman Capote published *In Cold Blood*. Andy Warhol floated silver pillows, exhibited silver bombs and Coca-Cola bottles and started making underground films. The first Velvet Underground album was recorded with songs by Lou Reed and John Cale. Russian satellite Luna 9 landed on the moon. Indira Gandhi became prime minister of India. In China, Chairman Mao launched the Cultural Revolution, setting the young against the old.

The first Australian conscripts were sent into battle in Vietnam; Japan replaced Britain as Australia's largest trading partner. In Australia, seatbelts were installed in cars; Sunday trading was permitted and six o'clock pub closing ended. US President Lyndon Johnson made a controversial visit and, as the vast tiled sails unfurled over the Sydney Opera House, Danish architect Jørn Utzon was forced to resign by Robert Askin's recently elected New South Wales Government. Utzon would never return to Australia.

Tamarama

THE RED SHOES

The game of chess is an ancient rite of move and counter-move, culminating in checkmate, the symbolic death of the king. Chess would provide the framework for my first opera production, Mozart's *Don Giovanni*, created at the age of twenty-one. The controversy that surrounded this production, the events that preceded it and some key players involved, would all have a lasting effect on my life and work.

It would take a generation raised on rock-and-roll to rediscover the true spirit of Mozart. In the 1960s, the nineteenth-century romantic approach was still in fashion, and Mozart productions tended to be slow, embellished, decorative and often lumpen. It would be decades before the early music movement wiped away the cobwebs, and conductors like John Eliot Gardiner and Rene Jacobs offered swift, light, unsentimental and playful readings that swung the pendulum back towards the excitement that accompanied original performances of these *drammi giocosi*, or serious comedies.

Opera Australia has a strong Mozart tradition. When the company was established in 1956, in an earlier incarnation as the Elizabethan Trust Opera, the first season consisted solely of Mozart operas. The uniquely ensemble nature of the company has lent itself to successful production of these works, and, even today, Mozart remains at the heart of its core repertoire.

My cousins John and Shirley Germain had arranged for me to see several of Mozart's operas at an early age, including *Don Giovanni*. As a NIDA student, I'd enjoyed a high-spirited *Cosi Fan Tutte*, and my reaction to Mozart's fidelity-testing, partner-swapping high jinks, beyond marvelling at the glorious music, was the realisation that enlightenment comedy offered rare insights into human nature. My particular memory is of Dorabella turning to her sister Fiordiligi with: *I will take the handsome dark one, if it's all the same to you.*

My cousins' encouragement had planted the opera seed, and it was nurtured at NIDA. As a rookie student, I was sent to Adelaide for work experience with the opera company at

Marcella Reale as Donna Anna

the 1964 Adelaide Festival of Arts. It marked the start of my initiation into the world of grand opera and offered my first experience of the revered Adelaide Festival, which I would one day direct. I stayed with my ever-generous cousins, the Germains, sharing their rented Adelaide apartment with a young NIDA graduate, Moffatt Oxenbould, then a stage manager but ultimately an artistic director of the company whose influence would decisively alter the course of opera production in Australia.

Neither Moffatt nor I had any sense of our future or our intertwining destinies as we shyly, awkwardly, faced each other, as student and recent graduate, across bowls of breakfast cereal. Thrown together by circumstances and our shared interests, we soon became good friends. On our days off we did the rounds of record, book and coffee shops. It was nice to have a soul mate on these expeditions, however briefly. A loose bond was formed, based on our enthusiasms and ambitions, peppered by occasional elbow-jostling rivalry. It is a friendship that I continue to value and enjoy to this day.

On arrival in Adelaide, my first work-experience chore was to sort several hundred seemingly identical sculptural grey costumes for a production of Verdi's *Macbeth*. It was part of the company's festival repertoire, along with *Carmen* and William Walton's *Troilus and Cressida*, another Shakespeare-based opera. *Macbeth* aspired to emulate contemporary trends in German opera production.

The innovation was to commission a design for this adventurous production from Adelaide sculptor Stan Ostoja-Kotkowski. A long, black, metal floating bridge became a curved staircase with jagged, angular steps that swept down to stage level. This was set against a vast curved cyclorama sky flooded with violently coloured abstract projections created by painted glass slides. The sculptural design was impressively stark and simple.

In *Macbeth*, Verdi is at his most rum-ti-tum, and the conductor seemed intent on emphasising this Italian organ-grinder aspect of the score. There was a startling contradiction between the sculptural abstraction onstage, which might have suited

Shakespeare's drama, and the toe-tapping *oom pa pa* emanating from the orchestra pit.

I had worked all night allocating grey-on-grey sculptural tunics, dresses and cloaks to the appropriate dressing rooms. The following morning, I settled, exhausted, into the auditorium stalls to observe my first-ever opera rehearsal. It proved an eye-opener. The generally unimaginative staging, which seemed to be putting old ideas into a modern design, became a background to the riveting onstage antics, which rivalled those of the Marx Brothers in *A Night at the Opera*. Arias were sung in Italian, the rest in English; this was both confusing and a harbinger of what lay ahead.

Difficulties were first signalled when an army of grey choristers entered at the top of the sculptural stairs and began singing their way downstage. Unfortunately, and hilariously, a few less arrived onstage than began the journey, several having fallen through an abstractly interesting but totally impractical missing step. Assistants materialised, and the grumbling grey army was herded offstage, swearing audibly.

A dumpy grey Hungarian woman next appeared in the spotlight, and, to suppressed titters from the stalls, read Lady Macbeth's letter, which memorably begins:

We met in the day of success …

Though what we heard was:

Ze met in da jay of zuk-zess!

This moment passed. Things settled down, give or take the odd abstract glass slide cracking from overheated projectors. Then, a vast sculptural cauldron was trundled on and a chorus of hefty witches entered and ran across the steel bridge. It wobbled in time to their less than dainty tread, as they sang:

We fly, we fly—we fly we fly we fly—we fly!

They managed to avoid the missing step and triumphantly reached their destination, which was the jumbo-sized smouldering cauldron. It promptly exploded with an overloaded smoke device that sent the cabal of singing witches coughing, reeling and spluttering into an outraged pile on the floor. At this point, a particularly plump and angry witch—possibly the union rep—stomped forward and in a broad Aussie accent broke the Verdian mood with:

Either that goes, or we go!

Not to be outdone, an equally rotund and taciturn representative of the opera administration leapt onstage and bellowed back:

We decide who comes and goes around here, Miss J—!

Promptly, Miss J— burst into tears and scurried into the wings, followed by a cluster of sympathetic witches.

Rebellion was in the air and the theatre was promptly cleared of all but essential personnel. I found myself dazed in daylight. No amount of directors and actors arguing over pauses in Pinter plays at NIDA had prepared me for this. I realised that, in opera, everything happens *big*. From melodramatic stage encounters to conventional offstage events, like a singer's birthday or a departure from the company, each event takes on an operatic dimension.

Far from being appalled by the continuing chaos, I was pretty excited. The scale and the seriousness of the endeavour, no matter how crazy the outcome, was impressive. My initiation into the drama of opera production was underway.

William Walton's new opera was a more sedate affair. Apart from an episode involving the diva demonstrably declining to wear a costume by cutting it to shreds and throwing it outside her dressing-room door, then locking herself inside and refusing to emerge and further discuss the matter, *Troilus and Cressida* was plain sailing and a relative success with critics and public alike.

I had the opportunity to observe a late-night lighting session for this production. As exhaustion set in after midnight, I volunteered to fetch coffee for the production team, which included the opera's director and my soon-to-be NIDA tutor, Robin Lovejoy.

The Pie Cart in King William Square is a 24-hour Adelaide institution. I'd become acquainted with it during rehearsal breaks; a quick pie and peas had often passed for dinner. It was not far from Her Majesty's Theatre, where the opera was performing. Here, I bought three take-away coffees, one more than I had hands to hold. In the days of thin cardboard take-away cups, this presented a problem.

Piling the cups on top of each other, I made an eager puppy dash to the stage door. As I arrived, two lids gave way, causing a volcano-like eruption that drenched me in hot coffee. A second trip followed, this time with two coffees in one hand, one in the other. Again: implosion and drenching. This time, only one lid gave way.

Desperate, as time ticked away, I returned for my third attempt. I walked very slowly, swapping the cups every block so the hot cup wouldn't have time to erode the lid below. Drenched in milky coffee, yet determined, I reached the now-darkened stage door, only to see the departing production team stepping into a shared cab.

What kept you? enquired one of them, with a wicked grin.

I did notice a sympathetic backward glance from the departing Robin Lovejoy. It was, perhaps, at this moment that Robin decided I might require a bit of extra NIDA mentoring.

I sat on the stage-door steps and drank the coffee as some form of consolation. In a swirl of memory combining the dropped beer bottle at my grandfather's house in Narellan with the imploding coffee in Adelaide, I wondered what hope I had as a director when I couldn't even manage liquid containers. Such sensitivities often consume the fragile temperaments of young and over-eager artistic aspirants.

It was therefore with some surprise that only a few years later, and after only one year of mostly experimental professional theatre production, not to mention the brief flirtation with substance abuse, that I found myself spick, span, alert and entering the offices and rehearsal rooms of the opera company to assume the role of an assistant director with the Elizabethan Trust Opera.

I was very excited and smartly dressed for the occasion and strode keenly down the corridor only to be confronted by Peter Smith, the urbane and supremely calm head of stage management. Peter drew a quick breath and smiled knowingly:

I see you're wearing the red shoes.

The Red Shoes, a classic dance film by Michael Powell, offers a veiled version of the story of the impresario Diaghilev and the dancer Nijinsky at a time when Diaghilev's Ballet Russe was redefining twentieth-century ballet. Moira Shearer starred as a feminised version of the Nijinsky character, a figure so consumed by dance that she ultimately dies performing the sacrificial ballet of *The Red Shoes*. I was unaware of the film at the time, or its implications, so I was nonplussed by the comment; though I was indeed wearing red shoes.

Yes. Bright, aren't they? was my unknowing riposte.

Peter showed me to the stage management office where I reacquainted myself with Moffatt Oxenbould, now well established in the ranks. To Moffatt's credit, he gave only the swiftest and subtlest of glances at the shoes. I was shown a desk, then proceeded upstairs to discuss my duties with the artistic director, Stefan Haag, the man responsible for my appointment. Before introducing Stefan, a little history …

Theatre in Australia was, and remains, controlled by a small band of people. At this time it was a modest affair. Two commercial managements, JC Williamson and Garnett Carroll, owned theatres and mostly imported Broadway or West End hits. The subsidised theatre sector was just emerging, being invented as it went along by Robert Quentin, Tom Brown and Robin Lovejoy at the NIDA / Old Tote complex—later the Sydney Theatre Company—and John Sumner at the Union Theatre Rep—later the Melbourne Theatre Company. In Sydney, others such as freelance director John Tasker, the elders Doris Fitton and Peter Summerton, and the new and dynamic American method guru Hayes Gordon struggled along on a semi-professional basis, as did their other capital city equivalents.

Subsidised theatre was established, funded and promoted by a man of great foresight, the economist and arts guru Dr HC *Nugget* Coombs. It was he who passionately championed the arts and advised governments of various persuasions— politically united only by their disinterest in the arts—to fund the future.

The consequences of Nugget Coombs' pioneering efforts were the formation of the Australia Council, the establishment of arts centres in every capital city of Australia, and the grand dream, inspired by the conductor and conservatorium director Eugene Goosens, that became Jørn Utzon's Sydney Opera House.

The Elizabethan Trust Opera had been founded by Hugh Hunt, an Englishman who restored an ex-vaudeville venue in the Sydney suburb of Newtown, renaming it the Elizabethan Theatre. Hunt chose Newtown as a local equivalent to Covent Garden, with its comparable working-class milieu and market gardens. Again, in the assimilation shuffle, the habits of older cultures initially defined the new, though they soon found their own shape.

Stefan Haag, who eventually took over the opera company, was an ex–Vienna Choir Boy. As a child on tour, Stefan had been stranded and interned in Australia after the outbreak of World War II. He grew up, married and settled here. After a brief return to Vienna, for experience, Stefan was appointed artistic director. He was smart, sophisticated and open to very bold ideas; some worked, others didn't.

My first duty as a fledgling assistant director was to work with Stefan on his new production of Donizetti's comic opera *Don Pasquale* and be resident director for a brief country tour. The travelling was fun and the opera tour offered a few enjoyable echoes of the sideshow circuit. The production had been designed in bright tour-able colours by Stefan's friend, Hungarian-born cartoonist Georg Molnar. The European connection was always strong in the opera world and much was decided over coffee at the few European-style cafés of the day.

Don Pasquale starred the Sadler's Wells soprano and home-coming queen June Bronhill. *Juney*, as she was affectionately known, had taken her surname from the town of Broken Hill, where she was born and whose residents had raised the funds for a scholarship that had taken her to London and on to a very successful career.

It was my job to supervise June's return to her birthplace for a performance of *Don Pasquale*, the planned highlight of the tour. The performance was fine and June was perfect as Norina, the soprano lead. It was the accompanying civic festivities that offered a swift and helpful initiation into backstage diplomacy.

We had flown in from performances at the recently established Perth Festival and arrived in Broken Hill late at night, after a long flight. Our diva was secreted in first class with her current beau. Curtained from our watchful eyes back in economy, *Juney* had taken full advantage of the complimentary drinks.

We disembarked near midnight to face an unexpected crowd bearing placards of welcome. A mayor materialised, decked out in the robes and chains of office. He had a press photographer in tow and was brandishing the keys to the city. The mayor was ready to escort us to a hastily planned official reception at the town hall, which would offer him a politically advantageous photo-op with the prodigal soprano. The diva was not pleased. June firmly gripped my arm and swayed her way, with a practised smile and wave, through the enthusiastic nocturnal crowd and into what passed for a limo.

At the town hall, we continued the imitation royal tour approach, and headed into a ballroom where CWA ladies had prepared a supper amid balloons and more banners, proclaiming: *Welcome Home—Our June!*

The other singers were delighted with the free food and grog, touring allowances being a pittance in those days, but something had further distressed our diva. It was the unmistakable sound of a cracked record, pumping out a jittery version of June's rendition of *Vilia* from *The Merry Widow*. With a frozen grin to the crowd, June leant across to me and hissed, in a slurred voice more Broken Hill than lyric soprano:

Get that off, or I won't sing a fucking note!

I summoned my diplomatic skills and settled the diva into her place of honour, then darted across the ballroom and took the needle from the vinyl myself. A few startled officials stared in my direction and a silence fell. Smiling encouragingly in June's direction, I explained:

Surely you'd prefer to hear from The Merry Widow herself?

Staring daggers at me, June, to her considerable credit, stood, swayed briefly, and saved the situation with a perfectly phrased chorus from *Vilia* to enthusiastic applause. Pleading exhaustion and the necessity of rest before the forthcoming performances, I escorted June and her beau to their hotel while the rest of the singers tucked into the CWA catering.

This was my first experience of diva wrangling, but it certainly wouldn't be the last. June and I bonded over amused recollections of the incident, and, after she retired from singing, I would occasionally run into her near Sydney's Kings Cross, where we both lived at the time. It was often outside the neon doors of bars and strip clubs, where June enjoyed an afternoon beer and a whirl on the pokies—sooner or later, everyone seemed to retire to the pokies. In June's case, I guess you could take the girl out of Broken Hill, but you couldn't take …

My other Perth Festival experience was lighting and supervising Stefan's personal project, an outdoor performance of ceremonial Aboriginal dance. Given the era, the performance was more folkloric than cultural. It served an important purpose, however, by providing a window into a culture that remained a mystery to most of white Australia.

Once *Don Pasquale* opened, Stefan was recalled to Sydney to confront some artistic crisis—probably budget issues, as the opera company operated on a shoestring—and I was entrusted to supervise and light the Aboriginal dance performance.

I got on well with representatives of the various tribes, who had journeyed to the festival from different parts of Western Australia. It was quite a corroboree, and many were whooping it up in the big city. My showground background helped assuage the fears of concerned officials. I assured them it would be *right on the night*—as it was. The dancers were diligent about their performance and took pride in a rare opportunity to demonstrate their culture. I chose to light the production in the spirit of its conception, and it had the visual flavour of a rock concert. A party of visiting anthropologists were appalled, but the Aboriginals, whose dancing became electric under atmospheric light, loved it, as did the audience.

Back in Sydney, I was assigned to assist Stefan Beinl, Herr B from my NIDA days, with his revival of a production of Puccini's *Tosca*, starring the gifted young Australian soprano Maureen Howard.

Herr B was up to his old push and shove tricks, which the veterans loved but I, along with the younger cast members, including Tosca, found limiting. Herr B was experienced at getting an opera up and running, but he was essentially an old man locked into revivals from his past. On this occasion, he was doing it in stage designs from an earlier production. My frustrations reached a peak on a day when, after sending Tosca out to buy his lunch because she was the youngest in the cast, he tried to stage a cathedral chorus entry through a door that didn't exist in the stage design.

I explained the difficulty as politely as possible, and he erupted, insisting there was always a door in that position in a European cathedral. I replied that we were dealing with a stage design, sans door. He lost his temper and started screaming in German, and I lost mine and hit him over the head with the very large score and stormed out.

Maybe I'd picked up a few diva tactics from June in Broken Hill, but my frustrations, involving old and new ideas, Europe and Australia, opera and reality, were brought to a head by this incident. I slumped in the stage management office where everyone, even Moffatt, gave me a wide berth. I waited for the inevitable phone call from Stefan Haag to *come upstairs*.

This time, I thought I'd really done it. Goodbye career.

And I had done it, though not in the way I had imagined. Far from sacking me on the spot, which I was expecting, Stefan was sympathetic and calm, pointing out that good directors did not necessarily make good assistant directors. He was taking me off the *Tosca* production and didn't have any further use for me as an assistant director. He's calm and understanding, I thought … but I'm still sacked.

There was a silence before he enquired: *Would you be interested in directing a repertoire production for next season?*

This was unexpected. I was cautious, though hope was returning.

Which opera?

Don Giovanni.

I was not so flabbergasted that I didn't quickly agree.

With that offer and my quick acceptance, my future would irrevocably change. It was a bold gesture of confidence from Stefan and a huge challenge for me. At twenty-one and with limited experience, what else could it be?

Stefan and I, sitting calmly in his office, didn't realise something had been set in motion that would require the French language to describe. In print and whispers it would become a *succès de scandale* or a *cause célèbre* and I would emerge from it as a fully qualified *enfant terrible*.

Don Giovanni is one of my favourite operas. Beyond its obvious musical bravura, there's a mystery and a paradox buried at its heart. As with Shakespeare's *Hamlet* and *King Lear*, the drama is embedded in its protagonist, a character who is both a vacuum and a force of nature. *Don Giovanni* seduces the mind and the senses in complex ways, which opens it to myriad interpretations.

The existing staging I had been invited to revive was an old Herr B production. It was based on a postwar romantic conception from Vienna, involving vistas of Spain on painted backcloths, trucked-on balconies woven with artificial flowers, and florid curtains that snapped shut for famous arias. It was the same production I had first experienced as a teenager.

Fortunately, everything was in disrepair, and while a new production was impossible because of the cost, my ears pricked up when I was told there would be a small budget available for the restoration of damaged sets and costumes. I realised that if I could come up with a conception so simple that it could be accommodated within that tiny budget, then I might be able to convince the opera management to let me stage a new version.

My mind worked overtime. There was a precedent. Stefan Haag had once faced a budget problem on Beethoven's *Fidelio*, which he solved with a simple series of black-on-black ramps that created the effect of a box burst open. It was one of the simplest, most modern and dramatically effective productions in the repertoire.

My idea for *Don Giovanni* was minimal, affordable, playful, dramatic and potentially effective. After listening to every available recording and thoroughly researching this most written-about opera, I came up with the idea of an extrovert Giovanni treating life as a game, something that the energy and symmetry of Mozart's eighteenth-century score enforces. Don Giovanni as the chessboard king who is finally checkmated by the ghost of the man he slays at the opera's outset, the Commendatore.

The steeply ramped chessboard would become an open stage, mostly lit white. The chess game would only be delineated during formal arias and certain ensembles. These would be sung directly to the audience from advancing positions of the game. The rest of the action would be more natural and realistic. The only additions to this essentially simple idea were tabloid images of Giovanni's crimes, in the gritty black-and-white style of New York crime photographer Weegee. These crime shots would background appropriate arias and become a montage of evidence, a kind of hell of his own creation that Giovanni faces at the opera's climax.

The idea was radical for the day, and almost the opposite of the romantic mock-Spanish revival that was expected. Many were cautious, but Stefan Haag was sufficiently convinced to allocate the available resources to a new version over a revival of a dated existing production. Thus began a tradition of offering low-budget productions to young directors to try their hand. It was an approach Baz Luhrmann would one day benefit from in a memorable staging of *La Bohème* that brought his considerable talents to public attention.

I directed and designed the sets and lighting for *Don Giovanni*. Ron Reid, my design collaborator from *A Taste of Honey*, created flamboyant costumes influenced by Sergei Eisenstein's 1944 film *Ivan the Terrible*. These weren't strictly necessary when everything else was so stark, but they went some way to appeasing the traditional opera audience's desire for spectacle. The fact that there was only one costume per character, each a chess piece, made them affordable. There may well have been a different outcome had we started with the resources of a new production, but this interpretation was inspired by chance, circumstance and economics.

The rehearsals were difficult, as my methods, which included improvisation, were new to many of the company's singers who were used to what they called *positioning*, which really meant push, shove and shout. I don't believe I once raised my voice, despite considerable provocation. I tried to be sensitive to the politics of established singers dealing with a young, raw and demanding director. I received initial support from most of the principal artists, including, to everyone's surprise, the imported guest Italian soprano, Marcella Reale.

In the title role was a wonderful singer and company stalwart, Neil Warren-Smith. Neil was, in truth, perfect casting for Giovanni's servant, Leporello, which he had already sung to great acclaim. Given a late career shot at the title role, he would have been more relaxed with a standard reading in a more conventional version. We attempted to accommodate each other, not always comfortably. The German-American conductor, Thomas Mayer, was an old-school pragmatist who only concerned himself with the production when it touched on musical matters.

We were scheduled to open in Melbourne, and the final rehearsals at Her Majesty's Theatre in Exhibition Street would have tested the patience of Job. The rehearsal schedule had been minimal, and insecurity prompted lazy arguments from singers. The *why don't we just give them what they want* school. Old lag stagehands, challenged by the youth of the director, kicked props slowly around the stage with a sneer, and swords were flung contemptuously. I remained deliberate and calm, while internally feeling that if I could survive this, I would survive anything. *Don Giovanni* was my initiation by fire.

The season had a youth emphasis with the worthy aim of opening up opera to young audiences; *Don Giovanni* opened on a youth night. Our onstage preparation time was as tight and exacting as the rehearsal period. Everything had been scheduled for a revival, not a new production. I was still lighting up to curtain time on opening night. I recall the mix of firm professionalism, tact and regret as Moffatt Oxenbould, who was stage manager, requested the obsessive director release the crew to prepare the stage for the premiere performance.

Older music critics had assumed that Mozart's finest opera had been given to a rock-and-roller in order to pander to young subscribers, and they resented the idea. As the performance progressed, older subscriber-type patrons walked out and their seats were quickly taken by enthusiastic younger audience members from the crowded standing room at the back of the stalls.

The performance ended in a raucous cacophony of cheers and boos. One critic, Kenneth Hince from the *Australian* newspaper, had already fled to the toilets and flung his head under a tap. He emerged, wet and dripping, lapelled a passing opera executive, and implored:

Tell me it's a joke!

Strangely, once the butterfly-in-stomach premiere was over, I was relatively calm. Stefan Haag graciously spent a moment with the singers and reassured them to stick with the production, come what may. By now, he had a fair idea of what to expect from the next day's newspaper reviews.

I woke the next morning with a sense of relief so strong it wasn't shaken by newspaper headlines that screamed *Desecration of a Masterpiece!* in the *Age* and *I Walked Out!* from the *Australian*'s head-under-the-tap critic. Had the reaction been more considered and less shrill, I would have taken it more seriously. However, for the first time in living memory, opera reviews were not in the arts section but on the front page. Lola Montez came briefly to mind.

I was due at the theatre around 11 a.m. to sort out some technical issues left unresolved by the race to curtain time. It was Moffatt's view, from the stage management corner, that the production was under-rehearsed and that if we were going to take a risk we needed to allocate the time and resources to best realise it. This was true, but I don't think it would have changed the outcome, which was really to do with a generational war between tradition and change, played out in the realm of opera. No, I suspect the critical storm was inevitable.

What wasn't inevitable was a young woman reporter who greeted me at the stage door. Her mission was to get a human interest story for the afternoon rag on what it felt like to be so young and to have to withstand such critical vitriol. My reply shocked her, as I wasn't about to cave in to self-pity or sentimentality. I ended up innocently fanning the flames with my dismissive remark:

Well, what would you expect in a provincial burgh like Melbourne?

The afternoon paper emerged with: *Director Strikes Back!*

That night I was asked to appear on *In Melbourne Tonight*, the popular television variety show. It was hosted on that occasion by singer-comedian Jimmy Hannan. I was joined by soprano *Marcella Reale*, who was happy to defend the production. We were to debate its merits with the *Age*'s critic Felix Werder. In 1967 it did seem amazing to be discussing culture on prime-time commercial television, and it would still be surprising today.

Werder was a rotund, old-style Viennese émigré with a superior smile and an attitude that suggested only he understood Mozart. I pointed out that Mozart had been closer to my age than his when he wrote the opera. It was obvious he saw himself as guardian of the classical flame, and that he'd concluded I knew nothing of Mozart. As his arguments dissolved under my relentlessness and Marcella added that productions like this were common in Europe and we were lucky to have one, he resorted to the oldest trick in the book and attempted to reassert his authority by patronising me.

I don't like what you did with Mozart young man, but ... smile ... I admire you.

The host turned to me with conciliation on his mind and a commercial break in sight:

And what do you say to that, Mr Sharman?

I summoned the take-no-prisoners attitude from show-grounds past.

I'm afraid I can't return the compliment.

The next day the box office turned from abysmal to lively. Young people bought the cheap seats and moved to the more expensive ones as older audience members walked out. The production travelled to Canberra, then Sydney, where the florid French epithets accompanied it.

The view from the opera company was that they had gotten away with it so far, but were about to meet their Waterloo in the guise of an informed and influential Sydney critic who found the company's musical and production standards mediocre and provincial. Kurt Prerauer was a former music librarian from the Staatsoper Berlin who had worked with some of the greats, including Wilhelm Furtwängler and Erich Kleiber. This critic knew his oats and he wrote for the small-circulation but influential *Nation* magazine. His observations on *Don Giovanni* were far from uncritical, but after putting on a brave face over all the pain associated with this production, his encouraging review was some kind of redemption and it felt good.

To such thin straws does one sometimes clutch.

After this iconoclastic production it would be many years before I directed another traditional opera: Benjamin Britten's *Death in Venice* at the 1980 Adelaide Festival. Instead, I became the director of a trio of musicals that helped define both their era and modern musical theatre. These came about as a direct consequence of *Don Giovanni*.

Stefan Haag left the opera company to join forces with a young entrepreneur who had been publicity advisor on the 1967 opera season: Harry M Miller. Harry would emerge as the smartest commercial producer Australia had ever seen. He and Stefan had a plan to stage a major new American musical and they wanted to break the mould of importing directors. The musical was *Hair*, and Harry strongly felt they needed a director who would engage young audiences. Thanks to *Don Giovanni*, they knew where to look.

After all the operatic dust had settled, I had a final encounter with Stefan Beinl. I received an invitation to meet him for a drink at the Rex Hotel in Kings Cross. Herr B proved to be a

wonderful conversationalist. Our chat turned to the controversial *Don Giovanni* production, and Stefan had some advice:

*I have seen such things before. The work of Bertolt Brecht and others,
of course, in Germany. But you don't do that here! They are far too com-
placent ... too stupid! Here ... you shovel them shit! I promise you, they
will lap it up with their fat tongues. That's my advice, young man.*

To be honest, I doubt if there's an Australian artist who hasn't,
albeit fleetingly, shared Herr B's cynical sentiments. However,
we'd been shovelled shit for far too long and it was time for
something else.

Despite this, I was grateful to Herr B. From him, I learnt a
lot—good and bad. As I walked away from that conciliatory
drink and his bitter pragmatic advice, I was also reflecting on
Kurt Prerauer's injunction to flee and work where real culture
existed—in Europe. But I had seen *The Season at Sarsaparilla*,
heard Richard Meale's *Clouds Now and Then*, signs of life that
suggested it was time we started looking more closely at ourselves and applying our skill and passion to our own culture.

I would, finally, address this question. I would also work outside Australia, but on the basis of what I'd achieved here, not in
some cultural job queue in a foreign land. How would things
ever change if everyone kept leaving? No, I decided, I would
stay and help work some magic, some transformation.

And I would never shovel them shit.

A new "Don Giovanni"

THE chessboard is a very old invention, and we have seen it also as the design for floors, from old paintings onwards. However, to employ it in the manner of Jim Sharman's "Don Giovanni" was new. It took away the mincing and put in the titan Mozart instead, by making each step appear a stride. Critics jeered at Sharman in Melbourne, as they jeered at the late Wieland Wagner in Germany. Now Wieland is being imitated everywhere, including Australia, and one day they may do the same to Jim Sharman. I do not know whether Sharman's production has been modified since it was in Melbourne ... if so, no one could be less surprised than I. Why did Sydney critics not get a chance of picking him to pieces, or lauding him? Australian music, and opera in particular, has every reason to be afraid of the Sharmans, as German philistines had with Wieland Wagner, whose work is now being distorted into true-blue Teutonism by his brother, Wolfgang. Take to your heels, Jim Sharman, if you don't get what you want. Learn in London, and with Rennert, not with Felsenstein, the greatest, for he has outlived his style. In ten years' time, between your contracts with Hamburg and Milan, perhaps you will consider making six weeks available for an Australian production.

Sharman was the first producer in this country, in my opinion, to make his audience aware of the problems in "Don Giovanni", of bridging the fearful abyss between Mozart's genius and da Ponte's childish jokes. Sharman even had the courage to present a Zerlina of the Kierkegaard brand: "Masetto or Don Giovanni, it doesn't matter to her", wrote the great philosopher about 125 years ago. When I read of it, I didn't think it could come off. Sharman made it come off. He gave the girl an unbecoming, cynical, perennial bridal veil ... or was it the hat of a female pawn on Giovanni's chessboard? This is only an isolated example: whole libraries have been written on the Giovanni problem.

Sharman shows even the most untalented singer ... not "how to act", but how to *be* the part. He can combine the characters to a logical pattern instead of inarticulate heaps. This is more difficult to bring off in Giovanni than anywhere else ... or if, outside Giovanni and Turandot, I have seen it in local opera, I must have forgotten. Elvira enters in carefully measured steps, one to each beat. Is it technique? No. Characterisation. Elvira's conformism as eternal opposition to Giovanni's non-conformism. Sharman had many hundreds of ideas like this. They offset the one hundred errors he committed (perhaps some of these were later additions "on request"), including the introduction of the characters towards the overture's last bars—an idea which fits Rossini, not Mozart. Mozart was of the Great Theatre. It worked as the instinct of his genius, which didn't go wrong. Our task is to search for Giovanni's solutions, though they offer almost insurmountable problems. Jim Sharman, in the first operatic production of his young life, has erected a signpost. He possesses zest, imagination, inventiveness that would make him the centre of heated debates between progressives and reactionaries in any culturally advanced country. That he was born in operatically innocent but eternally opera-prattling Australia, enhances his merit the more.

ABOVE: Neil Warren-Smith as Don Giovanni
OPPOSITE: Kurt Prerauer on *Don Giovanni*

2

Dancing

DANCING IN THE STREETS

In 1927 the curtain rose on Jerome Kern and Oscar Hammerstein's musical *Showboat* at the Florenz Ziegfeld Theatre, and the formally attired Broadway audience experienced the surprise of their theatre-going lives. First-nighters on *the great white way* were used to seeing blonde, leggy, powdered Ziegfeld showgirls descending spectacular mirrored staircases, while a debonair tenor in top hat and tails crooned:

A pretty girl is like a melody ...

Instead, they were confronted by surly black faces and music derived from work songs of Mississippi slaves:

Niggers all work on the Mississippi.
Niggers all work, while de white boss play ...

The shock was palpable, and the Broadway musical was born.

Showboat was the first musical to integrate song, dance and drama. The composer, Jerome Kern, was the New York descendant of German Jews with Viennese operetta in their blood. In collaboration with Hammerstein, he integrated operetta techniques with a hybrid of vaudeville, folk and work songs and created something unique. The musical was adapted from Edna Ferber's novel, and the theme, on page and stage, was miscegenation, or, in modern parlance, interracial sex. Integration, musically, dramatically and sexually, is the bloodline that links the more adventurous and often subversive Broadway musicals: from *Showboat* through *West Side Story* to *Hair*, *Ragtime* and *Hairspray*. These and other shows succeed in capturing the spirit of their times in an original and ultimately crowd-pleasing form.

Eras are often announced in song, either from the airwaves or the stage. *Oklahoma*'s popular opener *Oh What a Beautiful Morning* heralded the peace after World War II and trumpeted the United States' victory to a relieved public, while in ravaged Europe, Brecht's *Mother Courage* was left to drag her family, her goods and her chattels around in a cart, chanting bleak anthems to stoicism. The satirically bitter refrain *Life is all right in America / If you are white in America* revealed *West Side Story* as a harbinger of changing racial attitudes that would wipe

PREVIOUS PAGES: Let the sunshine in

black-faced vaudevillians and stereotyped Latino flunkies from the cultural map. The seemingly innocuous Motown pop hit *Dancing in the Street* became a coded call to arms for black activists in every American city. A tribe of soulful hippies encouraging their Broadway audience to *Let the Sunshine In* heralded something else again.

The youthful promise of the Kennedy era in the United States had played out to the tune of *The Peppermint Twist*. This sexy dance was brutally interrupted by the assassination of the young president. In 1968, following further assassinations— the inspirational civil rights leader Martin Luther King, black activist Malcolm X and the attorney-general Robert Kennedy— there was a more sombre mood on American streets. Youth culture had assimilated new beats from a swinging London, where The Beatles replaced their postwar diet of baked beans. An increasingly rebellious and hirsute younger generation, alienated by an unpopular war in Vietnam, racial disharmony, censorship and short-back-and-sides conformity, found expression in popular anthems expressing the contradictions of activism and pacifism. There was a hormonally driven youthful desire for greater sexual, personal and political freedom, and it found popular expression in the tribal-love-rock musical *Hair*.

The implications of all of this were swirling around me as I stood with the authors of *Hair*, James Rado and Gerome *Gerry* Ragni, in an elevator in Sunset Boulevard's Chateau Marmont hotel. It was around midnight, post-performance, on a clear night in 1968. We were accompanied for a few floors by Sal Mineo, James Dean's co-star from an earlier alienated youth flick *Rebel without a Cause*. As the elevator doors closed on the diminutive if still handsome actor, Gerome Ragni confided that Sal was currently jerking off, naked and nightly, in a downtown production of a tough prison play called *Fortune in Men's Eyes*. I was impressed, as I was meant to be. We briefly engaged in some surprisingly technical theatrical chitchat about how some things are hard to achieve on cue.

I had flown from Sydney to San Francisco at the behest of adventurous producer Harry M Miller on a *recce* to survey the various stagings of *Hair* prior to directing and designing the Australian production. It was my first trip out of Australia, and after witnessing a downtown Black Panther riot that obscured the Golden Gate with clouds of fumes from gas and stun-guns courtesy of the police militia combat force, I realised I was in a very violent country. The wild west might have been tamed but America seemed to be singing a new song to a very old tune.

After a day holed up in a city under curfew, I transited to Los Angeles, which struck me as a curiously unreal, almost fabricated city. My first sighting of *Hair* was at the renamed Aquarius Theatre. I was to discover that every city's production of this musical had a different quality. The Californian version had a laid-back feel and was probably the most hippy of them all. To my critical eyes, it seemed chaotic and under-powered. The exceptions were black performers like the young and obviously brilliant Ben Vereen, who would progress to stardom via Bob Fosse musicals; Jennifer Warnes, who went on to successfully interpret Leonard Cohen's extraordinary repertoire; and the actor–authors James Rado and Gerry Ragni, who had transferred from the original Broadway production to recreate the lead roles of Claude and Berger.

After the show, I met with the authors and our conversation continued over supper in their suite at the Chateau Marmont. I had barely arrived and had already witnessed a street riot, a curfew and a subversive musical that broke all the rules. I was excited and dazed, but James and Gerry were surprisingly sweet and solicitous and our conversation went for hours, until it was too late to go home. Gerry Ragni offered me the choice of the sofa or sharing their bed. Boringly, but wisely, I chose the sofa. More than once during my travels on the *Hair* tour, in this free love era, this option would present itself. I invariably chose the sofa. I guess that's why I'm a director and not an actor; for me, observation always prevails over the action. Tragically, AIDS was waiting in the wings for many who unthinkingly, or unknowingly, chose the action.

I took everything that emerged on my theatrical travels in my stride, which is odd considering I was naïve and twenty-four and a provincial tourist from a culturally invisible country on my first trip to the capitals of the world. Still, the ways of theatre are timeless and universal, and I've instinctively understood them since I first peered out from behind a stick of fairy floss as a showground toddler. Riots and subversion, stage nudity, drugs and sexual permissiveness all seemed par for the course; but there are human contradictions that challenge your expectations. One such contradiction caught me by surprise that night at the Chateau Marmont.

My innocent understanding of *Hair* was that it was by, for and about young hippies. Once out of the stage lights it became obvious that Rado and Ragni, while exemplifying these fashionable virtues onstage, were essentially two experienced actors who had researched and written a hit Broadway show with two great roles for themselves. Closer observation also revealed that the still handsome James Rado was closing in on forty and watching his weight. I had been so impressed by his youthful verve as Claude that when, prior to retiring, James matter-of-factly slid off his blond hippy wig to reveal very little hair underneath, I was stunned. This was nudity of an unexpected kind.

As one who later succumbed to premature baldness myself, I can understand the jibes that would have greeted the news that the creator of *Hair* was a *chrome dome*. I was reminded of the startling moment in Genet's *Our Lady of the Flowers* when a coronet of pearls cascades from Divine's head in an underworld bar in Montmartre. Divine pulls out her false teeth, pops them on her bald skull and calmly announces: *I'm still queen of you all.*

The morning after was all coffee, orange juice and polite farewells. My Harry M Miller–sponsored international *Hair* tour continued. Pop star and local heart-throb Julien Clerc starred in a chic Paris production. The London version was the warmest and most proficient, and I spent a few enjoyable days with the show's kindly resident director and choreographer David Toguri. His cast included Paul Nicholas, who would play Christ in my London production of *Jesus Christ Superstar*, and

Tim Curry, who years later would famously invest *The Rocky Horror Show* on stage and film with his considerable talents. Annabel Leventon and Oliver Tobias were the other outstanding leads in a staging that also featured svelte and sexy ex-model Marsha Hunt and future Evita, Elaine Page. Unknown to me, lurking in the wings of that fine production was the future creator of *Rocky Horror*, Richard O'Brien.

There was talent to burn, openness and a special energy among all of the *Hair* casts worldwide, but nothing I encountered in London, Los Angeles or Europe prepared me for what awaited at the Biltmore Theatre on West 47th Street in New York. That experience was unique, and it made clear to me why anyone contemplating staging Broadway musicals is well advised to experience the original production.

As I checked in to the mid-town Algonquin Hotel, a genteel oasis with literary credentials handy to the theatre, I was beginning to feel blasé about *Hair*. Exposure to a range of productions had given me all the information I needed to stage the Australian version; seeing another seemed a mere formality. I had been formulating my own ideas in between playing tourist and catching up with expatriate friends in each city I visited. In London, Martin Sharp, the Wizard of Oz, had put me in touch with an Australian journalist working for the *New York Post*, Lillian Roxon. I called Lillian and we arranged to meet later that night, after the show; a party was mentioned.

While I showered and readied myself for the theatre, my complacency, which probably involved an element of jet lag, gave way to anxiety and excitement. After all, I was in New York and about to see my first musical on Broadway. My childhood memories of endless Saturday matinees watching repros at the old Theatre Royal were about to be eclipsed by the bright light reality of *the great white way*.

Finding myself alone in a New York hotel room, I was suddenly struck by the enormity and responsibility of what lay ahead. Up until now, I had approached the prospect of staging *Hair* with determined detachment. It hit me in an adrenaline rush that this wasn't just another show but the most popular musical in the world, and that the expectations would be enormous. I calmed my insecurities, headed into the elevator and cruised through the Algonquin's tinkling foyer, with its ghosts of Dorothy Parker, Lillian Hellman and Candides past. A deep breath, then I glided along 44th and across Broadway. My feet were dodging crowds excitedly assembling under marquees, my eyes devouring neon names of shows I had previously encountered only on the covers of original cast recordings.

Hair begins with the cast, or Tribe, greeting the audience with flowers and chat before assembling onstage in a *slo-mo* haircutting ceremony that anticipates the ritual to follow—the sacrifice of conscripted American youth, represented by the Hamlet-like Claude, to the caskets daily returning from Vietnam. A series of William Burroughs–like cut-up vignettes tackle the hot-button issues of the era: sex, drugs, war and racism. The life force of the show is the anarchistic Berger, originally played by Gerry Ragni, who shares a three-way relationship with Sheila, originally Diane Keaton, a student radical and free-love exponent, and Claude, originally James Rado, whose decision whether or not to burn his draft card provides the only conventional narrative in the show. It ends with his sacrifice, a brief requiem for the young cannon fodder of the day and a passionate and powerful plea for peace: *Let the Sunshine In*.

Hair is often condemned for having no plot. Nor does it have stars in the traditional Broadway musical sense but rather a collective, led by the three principal performers. What caused it to resonate in a way that more conventionally structured musicals rarely achieve was the brilliant and original mix of ceremonial tribal staging, the street-wise behaviour of an engaging cast, the fast-paced revue-like progression of short, confronting songs and the final, almost operatic, transition into a passion play with revivalist fervour involving cast and audience. It was and remains a unique Broadway experience.

At the Biltmore, the pre-show chat wasn't trivial *hippy-dippy*. It was a barrage of street talk and wisecracks to which the audience responded in kind. Once they hit the *slo-mo* and Ronnie Dyson's ecstatic young voice intoned *When the moon is in the seventh house* ... you were in little doubt that the *Age of Aquarius* had already dawned.

What followed was a high-octane celebration the like of which I've rarely experienced in a theatre: a performance that acknowledged the nuance and invention of Tom O'Horgan's imaginative direction, properly realised by a young Broadway cast who understood the origins of these experimental techniques. After all, NYC was the mecca of experimentation and home to La Mama, the Playhouse of the Ridiculous, the Bread and Puppet Theatre and the hugely influential Living and Open theatres.

This was not only an attack by young dissidents on entrenched conservative and militaristic values; *Hair* also set out to challenge moribund Broadway traditions. It was the first musical to transfer from experimental Off-Broadway to tradition-bound Broadway and the first to use rock music and amplification. Musically, it was startling to hear a rock score in venues that previously harboured sentimental showtunes, and with the supremely gifted composer Galt MacDermot on keyboards, the sound was tight and powerful. As little hymns to *Coloured Spades*, *Sodomy* and interracial sex resounded, the mostly middle-class audience were in the position of their 1927 forebears during that initial run of *Showboat*. The cast boasted the voices of Dyson, Melba Moore, Lamont Washington, Lyn Kellog, Steve Curry, and Natalie Moscoe, who would later wend her way into the Australian production. I noted the crackling wit of Paul Jabara and Jonathan Kramer, both of whom would play Herod in my London *Superstar*, and Hiram Keller, who would soon star in Fellini's *Satyricon*.

I reeled out of the Biltmore Theatre and into a brief conversation with Galt MacDermot. Galt was, in many ways, the quiet spirit behind *Hair*. He was soft-spoken and looked more like a neatly attired jazz musician than a hippy. He was from Montreal, which intrigued me. Canada has given us a disproportionate number of gifted and curiously melancholy singer-songwriters: Leonard Cohen, kd lang, Neil Young, Joni Mitchell, and an entire family of Wainwrights, including the inspired Rufus.

Galt's family had been Canadian diplomats and were posted to apartheid-era South Africa, where his anti-racist passions and enthusiasm for African tribal music were born.

He confided that James and Gerry had called from Los Angeles to advise my presence, and that I was a serious young man and they now had great faith in prospects for the Australian production. Galt had informed the cast and, as a result, I witnessed one of their finest performances. On hearing the author's commendation, I realised that my uncomfortable night on a Chateau Marmont sofa might have been the right idea after all.

By the time my chat with Galt was over, the cast had disappeared into the shadows of the Broadway night. I headed downtown, near Union Square, to meet up with Lillian Roxon. Here, the streets looked like the show I'd just emerged from. It was hippy central: beads, bandanas, chanting, protest leaflets, astrology, numerology. Lillian was certainly no hippy but she proved to be a delight. She was a plump, middle-aged, bustling, Aussie-NYC talk-a-thon and she steered me to a table in her favourite eatery, Max's Kansas City. After being stuffed with pasta and filled in on rock gossip from Max's—how The Doors singer Jim Morrison had peed into a wine bottle and paid the waitress to drink it; what a lousy tipper Mick Jagger was etc.—we headed to the mysterious party.

Led by Lillian, I entered what resembled an art students' ball, but which turned out to be Andy Warhol's Factory. It was packed to the hilt with everything from socialites and business types to transvestites, a wide variety of exhibitionists and an excess of leather-clad hustlers. Beneath the glitzy surface, it was still drinks, music, chitchat and dancing; just like any other party.

Lillian, who had spent our supper time at Max's insisting how outrageous and decadent and sophisticated New York was, now turned personal publicist, and proceeded to talk me up to various seemingly important people. I had assumed that among this fashionable underground cabal, where *Hair* was already considered old hat, a virtual nobody directing it in culturally insignificant Australia would be dismissed as a total non-event. Not so. I was embraced with warmth and interest.

Decades later, I recalled this event to a friend who had experienced a similar reaction. He'd strolled casually into a gay bar during the AIDS era, and when the patrons discovered he was Australian, the cry went up: *Fresh meat!* I came to realise that in New York visitors are not viewed simply as human beings but as a potential opportunity—at least until they prove themselves otherwise. This has its advantages. As I was intimidated and, by now, weary from jet lag, I said little and observed a lot. Paul Morrissey, who directed many of Warhol's films, including *Flesh*, *Trash* and *Heat*, proved chatty, savvy and a tad shrill as he brayed about himself and introduced me to some muscular T-shirt who, Paul proudly announced, was *having sex in my next movie* ... and so it went.

As the party began to break up I had a brief encounter with Lou Reed. I was a great admirer of The Velvet Underground albums, mostly written and sung by Lou. On this occasion, Lou was skulking quietly in a corner with the recognisable look of an artist stranded *between engagements*. I sought him out and introduced myself. *Lou-Lou*, as he was affectionately addressed by Factory habitués, put aside his disdain for Broadway musicals in general, and *Hair* in particular, to chat enthusiastically. We were interrupted by Lillian, who transformed from daring NYC sophisticate into Aussie mother-protector as she whisked me into a cab and back to the Algonquin.

The one person I didn't meet that night was equally shy. He was always the still centre of the room but seemingly detached, almost motionless. Andy Warhol was like a Buddhist monk, and as pale as the walls. At a certain point in my conversation with Lou Reed, Warhol turned and we briefly caught each other's eye. In that look, which was part seductive, part forensic, part blank, there was a terrible recognition of something shared; something so personal we both instantly turned away. There was naked desire in this look like a whiplash. I'll never forget it. I still feel the physical stutter in my reaction racing across time.

I would never meet Andy Warhol and would only experience that look again on a few special occasions in my life: in a newsagency on London's Brompton Road, during a chance early morning encounter with the painter Francis Bacon; in Sydney, with the writer Patrick White, and in Germany, with the choreographer Pina Bausch.

I would get to meet and know Patrick, and through him I would come to better understand what that look meant. It was a look of shared recognition that seemed exclusively the province of carnivorous artists or *monstres sacré*. The look of impossible love shared between predatory vivisectors.

With that exchange firmly riveted to some emotional archive of my soul, I returned to the more sedate pleasures of the Algonquin, enjoyed a few more inspiring days checking out art galleries and street life in the Big Apple, then flew Pan Am and Qantas back to Sydney, where I turned my attentions to the matter at hand: the Down-under incarnation of a *tribal-love-rock musical*.

IN THE FOREST

Around 1995, I found myself in the village of Sanur, on the island of Bali, being tended by a blind masseur. As he sensually and expertly stroked away traveller tension, we got chatting and I hinted at my theatrical background and interest in Balinese dance, which I had witnessed in the mountain village of Ubud— a favourite destination in this magical retreat for interested or exhausted westerners seeking spiritual replenishment.

What you have seen is for tourists! It is entertainment for commerce. We need it, we live off it … but you should go into the forest at night when the whole village assembles and enters a state of trance … here we dance our ceremonies and our myths in our own time, in our traditional way.

I was reminded of Aboriginal corroboree, the very first Australian theatre.

In the townships and the hotel lobbies, we dance for show, but in the forest … we're dancing for the gods.

IN 1968 …

French students and workers rioted in Paris. In the United States, Black Power was on the rise, as were the women's movement and gay and lesbian liberation. Riots disrupted the Democratic Party Convention in Chicago. The protest leaders were arrested on conspiracy charges and activists in the Black Panther Party were jailed. Civil rights movements were under attack and their leaders assassinated. Richard Nixon became US president. After The Beatles broke up, John Lennon and his partner Yoko Ono were arrested on drug charges. John Gorton was elected prime minister of Australia. Apollo 8 transmitted the first pictures of earth as seen from outer space. The inventor of the geodesic dome, Buckminster Fuller, coined the term *spaceship earth*. Marshall McLuhan predicted an electronically retribalised global village where *the medium is the message*. *Hair* opened on Broadway, with its glib, yet accurate, catchcry:

The War is White people sending Black people to fight Yellow people to defend the land they stole from the Red people.

Banyan tree, Bali

GA-GA AT THE GO-GO

There was a spring in my 24-year-old step as I began rehearsals for the Australian production of *Hair*. The venue was a cavernous hall at the Sydney Showground, where we rehearsed for five weeks in the autumn of 1969. There was a sense of energy and expectation in the air. Outside, a neat, conservative society went about its business and its wars. Inside, we were preparing a Dionysian revolution.

The hall itself was only a short walk from the building that housed the family boxing troupe during each Royal Easter Show. Ironically, the same hall would become the site of the sexually anarchic dance parties of Sydney's Gay and Lesbian Mardi Gras, now part of Fox Film Studios, where *Moulin Rouge* and *The Matrix* were shot. Harry M Miller hired the hall to house the entire production. He had previously presented The Rolling Stones at a nearby venue, so the Sydney Showground offered history and familiarity to all concerned; it was also cheap.

My design for the raked circular stage, with its pacifist emblem and tiered quadrangle of sculpted scaffolding sur-round, had been erected in the main hall; pianos were wheeled into adjoining studios for music coaching. A wardrobe department was set up to transform the young cast's street clothes into the requisite hippy tribal wear. I had a tramp-oline installed to free up and energise the rehearsal room atmosphere. All of this was in stark contrast to the starched and formal rehearsal methods of the day, where tea was politely served at breaks and *Mr Smith* or *Miss Jones* would be kindly requested to *Commence the scene from your position by the door.* However, for all our T-shirt and jeans casualness, the rehearsals were long, hard and detailed. For a show about peace, it was planned and prepared with almost military precision and accompanied by professional expectations that were carefully nurtured, sustained and, when necessary, enforced.

It was all go as this much anticipated production took shape, and we rehearsed non-stop: six days a week, day and night. There were trust exercises involving racially mixed cast members falling weightlessly into each other's arms to build camaraderie, and blindfolded sensory explorations to awaken sensitivities and loosen inhibitions. Pianos pounded notes into the consciousness of a cast whose limited experience in garage bands, experimental theatre or street-busking had not necessarily acquainted them with the intricacies of music charts and complex harmonies. Politics played their part, and iconic war-zone images and documentation from *Ramparts* magazine were circulated and discussed to background the show's anti-war rhetoric.

The antiseptic aroma of the hall slowly gave way to the scent of incense and aromatic oils as the cast shed inhibitions and clothes, grew their flowing locks or sunbeam afros, and bounced around with growing confidence as songs and moves and attitudes became second nature. I drew out traits of each performer to meet the dramatic requirements of a particular song or situation and paid close attention to communicating unfamiliar states of mind via song, dance, action. My rehearsal approach favoured action over motive. I tended to be suspicious of rubbery motive, often a matter of opinion or conjecture. I preferred to emphasise action; it's more theatrically dynamic and closer to fact. I aimed for a rehearsal atmosphere where things emerged naturally, magically even—given that magic is a form of emotional science—rather than being intellectualised or applied, like make-up or a borrowed coat.

I encouraged improvisation, and individual roles were often swapped, a rehearsal practice that continued well into performance; though a long run ultimately restored a more conventional casting approach. Musically, I involved a popular underground band, Tully, to strengthen the rock aspect of the score and give it a less sanitised feel, though their embellishments would develop to a point where they were gradually replaced by more reliable session musicians. Freedom has its limits in a long-running show but, at the outset, there was a strong correlation between the ideas and ideals of *Hair* and those of its young cast, director and their rock muso colleagues.

My experimental and exploratory rehearsal techniques, which had been resisted at the opera, were eagerly embraced by my hand-picked cast of contemporaries. As it had in other countries, the success of *Hair* shifted many elements of these new rehearsal approaches from the underground into the mainstream. What had been sniffily dismissed as self-indulgent or offensive, or too challenging and confronting, would soon become part of the theatrical norm.

The original Broadway production of *Hair* was dominated by the energy of Gerry Ragni's performance of Berger as a raging hippy force of nature. Our version initially gave more emphasis to Claude, played by Wayne Matthews alternating with John Waters, as the dramatic fulcrum. Claude shifted between tribal enthusiasm with noisy anarchic songs like *I Got Life* and the Hamlet-like questioning of his Act One finale: *Where Do I Go?*. Here, Claude's indecision was contrasted by the certainty of *The Tribe* as they emerged naked from a mushroom cloud of billowing parachute silk with a heartfelt cry for freedom—the famous nude scene.

Keith Glass' Berger was Claude's friend and energising foil. Keith brought his scrawny sexy looks and the panache of a natural rock singer to the role. Six months into the run, the older, more experienced and physically charismatic Reg Livermore took over, and the balance swung more towards that of the Broadway original. *Hair* began its life in Australia very close in feeling and sound to the hippy idealism it espoused. Inevitably, as success and longevity kicked in, standards rose and professionalism took over where street cred had once held sway.

All this was yet to come. Huddled in our cave at the showground, we were still uncertain as to whether the show would open at all. In 1969, there was a chief secretary in New South Wales, a hangover from the role of the British colonial secretary sent from England to keep rowdy provincials in line. The chief secretary censored books, films and stage productions. There had already been embarrassing bans of now classic books like *Lolita* and *Lady Chatterley's Lover*. Jean-Claude van Italie's play *America Hurrah* had recently been closed by the police, and battle lines had been drawn in the public debate. *Hair*, with its nudity, anti-war rhetoric, subversion and expletives, would be a test case for censorship in Australia.

Harry M Miller was nervously sitting on a very expensive investment. *Hair* was a controversial show that HMM, urged on by his executive producer, my ex opera boss Stefan Haag, had placed in the hands of a relatively inexperienced young director. He must have had a few sleepless nights; if so, he never showed it. Harry was a courageous producer and well versed in nocturnal anxiety, having previously toured Judy Garland. Judy was prone to phoning HMM at 3 a.m.

RING-RING

HMM: *What's up, Judy?*

JG: *Nothing.*

HMM: *How can I help you?*

JG: *You can't! I just want you to know what it feels like!*

Click ... Ah, amphetamines.

The drug of choice on *Hair* was marijuana, which was popular with the cast and readily available. An ex-CIA agent in Australia had set up Kings Cross bars for US servicemen on R and R, and he reputedly imported narcotics in body bags from the battle zones of Vietnam and Cambodia. Drugs were a weapon in the Vietnam War, used by both sides. I was pretty much over them after my flirtation with speed and a brief if enjoyable and illuminating encounter with LSD, which I obtained from a student doctor with whom I'd had a short-lived fling. He was an advocate of the radical, if dodgy, theories of RD Laing and was prone to self-prescribing. He was later hospitalised. The rock musical era would have its casualties, onstage and off.

The popular rumour that the young cast of *Hair* were permanently stoned was wildly exaggerated. The show required a precision that simply wasn't possible if you were permanently out of it. To my eyes, the atmosphere backstage was surprisingly conventional, the hippy anarchy being mostly confined to the performance. It was often the audience whose imagination took them to places the hard-working cast would rarely venture; though, on one occasion, wandering past a dressing room, I did overhear after-show party preparations being eagerly discussed, and the phrase *You get the baby oil and I'll bring the plastic sheets* floated by my ears. Hippy or no, some chorus boys will be chorus boys.

As is often the case with performers, of whatever stripe, the cast tended towards clannishness and mostly kept to themselves. In rehearsal or onstage they had each other, but in the outside world they would daily confront hostility. Looking hip and having long hair might have seemed admirable to young fellow travellers, but taxi drivers would ignore them and they were refused service in shops. Their street walks would be accompanied by cries of *Get yer hair cut, yer fuckin' poofter!* and threats of violence. In 1969, fear and conformism still ruled.

A mixture of curiosity and prejudice was applied to the half-dozen black American artists I had cast in New York. They were conspicuous in the overwhelmingly white, provincial and overtly racist Australia of the time. The women mostly handled this better than the men, many of whom left as soon as their six-month work visas allowed. While black music was embraced in the discos and clubs of the day, black people on the street were seen as a much more challenging matter. This attitude slowly changed, and I'm happy to say that *Hair* played its part in that transformation. Later arrivals, notably the gifted and delightful soul singer Marcia Hines, still a teenager when I cast her in Boston, were to contribute much through their talent, visibility and appeal to the ever-so-slowly expanding cultural horizons of Australia.

If the outside world was often hostile, a more generous and liberated version of community was being nurtured inside the rehearsal room and, censorship willing, would soon be open for inspection by the Australian theatre-going public. In this space, I was definitely in my element. I was anywhere and everywhere as ringmaster to this anarchic carnival—coaxing, persuading, cajoling, demanding:

More energy on those spin-on-a-dime turns, everyone. Try somersaulting into that next line rather than just mumbling it. Imagine chains cutting through your body as you rasp out Prisoners in Niggertown, *it's a dirty little war.* When you're Walking in Space, *you're stoned and trying to travel a tightrope in slow motion.* Hair *is the title song;*

it's exciting, folks, but not yet electric. Berger, hit the consonants on There'll Be Ga-Ga at the Go-Go, *and twice the energy everyone, please. More vaudeville strut on that entrance, Donni. That hat looks great, Charlene, now try it on the angle—perfect. More angelic on* Sodomy, Terry, *and don't forget the C in* Cunnilingus.*Try it down an octave, Creenagh. Now again, everyone, you too, Clive, with your clothes off this time* ... Precision and anarchy alternated in this three-ring circus of a rehearsal room. It was calm, work-a-day, dynamic, tender, demanding and exhilarating. There had been nothing quite like it; we were all on the highwire without a net.

As opening night approached, we moved from our show-ground rehearsal barn to the theatre. During our early discussions, HMM, Stefan Haag and I had visited the old Minerva Theatre in Kings Cross and we all thought it perfect. Harry liked the idea of the show as an event and was prepared to finance renovations. He renamed the theatre the Metro, Kings Cross. I was dedicated to opening new theatre venues in a city that was better known for knocking them down. This decision played an important role in the ultimate success of the production. Harry was right—an exciting new venue made the show seem special. The audience, despite an absence of parking, enjoyed the frisson of finding themselves in the still bohemian Kings Cross for an adventure in entertainment. The reclaiming and refurbishment of old or disused theatres became part of the rock musical tradition. Each new show successively reopened venues like the Capitol in Sydney's Chinatown, the Valhalla in Glebe and the Metro in Bourke Street, Melbourne. Years later, a couple of soon-to-be-demolished cinemas on London's Kings Road were converted into theatres for *The Rocky Horror Show.*

Excitement narrowly outweighed nerves as our opening night drew closer. The new venue was slowly readied; sound amplification and a vast exposed lighting rig and other technical demands, mostly untried at the time, were gradually perfected. By now, there were run-throughs of the show at night and we resolved technical problems by day. As stage and lighting designer, I was also preoccupied with the look of the production. It was an exhausting and exhilarating process. Stefan Haag was a valuable ally during these stage rehearsals. Harry kept his distance until we had a run-through with an invited audience of university students. As this was the time of conscription for the Vietnam War, the audience and their contemporaries were all potential cannon fodder. The climactic anti-war crescendo of 3-5-0-0, always a highlight of our production, reduced them to tears; even Harry briefly disappeared behind a handkerchief.

After this rehearsal, which was powerful and uncompromising, shocking almost in its passion and directness, I noticed Harry loitering in the stalls. He waited until we were virtually the only two people left in the theatre. *Jimmy*, he called, using the diminutive, in a warm but *I want a word* kind of way.

Here it comes, I thought.

Pages of producer's notes, interventions, requests for cuts, self-censorship …

Yes, Harry? I replied, all affected innocence.

HMM: *It's very good.*

JS: *Thank you, Harry.*

Pause.

HMM: *You know that bit with the dress?*

I did. He was referring to the song *White Boys!*, delivered by three black women as a parody of all-girl Motown-via-Las-Vegas groups like The Supremes, with bouffed hair and pink-sequined hourglass dresses. The gag was that the costumes opened to reveal they were all bumping and grinding in the same huge dress.

HMM: *When they did that in New York, the audience stamped and cheered.*

JS: *Mm.*

HMM: *They didn't here.*

Pause.

HMM: *Think about it. Otherwise, terrific. Good night!*

It was immaculate and I was furious. No artistic intervention that I could argue about. Simply the producer seeing the show through the eyes of the audience and realising there was one moment that wasn't delivering on its potential. I stomped home and paced all night, worrying about it. I hit the phone in the morning and called a rehearsal for later that day, reworked the scene and at the preview that night, the audience went crazy.

Harry smiled and nodded: *Thanks, Jimmy!* Nothing else said.

Inevitably, there were areas of tension and difference between us, as Harry was certainly no hippy and represented the business side, while I represented the artists and the spirit of the work and its ideology. There was respect on both sides, however, and on a simple showbiz level there was more sympathy and understanding than I've encountered since with any other producer, commercial or subsidised. The ex–socks salesman from New Zealand, equipped with little more than a well-thumbed copy of *Memo from David O Selznick*, had set out to transform Australian theatre with this show and, in a different way, so had I, the grandson of a working-class sideshow proprietor. Without ever discussing the matter, we knew our respective roles. At the crunch, we kept our cool and our heads, and while I got on with the show, Harry got on with the business and the promotion. As a double act, it was a ripper.

The government of the day thought there would be political mileage in banning *Hair*, but increased air travel had opened Australia to the wider world and Harry orchestrated events so that the act of denying the city the opportunity to see this controversial show would confirm Australia's provincial status. His press campaign began to turn the censorious tide, and banning the show became a less appetising political option. The chief secretary and the state government, however, were entrenched conservatives, and their word would be law. While it was rarely discussed, the question of whether we were preparing for a long run or a single performance hung heavily in the air, unspoken and unanswered.

The big night approached. We shifted from rehearsals into previews. The chief secretary announced he would attend the final preview. Harry had a plan. He was a popular figure in local society and had befriended the lively and intelligent Zara Bate, former wife of the late conservative Prime Minister Harold Holt. Zara and her husband Jeff Bate were invited to the first preview; she was bowled over by the show. Harry invited her back for the final preview and seated her near the chief secretary. He loathed the show and was horrified by everything it represented. Influenced by public opinion and a vocal anti-censorship press campaign, and with the bubbling and enthusiastic Zara Bate in attendance, however, he was cornered. Avoiding the issue and needing to consult with his famously ruthless Premier, Sir Robert Askin, he informed Harry that he would make his decision the next morning and phone him.

The possible entry of Askin into the debate worried us all. During US President Lyndon B Johnson's visit three years earlier, when the presidential motorcade was blocked by a group of anti-war protestors, Askin had instructed his driver to *Run the bastards over!* As an Australian politician, Askin was used to kowtowing to Americans, but not to American musicals.

The next morning, in Harry's office, we discussed opening night protocol, after-show events, cast issues, in fact everything but censorship—which was the only issue on anyone's mind. Finally, the call came from the chief secretary's office and, after a terse nod from Harry, I stepped outside. Time passed and I started to worry. When the door opened, Harry, looking decidedly pale, motioned me back in.

We won! he said, grimly.

Then, why so pale? I wondered.

You won't believe what he said.

Frankly, I didn't think anything a politician could say would faze our Harry.

After he rabbited on about disrespect for law and order and family values and the war and patriotism and all the rest … he wanted to know if the black girl on the left in the nude scene was available for dinner.

I also went pale. Well, paler. Was this the pay-off?

I made it clear we were a theatre production company, not a dating service.

We both burst out laughing, partly in relief. Even Harry, who wasn't averse to cynicism about the ways of the world and had no doubt set up a dinner date or two in his day, well, even Harry was astonished. This incident banished any doubts I might have had about the ultimate hypocrisy of censorship.

The opening night of *Hair* was a triumph. A bomb threat meant the auditorium was cleared by police, which delayed the start and raised the stakes. Instead of the intended disruption it only heightened the sense of occasion. From the opening mingling of cast and audience, decked out in a curious mix of traditional finery overlaid with beads and bandanas, through the sassy and mischievous catalogue of rock anthems to the devastating 3-5-0-0 and ultimate cri de coeur of *Let the Sunshine In*, a mainstream Australian theatre audience had rarely been so directly involved in a public celebration of energy, emotion, outrage and idealism; it was electric and infectious. Dionysus was certainly in the house that night. I was almost too tense and exhausted to enjoy it but I emerged fulfilled and managed to convey my gratitude to the cast before indulging in the exorcism of a wind-down dance at Harry's elaborate *Hair*-themed post-show party; such events would become a feature of all future HMM productions.

I recall a long rambling conversation with Stefan Haag, who was wearing a Cheshire-cat grin. Stefan was the first person to make the name connection of *Sharman, Shaman, Showman*, and it was probably the right night to do so. There seemed a sudden logic in the journey Stefan had led me on—from Aboriginal tribal dance performances through *Don Giovanni* up to this amazing night. He was a wise, erratic, yet progressive man, with ideas often ahead of their time. In his maturity Stefan seemed satisfied to encourage artists of a new generation in their ambitions for theatrical progress.

The opening of *Hair* ended for me in a shabby, all-night Kings Cross diner, squashed into a lurid green vinyl banquette between an effusive Graham *Gra-Gra* Kennedy and several elated cast members. Unbeknown to me, Gra-Gra had been the major financial angel behind Harry's bold enterprise. After our night-cap, I walked, or rather floated, home—*Walking in Space*. In a reversal of my opera experience, I awoke the next morning to uniformly rave reviews and with an undisputed hit on my hands.

Hair was seen by around two million Australians over several years and was the harbinger of a more liberal climate and a more tolerant and less conservative society. We won the censorship debate in New South Wales and would continue to do so in every state in Australia where the musical was performed. It certainly helped to sway public opinion against conscription and an ill-considered war in Vietnam; the *Hair* cast led many a public rally to that end. It broke down prejudices regarding race and sex, and the songs provided anthems for a generation who would elect the reform-minded government of Gough Whitlam in 1972. This political change brought with it a sweeping, welcome and long overdue transformation of Australian society.

As a musical, *Hair*'s often naïve volatility and the sense of being hot-wired to the specific issues of the day make it a difficult show to revive. It's wedded to the culture of its time and now succeeds best in concert, where Galt McDermott's inventive and melodic score continues to surprise audiences. If one of its aims was to revolutionise the Broadway musical, the jury remains out on that score. Like a businessman getting back to conventional work after a holiday that revealed more interesting possibilities, Broadway swiftly reverted to more obviously commercial, formulaic, sentimental and escapist fare.

All this was yet to come as I sat, with a mild hangover and new-found confidence, nursing a mug of black coffee, surrounded by tabloid and broadsheet headlines and the detritus from opening night in my recently rented Surry Hills terrace house. *Hair* would go on to have its influence on society, but it had already changed me. It was more than simply acquiring fashionable long hair, hippy clothes and some pop-art furniture, though I was the proud possessor of all these props and costumes. Instinctively, I now knew that I would never become a jobbing journeyman, taking whatever production came my way, but a director who knew theatre should engage as well as entertain. I had a talent and therefore a responsibility to apply it where it would, in some way, move things on. *Hair* showed me the transformative possibilities of theatre. Like *Showboat* in 1927, *Hair* was a beginning, not an end.

The play's the thing / Wherein I'll catch the conscience of the King,
Shakespeare, through *Hamlet*, reminds us. My new-found commitment would become more resolute with time and often
be seen as contradictory, uncompromising, arrogant, stubborn. It was certainly single-minded. From now on, unless
there was the promise of some *ga-ga at the go-go*, for me it was
a no-no.

"Able Baby"

"Hello There"

"Let The Sunshine In"

"Hair"

"Walking In Space"

"My Conviction"

"Abie Baby"

"Eyes Look Your Last"

"Donna"

COLOURFUL CHARACTERS

When fame knocks on the door reality flies out the window. That's a showbiz truism. It happens. I would observe this flight from reality in others, shake my head in disbelief and swear to guard against it; but it creeps up on you. Sooner or later, the person who was chirpily walking and whistling to rehearsal is staring blankly at the world from behind the tinted window of a limousine chauffeuring them from an anonymous airport to an identikit hotel room. The airport lounge that was once an enjoyable holiday abstraction has become the void in which you feel most comfortable, the transit lounge of your soul.

Fame and friendship make for a curious mix: a cocktail that should be shaken gently lest it sour. I recall a late-night conversation between the King of The Velvet Underground, Lou Reed, and Mick Rock, a ruefully honest photographer. It was after Lou previewed his latest single, over a late-night drink. Mick failed to respond with the appropriate enthusiasm and even Lou, whose poet's eye made him more aware of the traps of fame and flattery than most, protested: *My friends all loved it!* Mick let out a long-suffering sigh: *I'd be careful of those friends if I were you, Lou … especially if they're on the payroll.*

I'd like to boast that I never succumbed to the temptations of success and always kept my feet on the ground, but I'm not so sure that's true, of either myself or any of the other garlanded members of the youth-quake generation who were elevated to premature fame. Before my reality bird had its feathers ruffled, let alone threatened to fly the coop, I was fortunate enough to establish a few friendships that would endure and sustain me over many years. These colleagues provided emotional and intellectual sustenance and the occasional and very necessary reality check—for which I am truly grateful.

Early schoolyard friendships rarely travelled the distance into my professional life. An exception was my old schoolfriend Ian Cookesley. Ian once holidayed on the road with the family boxing troupe, and he collaborated on my early G&S productions and became production manager on *Hair*. Ian and Sandra McKenzie, who was my assistant, confidante and the stage

PREVIOUS PAGES: The Australian cast of *Hair*

director of both *Hair* and *Superstar*, were exceptional companions during the rock musical period. We went our separate ways when those grand adventures concluded. Stage productions tend to be like that. Intense relationships form, and a family atmosphere is artificially created. Then the family members disperse when the curtain falls, rarely to meet again.

There were early mentors, like the composer Richard Meale, whose opera of *Voss* I would later direct and who broadened my musical tastes. This formative encounter encouraged me to always be on the lookout for the smartest eyes in the room when seeking future friends and collaborators. Some of these were fellow travellers, others were artistic colleagues and, of course, there were personal relationships too.

The Brissie Mob

Perhaps it was the warmth in his eyes or the studied intelligence behind them that first drew me to Rex Cramphorn. In my first professional year I had been invited back to NIDA to direct plays and tutor students in theatre production. The directing was fine but, with the ink barely dry on my diploma, my tutoring role was complicated by the fact that I was often teaching students older than myself.

Rex was a mature-aged student and part of a small group studying theatre production. He was approaching thirty and definitely the smartest person in the room. When you're in your early twenties, a few years' age difference can seem an eternity. Later in life, a decade means little, but to twenty-somethings —whose anthem was The Who's *My Generation* with the pay-off line: *Hope I die before I get old!* and old meant thirty—it was a barrier. Rex was also an honours graduate from the University of Queensland, another reason to feel uncomfortable; his academic qualifications were considerable, mine zero. He was discreetly gay, though this was not immediately apparent. In that era, sexuality often remained something unspoken even among friends. We slowly struck up a conversation that took us beyond the artificial student–tutor relationship and out and about together. It was our differences that informed our friendship, not our similarities. At this stage I was a radical populist while Rex was conservative and scholarly. I had barely heard of Racine and Corneille, yet these classical dramatists, along with a few equally obscure Jacobean playwrights, were Rex's great enthusiasms.

I suspect we had both privately decided that theatre was a way of life: a vocation and not just a profession. We shared a crypto-mystical interest in the interplay between reality and illusion. In different ways we were both seekers and explorers. Rex was subtle and seductive in his directorial style. It was a trait Woody Allen would amusingly popularise as passive-aggressive. In other words, Rex got his own way without ever appearing to, whereas I tended to lead from the front. He displayed qualities I associate with those eternal students in the plays of Chekov, like Trofimov in *The Cherry Orchard*. Rex's interests were often academic and yet he privately feared that taking the academic path would lead him into a sterile cul-de-sac. I was the opposite: a practitioner hungry for the stimulus that only self-education and knowledge could provide. There was mutual fascination at play in our developing friendship.

By now, NIDA was better established and attracting a high standard of acting student. These spirited young actors proved to be the catalyst in our relationship. It was the right time and the right place. Their craft and the idea of transforming it into something less prosaic and more poetic engaged us.

My daily walk to NIDA timed with that of one such actress-to-be, an attractive and loquacious young woman who assumed, because of my youth, that I was a fellow student. I didn't contradict this impression and was therefore privy to a daily stream of unedited gossip about her colleagues and the staff. When I finally took a rehearsal and my staff role as a NIDA tutor was revealed, it was accompanied by a look of shocked surprise on the usually composed and exquisitely proportioned face of Kate Fitzpatrick.

Even as a student, Kate trailed something glamorous, classic and ancient in her wake. Her lunch-time strolls to the university

cafeteria were accompanied by looks from passing engineer-
ing students that would have made Helen of Troy blush. Kate
would become the envy of other actresses, the butt of their
jokes, and the source of their jealousy as she blithely paraded
her contradictions in a seemingly unending chatterbox tone
that often made me wonder if her retinue of male admirers
ever found pause to consummate their all-to-obvious desire.

Kate was self-absorbed yet generous to a fault, gifted yet
frivolous, elegant yet earthy, beautiful yet ferociously self-
critical of both her look and her persona. She was also a
Francophile and conversant in the language. This, and her
classical actress demeanour, meant she was irresistible to Rex
and they became fast friends. Kate and I also struck a chord,
and both Rex and I directed her in some of her finest performances. Rex, in classic mode, cast Kate in Racine and as Violetta
in *The Lady of the Camellias*, while I favoured her earthier side
as Pirate Jenny in *The Threepenny Opera* and Nola Boyle in *The
Season at Sarsaparilla*. Mention must also be made of a Nimrod
Theatre outing for John Bell, Kate dazzling in doublet and
pantomime hose in *Hamlet on Ice*.

Kate could muck in with an ensemble but, at heart, she was
from the diva school. It's a special category of actress. Divas
tend to flatter potential directors as one might encourage a
witty hairdresser or stylish couturier who would reciprocally
enhance one's stage appearance. Our friendship with Kate was
nonetheless genuine and longstanding. It was fuelled by mutual
admiration, discreet understanding and a minimum of sexual
intrusion. Rex and I knew that underneath all Kate's glamour,
assumed promiscuity and social and theatrical flamboyance
lurked *the smarts*—that steely intelligence and survivor soul of
a tough-minded middle-class Irish Catholic girl from Adelaide,
educated by nuns. Kate was like a wonderful character straight
out of Balzac.

But I've drifted, as the contemplation of beautiful women
encourages you to do. Rex was another who, in the words of
Leonard Cohen, was *oppressed by the figures of beauty*—a fatal
flaw we both shared and relished. As I got to know him better,

I discovered this was also the source of his fascination with all things French, including the handsome Parisian film star and sometime Marseilles gangster Alain Delon.

Sex was more important to Rex than it was to me; I tended to sublimate it into my productions. He was mysterious about his nocturnal diversions, though they seemed to involve a stream of suitors that would have done Kate proud, and late-night shifts at leather bars, a novelty in the late 1960s. On one or two occasions I was summoned to accompany him as he retrieved possessions from a household he was departing. Apparently my presence was insurance that his exit wouldn't be accompanied by violent retribution.

I recall Rex's NIDA graduation production, a revenge tragedy by the Jacobean dramatist John Ford, expressed in an elegant flurry of white sheets, white light, hot, sexually charged acting and geysers of stage blood. It was called *The Broken Heart*, and one sensed there might have been a few in Rex's wake; maybe he was nursing one himself.

Through Rex, I was introduced to French cinema and was inspired by the radical playfulness of Jean-Luc Godard and the nocturnal Parisian streets of Jean-Pierre Melville, whose *Le Samouraï*, starring Delon, was a shared favourite. Other discoveries included Japanese cinema and writing. Rex was a fan of Yukio Mishima, with his gym-pumped midget frame, florid prose, self-destructive protagonists and Francophile flourishes. Reading Mishima's *The Temple of the Golden Pavilion* set me on the path to Yasunari Kawabata, whose spare prose I preferred. Kawabata's *Beauty and Sadness* and *Snow Country* became literary signposts on the road that would eventually lead me to Japan.

On a breezier note, Rex introduced me to the all-black pop sounds of Tamla Motown. The Motown sound was fashionable at the time, and many intense conversations at Rex's rented Glebe terrace house were relieved by a dance track from Martha and the Vandellas, The Four Tops, The Supremes or Marvin Gaye singing *What's Goin' On?*

In return, my NIDA experiments with improvisation and adventurous acting styles were a great influence on Rex. Gifted, demanding and audacious young NIDA actors like Nicholas Lathouris, who played Prospero for Rex, Gillian Jones and David Cameron his memorable Miranda and Ferdinand, and Terry O'Brien in a series of inspired comic cameos, were hungry for alternatives to the hidebound naturalistic acting styles that were the staple of the day.

It was with these imaginative young actors, some of whom later joined the cast of *Hair*, that Rex went on to form the Performance Syndicate, and over many years, he created some of the most exciting experimental theatre Australia had yet seen. The techniques of Japanese theatre, the Polish director Jerzy Grotowski and the collective audacity of the Living Theatre all played a role in creating a new theatrical language. Rex produced his best work with this group, including his elegant new readings of Shakespeare's *The Tempest*, some classic Racine and an athletic marathon-running exploratory work, *10 000 Miles*, written by William Yang and staged in a theatre converted into a mini-velodrome.

Rex had travelled to Sydney to seek out his vocation and, through NIDA, he found it. As well as seeking, he was also fleeing. He was leaving behind a tropical small-town mentality and the governance of one of the more conservative and oppressive regimes Australia had known—that of Queensland Premier Joh Bjelke-Petersen. In choosing to cross state borders in search of cultural advancement Rex was not alone. Fellow exiles included Queensland poet and novelist David Malouf, theatre director Rodney Fisher, literary and theatre agent Jane Cameron and the writer, actor and later photographer William Yang.

I privately called them *The Brissie Mob*. As Hollywood's fortunes were bolstered by the arrival of some of the world's greatest film-makers courtesy of Hitler's purge of German Jews, Australia's cultural life was greatly enhanced by this group of young Queenslanders in exile from an economically prosperous, yet endemically corrupt, voraciously anti-intellectual and stridently anti-gay political regime in sunny Queensland.

I met *The Brissie Mob* through Rex, and over time our lives and professional involvements variously overlapped. I premiered

David Malouf's play *Blood Relations*, and the opera of *Voss,* for which David wrote an inspiring libretto. The success that greeted *Johnno*, his first novella, launched his career as an international writer. Over time, I became friends with William Yang. William was the late starter of the group and finally emerged from a decade's foreplay involving architecture, playwriting and acting to astonish us with his startlingly original photographs that documented the underbelly of Sydney society. He subsequently created a new role for himself as a popular and original onstage diarist. I often observed: *William will outlive us all—and he's got the negatives!*

William's surge to photographic prominence was heralded by his first major photographic exhibition, *Sydneyphiles*. It consisted of raw images that exposed the local demimonde at play. Many of his subjects were present at the opening, on the walls and in person. William was very nervous about the potential for confrontation at this event, and as his friend and supporter, I had to supply a few fortifying drinks and a deal of encouragement to get him to the gallery. He needn't have worried. Despite his disturbing images of well-known social icons exposing their often naked bodies and fragile souls, their slashed wrists, sexual encounters and drugged excesses, the only complaints came from those that were not represented:

I was at that party and did far worse than that! Why aren't I there?

William's career never looked back. That night confirmed that self-respect is a less desirable human ambition than fame and notoriety. It was a chilling revelation.

Rex's mother, Ivy Cramphorn, was a less popular force-to-be-reckoned-with among *The Brissie Mob*. Known pejoratively as *Poison Ivy*, after a popular song, Ivy was a war widow with attitude. I got on surprisingly well with her and recall a memorable chance encounter at a city bus stop where Ivy dropped her often acerbic veneer and revealed herself as a troubled and essentially lonely soul who lived through and for her only son.

Rex and I had only one collaborative venture, and, while short-lived, it proved instructive. After both our careers had flourished in different ways, we were invited to put together a season of contemporary work for the Old Tote Theatre.

The company had already survived one palace coup, which resulted in artists leaving and forming the now flourishing Nimrod Theatre. The Old Tote was past its use-by, losing audiences and public support. This was a last-ditch attempt by a beleaguered board and management to appear modern. However, when funding became an issue, they decided to proceed with their conventional season of classics and commercial standards but slash our contemporary repertoire and cancel our planned productions of Australian plays, including new commissions and a revival of Patrick White's *A Cheery Soul*. Shocked by this retrograde step, we very publicly and deliberately resigned, in the knowledge that it might trigger the company's demise. The Old Tote had a remarkable history and established the idea of quality mainstream subsidised theatre in Sydney, but it was time for more progressive thinking, and passions ran high. What Rex and I did was iconoclastic, but necessary. To salvage at least some of our planned repertoire, we created a theatre company in an old Walter Burley Griffin–designed cinema, the Paris, near what is now Whitlam Square. Adopting the motto *Paris is the heart of Sydney*, we assembled a group of outstanding actors, writers and designers and managed to premiere two of the new Australian works: Dorothy Hewett's *Pandora's Cross* and Louis Nowra's *Visions*.

The Paris became an all-consuming obsession during its short life. Dorothy Hewett's play opened the season and it was set around the strip clubs, underworld and bohemian subculture of Kings Cross. During rehearsals for *Pandora's Cross*, Rex and I shared an enjoyable and absurdly memorable experience. Fortified by a few drinks, we decided on a spontaneous strip-club crawl as research. The clubs and their acts were mostly predictable, though we were fascinated to discover that several clubs were linked by underground tunnels, so the same strippers could perform identical routines in multiple venues. It was at the Pink Pussycat, the last club we visited, that a few surprises awaited.

The Paris Theatre
Company:

1. Martin Sharp
2. Roy Ritchie
3. Julie McGregor
4. Elisabeth Knight
5. Brian Thomson
6. Bill Walker
7. Jono Enemark

8. Ralph Tyrell
9. Arthur Dignam
10. Jim Sharman
11. Bill Harding
12. Fran Moore
13. John Paramor
14. Sally Campbell

15. John Gaden
16. Geraldine Turner
17. Neil Redfern
18. Rex Cramphorn
19. Gillian Appleton
20. Dorothy Hewitt
21. Luciana Arrighi

22. Anna Senior
23. Kate Fitzpatrick
24. Jennifer Claire
25. Robyn Nevin

A bored, naked stripper was doing her sitting-on-a-candle act when a busload of Newcastle miners were ushered in. They were tanked up and became boisterous. The stripper was unimpressed. She leapt off her candle and, with a voice that would cut crystal, shouted:

Music! The music stopped.

Silence.

I am an artiste! she volunteered. *And do not appreciate rowdies!*

Rex held his mirth in check courtesy of a handkerchief.

There were unsympathetic sniggers from the miners, then: *Think of your mothers!*

To our amazement, they all did. Like chastened children this army of hulks went quiet and bowed their heads in reverence. Or was it shame?

Music! she shrieked. The bump-and-grind of Tina Turner lurched back to life. Descending onto the candle, she resumed her act in an atmosphere of silence and awe. Rex and I slid discreetly into the street, in convulsions, knowing that nothing in *Pandora's Cross* would ever match that.

The Paris was a site of great hope, aspiration, hard work and finally some heartbreak. It was part of the process of shifting quality theatre in Sydney from its provincial English repertory roots and also physically moving it from the sheltered university-based fringe and into the life of the city. There was much goodwill surrounding the venture, but it was over-ambitious given the lack of resources and the weight of new ideas—new productions, new plays, new venue, new company, too much idealism and not enough money. The odds were against us and the venture failed. However, it cleared the decks, established some new criteria for what a progressive theatre might achieve and paved the way for the creation of the Sydney Theatre Company.

The theatre was subsequently demolished and replaced by an apartment block overlooking Hyde Park. It was probably the last gasp of the collective mentality that had its roots in 1960s politics and idealism. As the venture involved many leading artists of the day, its ripples are still felt within a generation for whom theatre remains more than a business or mere entertainment. After this, theatre in Sydney became more pragmatic and, it must be said, better funded and more professional. If there was a lesson from the venture, it's that in theatre you should offer the public only one new idea at a time. If it's a new play, it needs a known venue, and a new venue requires a known play. In retrospect, this is obvious. At the time, this tough lesson in balancing vision with pragmatism came at some personal cost to Rex, myself and all those closely involved.

Our dented idealism and new-found knowledge would fuel other ventures. Rex became artistic director of Melbourne's Playbox Theatre and, after directing the 1982 Adelaide Festival, I would create an ensemble company, Lighthouse, for the State Theatre of South Australia. The well subsidised and fully resourced Sydney Theatre Company was soon established and began its life by inviting me to mount the third of our planned Paris Theatre productions: Patrick White's *A Cheery Soul*. Ironically, it became the success that had eluded us in Whitlam Square.

We never collaborated again, but my friendship with Rex continued off and on over the decades until we drifted apart with the inevitable play of time and circumstances. Rex was one of those rare friends who remain so close you can take up where you left off, no matter what the time gap. It was a shock then to discover in the early 1990s that Rex had contracted AIDS. Some months later, aged fifty, he died—the first in my circle of friends to do so.

In 1995, it was with a mix of sorrow and pleasure that I accepted an invitation to give the first of an annual series of Rex Cramphorn lectures—a memorial set up by his friends and colleagues. That lecture became, in its way, the starting point for this book. The occasion was also the last time I saw Rex's mother. We shared a brief and quietly emotional reverie. Ivy Cramphorn, deprived of her son and purpose, died shortly after.

Rex's funeral had been well attended at St Stephen's Church in Newtown. *The Brissie Mob* rallied to their old friend's farewell and an unsettled, if eloquent, Rodney Fisher read a most moving eulogy in which he suggested that, among Rex's many considerable achievements, he was at least partly a model for David Malouf's *Johnno*.

After the service I found myself outside the church feeling oddly dizzy. I set off alone and on foot. Turning a corner, I stumbled, tumbling into the gutter of a laneway adjoining the church. I dissolved into floods of tears before being rescued by a passing friend, Louis Nowra. Louis had been another of Rex's close collaborators. He discreetly led me to a nearby coffee shop, where we sat, silently, until I was sufficiently composed to make my way home.

It was only after twenty years and when I was reduced to sobbing in the gutter that I finally realised that, along with many others, I must have loved the man.

With Rex Cramphorn, Bondi

The Architect

Oxford Street is an arterial chunk of asphalt that links the city and the eastern suburbs of Sydney. In an era before it became home to dance clubs and Mardi Gras parades, it housed modest emporiums selling menswear and a few Greek and Italian delicatessens. As the 1960s youth-quake began to grip the inner city, and students and young artists started colonising the cheap rental terraces and converted stables, a new phenomenon began to emerge to service their hunger, their impatience and their lack of culinary skills: the take-away.

An early, short-lived example of this species, with the inviting name of Hamburger Heaven, opened its bi-fold doors onto Oxford Street. Living in nearby Surry Hills, I would often drop by on my way home from rehearsals, for a burger with extra beetroot and fries. As I stood in line on one such occasion, a large and appealingly awkward figure hovered in the queue, glowing brightly under fluorescent light.

Brian Thomson was a drop-out architecture student. He was standing in line with his arms folded, impatiently tapping one of his bare feet. He sported the conventional uniform of the era: frayed jeans and khaki shirt. Framing his warm and open face was a helmet of hair, dyed bright pink.

Within moments of our being introduced by mutual friends, Brian flicked back a few strands of his electric mane and confided that he despised conventional theatre, was a disciple of the American architect Buckminster Fuller and his geodesic domes, an enthusiast for Andy Warhol, and had assisted sculptor Christo shroud the coast of Little Bay. Brian had stormed out of the architecture faculty of the University of New South Wales after a series of brightly coloured *Noddy Villages* he had enthusiastically designed for a project on housing for the aged had been dismissed as trivial.

Brian had a sense of fun and a rare energy about him. He also had the smartest eyes in Hamburger Heaven. A later revelation that his favourite song was *New York Mining Disaster 1941*, on account of Robin Gibb's heart-stopping falsetto, only added to my enthusiasm.

PREVIOUS PAGES: Brian Thomson, 1969 (LEFT); Brian Thomson, 1980 (RIGHT).

I couldn't believe my luck. I was on the lookout for a designer whose radicalism would chime with my own and who would help rescue the theatre from its pictorial rut. In front of me was no mealy-mouthed taste-obsessed thespian but a pop-addicted zealot with a generous spirit and an unapologetically ambitious streak. Brian had the take-no-prisoners attitude of a born diva, and pink hair to boot. I sensed I'd found a soul mate.

Our conversation continued as we strolled up Oxford Street, munching our burgers all the way, until we found ourselves at Brian's rented two-storey studio tucked away behind Taylor Square. At first glance, it seemed like the Aladdin's cave of a mad inventor. Upstairs was his work desk and architectural drawing board. They floated in a pool of light, like a meticulous white island surrounded by a sea of neon, pop sculptures and an array of small television sets, each tuned to a different channel. Order in the midst of chaos. Downstairs were more conventional living quarters and his patient partner. Over the years of our collaboration, Brian's partners would come and go. They would vary in age, nationality and gender but, like a renaissance artist with a stable of apprentices, the principle remained as it was on that first visit: one tap on the floor for tea and two for coffee. The tapping disappeared with time and the acquisition of middle-class manners, but the principle remained. Personally, I liked the tapping, as, I suspect, did its recipients.

The sometimes difficult transitions in his partner regime were often accompanied by drama played out at opera pitch. The more complex Brian's personal life became, the more inspired, precise, imaginative and brilliant were his designs. Whereas I had been reared in solitude and often sought inspiration in isolation, which made domestic life difficult for any prospective partner, Brian was just the opposite. He enjoyed company, companionship, and the emotional support it offered; domestic stimuli inspired him.

As I was in the midst of *Hair* preparations, I introduced Brian to Harry M Miller, who was only slightly startled by the pink hair. My producer was getting used to unlikely yet gifted suspects being ushered into his executive suite. Brian presented Harry with a tiny box of tricks called a *Hair Kit*. On the basis of this minimalist Duchamp-inspired gem, Brian was commissioned to visually transform the foyer of the Metro Theatre, a task he swiftly organised with enthusiasm and bravura.

It was a modest start but a foot in the door. Brian would later design the Melbourne production of *Hair*, adding a seven-strand rainbow flourish of lights that arched around the high proscenium. With this, Brian entered the world of the rock musical, where he felt right at home. He went on to design *Jesus Christ Superstar* and the apogee of our musical adventures, *The Rocky Horror Show*, and its cult movie sequel.

After *Hair* opened in Sydney, we embarked on our first collaboration: a surreal, gift-wrapped production of Shakespeare's *As You Like It*. The set was an offering to the audience, who responded with applause. Brian's white box of under-lit floors and floating clouds was a calling card for what lay ahead. The production didn't pretend to be set anywhere but on a stage and was devoid of any faux historicism. The concept was as modernist in its elegance and simplicity as the Greek and Elizabethan stages that had inspired it.

Brian's architectural training meant he possessed an innate sense of how to define stage space. It also meant his technical drawings were precise and all scale models were beautifully made. *It looks just like the model, only bigger* was a phrase that admiring and sometimes envious fellow designers used to compliment his work. His attention to detail was meticulous. *No one will notice* was an explanation often proffered by budget-conscious production managers suggesting how a corner might be cut in materials or construction. *I will*, replied the uncompromising but never impractical designer.

Our collaborations continued, off and on, for over thirty years. In this time, we played our role in furthering the visual dynamics of theatre in Australia and, on occasion, internationally as well. The best of our work appeared seamless, and it was generally assumed the process was breezy. Sometimes it was, but just as often it involved heated arguments, smashed models, midnight phone calls, sleepless nights, much tapping for tea and coffee and constant challenges to each other's sensibilities—until the best possible outcome was realised. Simplicity was always our aim, and this is the toughest goal. You never start with simplicity or the results are simple-minded. Simplicity is a hard-won achievement and reveals itself only after every imagined option has been tested, evaluated, discarded or embraced.

Our working process involved an intense relationship over a long period of time, and it had all the passion, tears, ennui and joy of an odd-couple marriage. We were sensitive to each other's finer qualities and just as aware of our shared capacity for self-delusion. I'm sure divorce often crossed both our minds, but something always kept us back from the brink and, before we knew it, we were onto another show.

When we began, stage design was often referred to as *décor* and tended towards pictorial charm-school clutter. It reflected the repro-antique-filled domestic world of its provincial audience. In this context, Brian's anti-realist and minimalist approach and his construction-site aesthetics were as startling as pink hair and bare feet had been at that first encounter.

We aimed to create a new visual vocabulary for the stage and it reached its stark and beautiful zenith on productions like Patrick White's *A Cheery Soul* and Brian's labyrinthine design for Benjamin Britten's *Death in Venice*. This landmark production, initially created for the 1980 Adelaide Festival, remained in the national operatic repertoire for twenty-five years.

Through Brian I met his brother Ken Thomson, a great friend of Barry Humphries and the namesake for Dame Edna Everage's fictional son, Kenny. Brian, with this enthusiasm for satirical writers like Tom Wolfe (*The Electric Kool-Aid Acid Test* adorned Brian's desk at our earliest meetings), was destined to design for Barry-Edna, and so he did. In time, other pop icons also attracted his eye and he created great public art: neon hearts for the Sydney Harbour Bridge and memorable images for the Olympic Games ceremonies. Tony Awards and many other honours would come his way, new and equally rewarding collaborations would develop and international commissions would beckon.

For me, at least, nothing has ever quite replaced the excitement of those formative years, when everything seemed fresh and balanced on a knife edge and required explanation and justification and aggression and courage. Very few people get to live out their dreams, but we did, and our encounter gave us the opportunity to exercise our imaginations to the full. Through our collaboration, we learnt how to make each new production another grand journey into the great imaginative unknown. That privilege, and the attendant lifelong friendship, with all its tensions and joys, was a supreme stroke of good fortune.

We met by chance, and chance holds a sacred place in architecture, in theatre and, above all, in life. Like entering Aladdin's cave, it simply requires an awareness of when to use the magic words: *Open Sesame*.

All About Eve

From time to time any artist worthy of the name will find themselves in the gutter and they won't necessarily be looking at the stars. Artists can scale dizzying heights but they can also crash like Icarus. The fragile glue that supports their little bipolar wings melts when they fly too close to the sun.

At such times, friends can mysteriously disappear, fearful that the downward spiral may prove catching. As fairweather friends evaporate, angels often appear in the guise of those more experienced in ambition's game of snakes and ladders—colleagues who offer comfort, kindness and perspective.

In 1995, I found myself walking distractedly down Macleay Street, Kings Cross, with a carton of A4 paper under my arm and an intense expression suggesting that all was less than well. A tall, familiar figure strode into view. He took in the writing paper and my blank expression and frowned:

If you think that'll help, you've got a surprise in store.

Stephen Maclean and I had once lived together. We hadn't been in close contact for many years but for the occasional smile and how-are-you-going exchange in the street. Faced with the sight of his old friend suffering an obvious case of the blues, Stephen decided to intervene. He did so in a typically abrasive way. It was his warm but unsentimental gaze that had first endeared him to me, as it revealed a good heart and a genuine nature that I found very appealing. I was very pleased to see him.

Stephen was a man who believed in simple remedies, and his cure for an attack of the blues was a roast dinner, a glass of wine, friendly gossip and a volley of showtunes. A few hours later, I found myself perched on the roof of an Elizabeth Bay high-rise that had seen better days, in a tiny caretaker flat that canny Stephen had stumbled upon—in his low-on-rent, high-on-atmosphere, Scottish-descendant kind of way. I found myself enjoying the wintry indigo view of the harbour at twilight, some undercooked roast lamb and vegetables, bargain-bin shiraz and a non-stop monologue on faded film stars, accompanied in stereo by the strident tones of *Judy Garland at Carnegie Hall.*

For many this would seem like a stopover in a suburb of hell but for me, on this occasion, it was well judged and did the trick. The highlight of the evening was an impromptu phone call from Stephen's favourite jazz singer, Peggy Lee, in Los Angeles. As an ex-journalist and now showbiz biographer and film-maker, Stephen had been trying to finance a documentary on Peggy, and his subject, now seventy-five and in her final years, was checking on progress. There was none.

I'm afraid they prefer them dead, Peg!

There was laughter down the line. Peggy obliged by dying a few years later, aged eighty-two. By then, the documentary was beyond saving. Stephen Maclean, who was a lively forty-five at the time of our dinner, followed suit in 2006, aged fifty-six, from throat cancer. It was a death way too soon, as was the case with several in my circle.

A decade after our Macleay Street encounter, I was attending his wake at the Clovelly Bowling Club, with an endless panorama of the Pacific Ocean stretching before me through vast picture windows. I was sad and contemplating Stephen's missed opportunities, including the documentary. It would have been a rare insight into that great jazz singer's life; Stephen had stayed with the ageing star in her Los Angeles apartment. He was Peggy's in-house diarist. As in Billy Wilder's film *Sunset Boulevard*, he had played screenwriter Joe Gillis to her Norma Desmond.

Not the least of the insights into fading stardom that Stephen's documentary might have provided, enthusiastically related over the undercooked dinner, were Peggy's bridge nights involving movie veterans and legendary film composer Henry Mancini, and Peggy waving to her old pal Mae West. Mae lived in the adjoining apartment block, but, according to Stephen, you could never tell if it was really Mae on the balcony, as she took delight in hiring drag queens to impersonate her and wave to fans in passing tour-of-the-stars'-homes buses, while Mae chortled like a mischievous child behind the curtains.

Our night on the rooftop in Elizabeth Bay in many ways defined the world of Stephen Maclean, author of *The Boy from Oz*.

Stephen Maclean, 1976

Some wit, warmth, gossip, abrasive insight, a few unfinanceable projects, a fading chanteuse on the line and *The Man that Got Away* on the stereo.

Was it always thus? Was it like that in 1971 when we first met? Stephen was a handsome young hired-hand journalist for *Go-Set* magazine sent to interview me for the forthcoming production of *Jesus Christ Superstar* in an anonymous rehearsal room in Sydney. We would later dine by candlelight, at a nearby French restaurant. It was a time when French cuisine briefly held sway and Edith Piaf anthems accompanied so many meals that you wanted to take aim at the speakers and silence *the little sparrow*. Of course, that was before Mediterranean and Thai cuisine took over. Thai means free. Stephen died in Thailand. Freeland. Pattaya Beach, to be precise. Grief encourages these rambling free-associations.

After that first dinner, we survived a crazy night when Stephen's furious and soon-to-be-ex boyfriend became so enraged he sent all manner of emergency services—Fire, Ambulance, Police—to interrupt our night together. We subsequently settled into an on-again, off-again relationship that would last several years.

As Stephen lazed beside the sun-drenched pool in a rented colonial mansion in the Adelaide Hills, occasionally tapping away on his portable typewriter, and while I rehearsed the concert version of *Jesus Christ Superstar* for the Adelaide Festival premiere, I had no idea he might be rehearsing some future scenario staring himself as Joe Gillis and another, better-cast and more qualified Norma Desmond. *Starstruck*, a film he later wrote, which Gillian Armstrong, another friend, directed, was based on the same idea.

In the age of rock-and-roll, Stephen was a throw back to an earlier era. A movie buff, he never stopped talking about Joe Mankiewicz's *All About Eve*, whose ambitious heroines Stephen admired and whose tall, dark and stylish Addison De Witt he often resembled. George Sanders, who played the acerbic critic in the film, wrote *Memoirs of a Professional Cad* and OD'd in Barcelona. He left a note: *I'm so bored.*

At the Clovelly Bowling Club, eulogies and testimonials mingled with memories of my time with Stephen.

Our affair survived *Superstar* but not the move to London. I moved into Chelsea, then Pimlico; Stephen to Earl's Court. He liked it there. It was cheap and he was close to the Gigolo and the Sombrero. The latter was a clandestine dance club where Stephen met two Venezuelans, Gonzalo and Gustavo. Handsome Gonzalo he kept for himself; the spikier, smarter Gustavo he introduced to me.

We still made occasional trips together, including for *Rocky Horror* in Los Angeles, where, coming back after midnight from rehearsal at the Roxy on Sunset, I found Stephen wrapped in a towel and urgently hunched in front of a late-night television movie in our shared suite at the Chateau Marmont. He was surrounded by an empty wine bottle and a multitude of chip packets from the Liquor Locker. Switching channels, he'd discovered a mysterious movie: *You gotta see this!*

It was a baroque melodrama played at *Rocky Horror* pitch. As it progressed our jaws dropped. Orson Welles' *A Touch of Evil* became one of our all-time favourites. Anyone seeing this film, now hailed as a masterpiece, would be as amazed as we were that night, watching Marlene Dietrich preside over the bloated corpse of Hank Quinlan, played by Welles, and her offhand remark before she sashayed into the shadows:

He was some kind of man. What does it matter what you say about people?

I often think of Stephen when I see films, especially backstage movies. I wonder what he would have made of David Lynch's *Mulholland Drive*. Would he love Johnny Depp as *The Libertine*? I think so. I'm sure so.

At Clovelly, I commiserated with Stephen's old friend, the producer Ben Gannon. Ben and Stephen were two for the road. No romance there but they linked arms and did the Aussie showbiz kids in London routine, partying endlessly and wining and dining with English impresarios and expat Aussie glamour girls. London society with its movie and rock stars suited Stephen, with its echo of Evelyn Waugh's *bright young things*.

When Stephen finally became an author and Ben emerged as a successful producer and they both returned to Australia, Ben produced Stephen's documentary and then the musical from his biography of Peter Allen: *The Boy from Oz*. They saw it succeed in Australia and, with Hugh Jackman in the lead, its transfer to Broadway.

I watched it in concert in Sydney, and Hugh Jackman, who was remarkable, reminded me more of the stylish and waspish Stephen than the gawkier Peter Allen. It must have made Stephen so happy to see something he began on *the great white way.*

Ben would die within months of Stephen's wake at Clovelly. This would be our last contact. He had started his showbiz life as a student assistant with me on *As You Like It*. Ben wrote notes in such glorious copperplate you knew he would travel far. He progressed through the rock musical ranks and became a successful London agent, then a discerning producer in Oz. Again, it was cancer. Again, too young. *Sad Song ...* as Lou Reed chanted on the fateful album *Berlin*, which Ben and Stephen and I would first hear in a little Pimlico flat in London in 1973.

The last time I saw Stephen was outside Morgan's Café in Victoria Street, Kings Cross. Ah, the eternal Cross. It had been our point of connection since *Superstar*. Stephen was croaking and bandaged but in good spirits. He had just come from St Vincent's Hospital and a final post-op check-up before he departed for Thailand.

I walked him back to Regents Court, a small hotel popular with artists, where the two wonderful women who ran it and who loved artists had allowed him to run up a tab; they knew he would never pay it. Ben might oblige. Ben was loyal and prosperous and special; he would often discreetly settle his old pal's debts.

Stephen could be demanding, and the cancer and all the croaking made him more so. It must have been so very painful but it was not in his nature to let you know that. Faced with a barrage of high-octane complaint from Stephen, the desk clerk looked as if the plane for Thailand couldn't leave fast enough.

Stephen and I made our farewells and he hurried back to his room to pack. I would never see him again.

Fran Moore wrapped things up at Clovelly.

Franny was Stephen's friend and sometime agent and another angel. She often picked up the pieces from the trail of hellfire left by Stephen, who could be a devil. He was high maintenance but worth it. Fran had dealt with Stephen's last requests: the Buddhist ceremonies and the Pattaya friends and the formalities in Thailand. In this instance, Stephen knew what was coming and had everything in order.

Fran looked ghostly pale but perked up as she spoke of his final moments; they were worthy of Genet. Stephen had passed away in the back of a Thai ambulance tearing through the streets of Pattaya towards the hospital. He was accompanied in the back of the speeding vehicle by a veritable chorus of attentive Thai ladyboys, some brandishing amyl nitrate. He died, as they say, with a smile.

It was a fitting end to Stephen's life, with *flights of angels to sing him to his rest*.

A little part of me was even jealous: the subterranean private part that wisely or foolishly lacks the courage to really live my life to the hilt. Stephen did, just like *The Boy from Oz*. He was so full of mischief and wit and *beans*, and that's why so many people loved him.

SHINJUKU SHUFFLE

1970: The cherry blossoms fluttered onto the lake in Shinjuku Goen. It was twilight and I paused to savour this traditional Japanese sight. It offered a welcome respite from the bustle of Tokyo. A deep breath before I returned to the noisy shopping and nightlife precinct of Shinjuku with its famously busy train station. I was accompanied on my walk by the sound of a lone violin. It floated over traffic and pierced the evening air. The violinist was probably a student practising. Everyone was practising in 1970 as Tokyo emerged from twenty-five years of postwar reconstruction. Japan was in the process of transforming itself into an economic and technological powerhouse. Soon it would host an international trade fair in Osaka —Expo 1970—and shake its techno-rattle at the world.

A future and more prosperous generation of Tokyoites would throw tradition to the wind and trade their tatami for carpet and swap their cushions for chairs; they would supplement their fish diets with high-carb, and add height and swagger to their previously modest demeanour. In 1970, tatami, fish and modesty were still on the menu. I was enjoying my first visit to Japan, and especially the performing arts: the spectacular soap opera of Kabuki, the visible puppeteers of Bunraku, and the provocative underground theatre of Shuji Terayama's company, Tenjo Sajiki, and its offshoot, the Tokyo Kid Brothers. Above all, I was transfixed by the spirit, symbol and sideshow that contributed to the ancient and hypnotic ritual of Japanese Nō.

For all the neon and glitter illuminating modern Tokyo, the Japan that most intrigued me was a place of ghosts, spirits, ancestors, Shinto animism and Buddhist contemplation. This aspect was superbly captured in the art of Nō; with its stately pace, polished wooden stages, ceremonial costumes, centuries-old ritual and deep soul, Nō subtly captured the splendour of the Japanese yang and the shadow play of its yin.

I had been in Tokyo for some weeks on a Churchill Fellowship, studying theatre, drifting around and living modestly. Then a call came from Australia asking if I was interested in directing the Japanese production of *Hair*. Gerry Ragni's sister, the author's representative, had seen the Australian production and pronounced it one of the best, hence the invitation.

That I was already in Tokyo seemed fateful. Accepting this invitation would mean tossing in my travel scholarship, but I quickly agreed. It offered a unique opportunity to work inside a culture to which I was already in thrall. I did a quick role change from cultural tourist to travelling director and soon found myself being entertained by the Japanese producers, the prosperous and fashionable Kawazoe family, at their Italian-styled Chianti restaurant. The Kawazoes were to be among the most intriguing people I met in Tokyo, and their distinguished pedigree interested me.

The family was descended from an elder statesman who had been foreign minister in the Meiji government and had helped to open Japan to the West. It had been a Kawazoe who shopped in Europe for educational and legal systems for modern Japan. For generations the family had helped to shape Japan's future. I was dining with history at the Chianti as I met with the elderly Hiroshi Kawazoe, his darkly beautiful second wife—who represented the French couturier Yves St Laurent in Tokyo— and his son from an earlier marriage, Shotaro Kawazoe, the producer-to-be of *Hair*.

The personable Shotaro, or Shoro as I came to know him, was in his late twenties and had the educated authority of a fashionable young man about town. Seated across the table from him during that first dinner, I noted that his elegantly tailored suit was adorned with hippy beads, suggesting conflicted interests. Shoro played flamenco guitar, was fluent in several languages and was a successful record producer. His well-known actress partner, Jun Fubuki, was to become the first of his three wives. Shoro had inherited his father's fine hands, though he was more abrasive and regarded his father's formality and aristocratic restraint with youthful, westernised impatience.

Hiroshi Kawazoe was a willowy, silver-haired sophisticate in his sixties, with beautiful parchment skin. I sensed his strength and gentility as we formally bowed and then casually shook hands. I was somewhat in awe of his elegant east-west manner. He seemed to be a throw back to the Taisho Era, that brief, wonderful, urbane and democratic period between the Meiji Era and Japan's disastrous descent into militarism in the 1930s. Hiroshi had continued the Kawazoe fascination with European cultural exchange, opening Chianti in the 1960s at the suggestion of his socially ambitious, much younger wife. Their restaurant played host to writers and intellectuals like Mishima and Kawabata, designer Issey Miyake, film-maker Oshima and young composers like Ryiuchi Sakamoto; it was popular with the fashionable, the educated, the talented and the discerning international visitor to Tokyo.

Shoro and his singer and musician accomplice Katsumi— a pop star and local idol—aimed to take the Kawazoe modern-ising tradition a step further by staging *Hair* in Japan. Shoro and I would often meet at Chianti to discuss both the practical details of the production and its relevance for young Japanese. In 1970, young Tokyoites, like Shoro himself, were caught in a riddle exemplified by the tension between bows and hand-shakes, suits and beads. They faced the culturally difficult choice between an independent lifestyle and a corporate future. I real-ised that the *Where Do I Go?* theme of *Hair* would become the defining aspect of the Tokyo production. Other elements, such as the anti-war issue, took on a different meaning in a warrior culture recently subject to nuclear holocaust.

We Japanese are already hippies was Shoro's assertion.

I wasn't so sure. My time in Tokyo hadn't been solely de-voted to studying the elegant rituals of Nō. I was street-wise enough to be aware of clashes between students and authorities and the passionate advocacy of extreme right and left ortho-doxies. Nor had I entirely bought the chrysanthemum- and nature-loving tourist image being promoted. I was aware that the Japanese preferred their nature clipped, controlled and manicured to Japanese specifications, like bonsai.

However, I enjoyed my new-found friends at Chianti; they became like family to me, and through them I grew to love Tokyo even more. It's an acquired taste, this fortress city, where everything happens on the inside, behind the façade. I experienced an odd convergence of feeling with Tokyo in transition. As I moved from my modest Churchill Fellowship accommodation to an international hotel, I decided to embrace the city. Many westerners leave it, while others are seduced and want to become Japanese. This is difficult in a country where everyone is encouraged to believe in mono-cultural uniqueness: that Japanese rice is like no other, which it isn't, and where a westerner speaking fluent Japanese is greeted with shock, because the Japanese language is a secret code that guarantees membership of an exclusive club.

This raised a tricky question. How would I approach directing *Hair* without the language? I decided the production would be best served by simply being myself, not by attempting to be Japanese, sympathetic as I was to the everyday poetry of the culture. Ironically, on my occasional return visits to Australia, my already narrow eyes and increasingly enigmatic manner encouraged my friends to observe:

You've become Japanese!

Our planning meetings at Chianti gave way to the more familiar world of auditions and rehearsals, and meals grabbed at the local noodle bar. The city was often in turmoil, with student riots in Shinjuku and downtown Hibiya Park. I was becoming something of a connoisseur of street action, and the Tokyo variety was the most formal and ritualised I had encountered; everyone knew their roles and had their uniforms. Later that year, one of Chianti's most illustrious diners, the right-wing author Mishima, led a small, self-funded army in a failed coup at the headquarters of the self defence forces —a polite term for the army. Mishima would go on to commit ritual suicide rather than face defeat. It was the uncertainty and volatility of this alarming era that kept us all on our toes; with our production of *Hair*, we were in the thick of it.

Theatre contributed mightily to the frenzy of change in Tokyo. The influence of New York and the Greenwich Village underground scene, of new wave cinema and Parisian student unrest, found their local equivalent in the little Shinjuku café-theatre of popular playwright and director ShujiTerayama. Here they performed incendiary works like *Throw Away Your Books and Take to the Streets!*. I felt happy and at home in Shinjuku and became friendly with Terayama, whose agitprop plays and films I always enjoyed, usually sitting hunched with my legs crossed on a cushion in his basement theatre. He was older, but a kindred spirit and introduced me to the Tokyo Kid Brothers, a group of theatrical rebels and my contemporaries. Their backstreet productions were even wilder than Terayama's, and their radical young director, Yutaka Higashi, became a close friend and ally. I cast their lead actor, Ryusaku Shinsui, as Berger in *Hair*.

I began to enjoy my double life in Tokyo as I moved effort-lessly back and forth between the alleys of Shinjuku and the sophistication of Chianti, doing the *Shinjuku Shuffle*. In an attempt to link the two worlds, I encouraged Shoro to com-mission a Japanese adaptation of *Hair* from Terayama, who was a provocative writer. In the words of Shoro, it proved to be ... *a little extreme*. We ended up with a more straightforward translation put together by Shoro himself and Katsumi, who, in addition to being a pop idol, was an accomplished lyricist.

It was challenging to be in the midst of all this political and artistic ferment. Even if you spoke the language it was con-fusing. I didn't, so the situation was often incomprehensible. The cast coped well with their foreign director. For translation I depended on the multilingual skills of Shoro. He dealt with the cast in Japanese, the European producer, Bertrand Castelli, in French, and me in English. At times it must have been hellish, but Shoro managed to keep all the balls in the air—well, most of the time.

Living and working in another country with a different cul-ture and without access to language was an experience that offered a different perspective, and it gave me insight into an emotion that I had previously felt uncomfortable about: the sensation of being both inside and outside events. I entered Japan via the *Alien* queue. Being a bona fide alien meant I could feel relaxed about the idea. This feeling had been with me long before I travelled to Japan but it was crystallised in Tokyo. It was no surprise that when I returned to Australia, I directed a film called *Shirley Thompson Versus the Aliens*. In truth, I felt less alien in Tokyo than I often did in Australia. In Japan I learnt to push past homesickness and loneliness into the deeper, more rewarding realm of solitude.

However, I wasn't short of company in the *Hair* rehearsal room. One night, I accepted an invitation from some of the cast to eat and drink with them among the fumes and camaraderie in one of Shinjuku's smoky, crowded, back alley workers' bars. I loved the atmosphere and was thrilled to be granted insider status after passing my initiation test of eating *fugu*, a potentially poisonous seafood delicacy. We settled into a riotous meal, and after a few weeks of self-imposed isolation and diligent rehearsal preparation in my hotel, I relished the very ordinariness of the experience. It was a rare, sweet taste of exuberant young Japanese life. We sang and danced our way back towards a nightcap in one of my fellow diner's dormitory rooms and, somewhere along the way, we realised we were out of cigarettes. A vending machine materialised at the end of an alley, blinking fluorescently in the darkness. *Peace* is a brand of Japanese cigarette no longer in fashion but, given the war, Japan's nuclear history and our youthful zeal and anti-war commitment, it was a tantalising moment as *Peace* glowed through the fog of the Tokyo night. After the farewell drink, the ever-punctual Yamanote Line sped me back to my hotel, neon flickering on the train windows. The next day we were in rehearsal, as if nothing had happened. The camaraderie was history and I was director-san again.

We rehearsed at high velocity, twelve hours a day, seven days a week. I was amazed by the energy and commitment of the Japanese cast. The chaos and contradictions of the day were reflected in the rehearsal room. Pop idol Katsumi, who played Claude, arrived in a limo with an assistant to light his cigarettes. He mixed it with African-American singers from Chicago and a Tokyo Tribe who had been mostly cast from the streets and arrived in frayed jeans and thongs. Ambivalence was also apparent in official attitudes to the production. It was a Broadway musical, which made it desirable in an Expo year presenting a new, democratised and prosperous image of Japan to the world. However, it incited a dangerous empowering fervour in the young, which was seen as a threat. Cast members were hauled out of rehearsals for police interrogation sessions and I was strip-searched by customs on every to-and-fro trip to Australia. The authorities didn't ban *Hair* but they didn't like it, and they made life as difficult as possible for all of us.

The fact that *Hair* premiered in a strange theatre located on a mid-floor of the Socialist Party Building in Shibuya added fuel to the fire. It must be said that my production had a harder political edge, especially in the anti-war scenes, than the Broadway original. This fact became an issue when I subsequently staged *Hair* in the United States and my Boston production was banned and prosecuted under the *Mann Act*—US legislation aimed at preventing anyone from crossing state borders for the purposes of subversion. I was hurried back to New York and the offending anti-war scenes were hastily restaged before the Boston production resumed its successful season. Italian film-maker Antonioni was prosecuted under the *Mann Act* at the same time for *Zabriskie Point*. The governments of many countries were taking a surprising interest in the arts in 1970.

The Tokyo production opened successfully, and the cast made up in passion, commitment and energy what they might have lacked in finesse. It had been playing for some months when I made a return visit to check on its progress. My visit coincided with the funeral of Shoro's aristocratic father, Hiroshi Kawazoe. I was shaken by the news of his sudden death and felt a deep sense of loss at the absence of such a dignified man. I attended some of the rites of his Shinto funeral, and Shoro was both stoic and polite as he took me through the ceremony; unbeknown to either of us, Shoro's world was about to implode.

I had returned to Australia when I heard of Shoro's step-mother's death after a reported nervous breakdown. In a city that thrives on rumours, there were murmurs of a dangerous liaison between her and a cast member, which might have pre-cipitated suicide. Or was it simply grief? Confusion and gossip swirled and circulated. To me, Tokyo became a nightmare of intrigue, politics and deaths. The aristocratic Kawazoes had been generous, my time in Tokyo extraordinarily fulfilling, and suddenly it was no longer. The curtain had descended and corpses littered the stage. It was a Greek tragedy, a Japanese *Orestia*. The dramatic trajectory continued its downward spiral when Shoro was arrested on drug charges, along with Katsumi and some cast members. It felt like the fall of the House of Atreus; only it was the house of Kawazoe.

The Expo tour of *Hair* to Osaka was swiftly cancelled. Once that was announced, the drug charges were mysteriously dropped. To me, the conclusion was obvious: the authorities didn't want subversive musicals ruining their made-for-Expo image. There is a sense of freedom and generosity in Japan but cross the line and it can swiftly become a feudal and authoritarian place. In its capacity to suddenly revert to a xenophobic island mentality it often reminded me of Australia.

In a final scene in Terayama's film of *Throw Away Your Books and Take to the Streets!*, an old-style Japanese family is dining quietly in a traditional wooden house. The walls suddenly collapse around them and they find themselves flung into the chaos of modern urban life, surrounded by the world's busiest thoroughfare: Shinjuku Station.

It was an extraordinary privilege to find myself in Tokyo in 1970, a cultural tourist turned participant in a transitional moment in the life of a city and its people, experiencing old-new, east-west tensions, suits and beads, staging anthems to life as its shadow hovered in the wings, and revelling in the *Shinjuku Shuffle*.

TOKYO REUNION

2005: The limo pulled into the valet parking at the Park Hyatt in Shinjuku, and white-gloved hands ushered us into the elevator and up to the New York Grill, with its panoramic views of a Tokyo night swathed in fog cut by blinking lights requesting passing jets to *please consider* not crashing into the skyscrapers.

We were shown to our table at this understated landmark, the central location for Sofia Coppola's film *Lost in Translation*. My Tokyo friends, film producers Kenji Isamura and Georgina Pope, were the architects of this reunion, deeming it *special* ... which, once our guest arrived, it turned out to be.

I'd heard he died a junkie, which wasn't true; that he'd died of cancer, also false. When Shoro Kawazoe strolled in to dinner on the forty-third floor of the Park Hyatt he looked relaxed, dapper, sophisticated and very much like his old self, or the ghost of Hiroshi, his late father, for Shoro had adopted the courtesy and restraint he once abjured.

We forgot the bows and handshakes and simply embraced.

It had been thirty-five years since we worked together. At that time, we were rookies—a 25-year-old director from Australia and the 29-year-old scion of an established Tokyo family. Together, we once contributed to a small cultural revolution with Tokyo *Hair*. Now, we were just two mature diners brought together by mutual friends at a venue that was no accident. The Park Hyatt had been deliberately chosen by Kenji and Georgina: the sophisticated atmosphere where food, fashion and Tokyo society intersected was a perfect echo of Chianti in 1970.

Our small group huddled around the low-lit table as memories of the days of Tokyo *Hair* flooded back. The talk was casual; warm reminiscences of *Hair* and cast members past; no drug busts, interrogations, riots or deaths. The rise of China was a popular topic, accompanied by predictions that Shanghai would be the Tokyo of tomorrow. Shoro spoke, for the first time in my experience, of his birth mother, the famous concert pianist Chieko Hara, and her life in Italy with cellist husband Gaspar Cassado. No mention of the deaths of his late father or stepmother. The food was great, the conversation convivial.

In the silences sat something else.

The Japanese understand the poetry of loss and the drama of time but, above all, the need for lightness in dealing with them. It's the upside of withstanding earthquakes, tsunamis, fire-bombs and being nuked twice. Lightness is what I love about Japan and what I learnt from it.

Japanese culture also inspired some of the most original and compelling moments in the productions that followed my 1970 visit. The rivers of fluttering blood-red silk that welcomed Christ into Jerusalem. The *Hanomachi* ramp from Nō that became a runway to reveal a stiletto-heeled transvestite Frankenstein in *Rocky Horror*. Ritual. Magic. Above all, the understanding that emerged from directing in a language I could comprehend only through rhythm and pitch and the realisation that audiences see before they hear; and that if you distil an idea visually then an audience will open their ears and listen and engage, not superficially, but emotionally and intellectually.

The seeds of these ideas lay in my childhood and were nurtured by Duchamp's ready-mades, Christo's shapes and Kubrick's galaxies; but it was in Japan that I began to truly understand the deeper rules of engagement in life and art. My eyes were opened by rituals of Nō, the alleys of Shinjuku, a glimpse of Mishima and his transvestite partner at a Chianti table and the fateful dramas and excitements that surrounded Tokyo *Hair*. It was something I couldn't share with others, but it would achieve outward expression through my work.

As the silence and conversation and fine dining drew to a close and we were about to depart, a group of visiting Germans at the next table enquired whether Shoro was the architect of the Park Hyatt.

Not missing the irony, for in truth the Kawazoes were among the architects of modern Tokyo, the dignified Shoro smiled, offered them his business card and, without a blink:

If you ever want a tall building ... call me!

And then Shoro Kawazoe was gone.

It had been an extraordinary reunion and I was spiralling through time. I took in the panorama of mist and blinking red lights outside. The Tokyo landscape of my past had provided the tarmac for the jet that was about to take off. It had taken me decades to digest something I once understood instinctively, at a deep, less articulate level, at twenty-five.

My experience in Japan was one of shedding, of opening up to silence, to nothing, to emptiness. It was as if in Japan I had opened a window and let my imagination in.

IN 1972 ...

Gough Whitlam was elected prime minister of Australia, heading the first Labor government since 1949. Australia became the first western democracy to recognise China. Negotiations towards Aboriginal reconciliation were begun. In Germany, terrorism increased and members of the Baader Meinhof Gang were convicted and imprisoned for bombing banks, police stations and media outlets, and for kidnapping. The Palestinian group Black September took Israeli athletes hostage at the Olympic village, resulting in the Munich Massacre. Security checks were introduced at international airports. The Northern Ireland parliament was suspended following Bloody Sunday, when protestors were shot by the British army. *Deep Throat* became the world's most talked about pornographic film. Bertolucci's *Last Tango in Paris* opened. The last Apollo mission landed on the moon. The carpet bombing of Vietnam was ordered by US President Nixon, who visited China, leading to diplomatic recognition. The SALT talks, aimed at limiting nuclear proliferation, helped to ease Cold War tension. The *Washington Post* published an exposure of the Watergate break-in, which led to the eventual impeachment and resignation of Richard Nixon.

Rehearsal break, Capitol Theatre, 1971

THE KINGDOM OF HEAVEN

Eastern paintings derive from the scroll. They unfurl or flow, like a river, defying time. Their philosophical origins are in religion, notably Buddhism. Western paintings tend to the rectangular frame and the manipulation of a perspective that leads the eye to a central idea, drama or passion; their philosophical origins are essentially Christian and their perspective can be traced to the geometry of the cross and the symbolism of the crucifixion.

The vision of a broken and bleeding man with a lopsided crown of thorns, strung up on two planks and silhouetted on a visible hilltop, was ordained by a Roman governor, Pontius Pilate. It was meant as a humiliation and a political warning. It deliberately derided an upstart carpenter and religious cult leader from the terrorist province of Galilee, who many in Jerusalem claimed was King of the Jews. Jesus never endorsed this claim but it threatened the entrenched interests of the local priests and undermined Roman sovereignty. Romans would allow *no King but Caesar* in the occupied territory of Judea.

The idea of embracing, inverting and elevating the despised image of a crucified man had its historical origins at the Council of Nicea in 3 2 5 AD and, as a marketing exercise aimed at popular ising a marginal religious cult, it has been an enduring success.

This idea was taken up in the twentieth century by the controversial French writer Genet, who transformed criminals into saints—*You're only a judge because I am a thief; without me, you don't exist.* The idea of deifying the previously derided was also advocated by various political movements: women's liberation, gay rights groups and the black liberation movement. *Black* had previously been a term of abuse. *Say it loud, I'm black and I'm proud* became a rallying cry for African-Americans.

Genet promoted the idea of divine love being inspired by betrayal. The origin of this provocative idea is in the betrayal of Jesus Christ by his close friend and disciple Judas Iscariot. Judas loved, then betrayed; that betrayal led to Jesus' death and martyrdom. Without Judas, Christianity would be robbed of its divine sacrifice—mythologised in the iconic image of the crucifixion—and wouldn't exist in the form we know it today.

Jesus Christ Superstar: Palace Theatre, London

I pondered all this in 1972, when I directed the Tim Rice and Andrew Lloyd Webber rock opera *Jesus Christ Superstar*, initially in Australia for Harry M Miller and, later, in London. *Superstar* began its life as a hugely successful recording, yet it had faltered onstage in Paris and on Broadway. It was challenging and unconventional, and there were issues of taste and a degree of theatrical condescension surrounding the idea of a biblical rock-and-roll opera. I liked it and took it seriously, and after a successful national Australian concert tour—with rock stars Trevor White and Jon English as Jesus and Judas, Michelle Fawdon and, later, Marcia Hines as Mary and Robin Ramsay as a memorable Pilate—and a visually striking theatre version, the producer Robert Stigwood invited me to stage it in the West End. I agreed, providing I could continue my collaboration with Brian Thomson, whose spectacular dodecahedron, tubular elevators and floating ramps had contributed mightily to the Australian production's success. Robert agreed to my choice of designer, and Brian and I set off to create a new production in London.

Brian and I, influenced by discussions with Robert, Andrew and, especially, Tim Rice, did *Superstar* the great service of treating it simply. We allowed for a little spectacle, though much less than in the overblown Broadway version or in our more flamboyant Australian staging. From the concert version, I retained the direct-to-audience communication of songs and interwove this with a more realistic narrative in the dramatic scenes. Influenced by Pasolini's film *The Gospel According to St Matthew*, the London version had a starker, more human dimension. The musical drama of the shattering Stravinsky-inspired *Trial before Pilate* was allowed its full operatic power, but the focus remained with Paul Nicholas' provocative and powerfully sung Jesus and Stephen Tate's troubled Judas. It became the longest running British musical of its day, playing for nine years at the Palace Theatre, and it set in train the renaissance of the British musical which continues to this day.

Swedish dramatist August Strindberg once suggested that theatre is essentially Bible stories with pictures. *Superstar* is a classic Bible story, conveyed through incisive lyrics and a vibrant score—possibly Andrew's best. We had a great cast to perform it. However, these elements were present in other versions, so it's interesting to speculate on what caused the London production to engage the public's imagination over nine years.

One factor was generational. In this production of *Superstar* the creative team were roughly the same age as its creators, with similar strengths, weaknesses and enthusiasms. In that sense we captured something of the spirit of the times. I never asked Tim if he was influenced by John Lennon's observation that The Beatles were *more popular than Jesus*; I simply assumed this idea informed the ironic title song. I was similarly sympathetic to the pop ethos. This version reflected a generation raised on rock music rather than Broadway showtunes.

The London production addressed the interesting dramatic contradiction at the heart of the work. *Superstar* has Tim's original, witty, sceptical libretto telling the story of the passion from Judas' point of view. This is enhanced yet also contradicted by the emotive musical score. Andrew's music expresses the passion but, excepting King Herod's vaudeville turn, without irony. This tension between the lyrics and the music was also present in the collaborations of Mozart and Da Ponte, Gilbert and Sullivan, Brecht and Weill. It echoes the contradiction between Judas' rational intelligence and Jesus' singular faith, and, not to draw too long a bow, something of that between cricket-loving pop stylist Tim Rice and the gifted, temperamental son of the then head of the Royal Academy of Music, Andrew Lloyd Webber.

A less obvious factor in its success related to the placement of the interval. This was never specified, and varied from production to production, but I felt that the scene in the garden of Gethsemane, climaxing in Christ's great *Why me?* anthem, sat at the heart of *Superstar* and was the logical climax of Act One. By placing the Gethsemane aria just before interval and leaving the audience to ponder Christ's deeply human dilemma, and have them return to The Last Supper and the showdown between Jesus and Judas—a scene where Jesus seems to provoke Judas into betraying him—opened the bleeding wound at the heart of this modern passion play. The incision became a door through which the audience could enter and deepen their engagement with this rock-operatic drama of love, sacrifice and betrayal.

A Texan producer whom I met soon after *Superstar* opened in London, a large goatee-bearded man with a generous laugh, wanted to buy the production. It wasn't for sale. However, he loved *Superstar* and had seen every version. In passing, he observed that mine was the only production that left a window open to the possibility of faith. In his opinion, this was part of its appeal to the public.

This last consideration could also have influenced the leading theatre critic of the day, Harold Hobson, when he trumpeted in the *Sunday Times*, no doubt to the relief of the publicist: *The kingdom of heaven will open to receive this production.*

It was not always thus. Some months earlier, it had been a very different story.

When we heard we were getting the Australian production ... well ... my dear... you can imagine ... we all just roared with laughter!

I was nursing a drink in the Soho pub next door to the Palace Theatre, sitting with Brian Thomson. The pub owner, a cheerfully waspish old theatre queen, was entertaining us with a frank assessment of Australia's cultural credentials circa 1972.

There was no shortage of Australian talent in London at this time; it remained *home* and an artistic hive for many colonial bees. There were exceptional artists like Barry Humphries, Sidney Nolan, Joan Sutherland, Michael Blakemore and Charles Mackerras. Beyond these individuals there were more ordinary talents who had simply jettisoned their derided accents and blended in, aiming to achieve success as surrogate English.

The difference in 1972 was that Australia was beginning to export talent rather than merely import it, in some branch-office imitation of outpost Empire. The election of the Whitlam government signalled a new spirit of independence and a more assertive national voice. Like the Wizards of Oz that had preceded us, we were part of this new generation that displayed a take-it-or-leave-it approach. We hadn't come to stay. For us, the real game wasn't centred in what earlier arrivals termed *The Old Country*. For many of us, Britain was simply that: old ... and often patronising.

The brashness and arrogance that were part and parcel of this newly assertive approach seemed acceptably energising in a British culture now bereft of colonies and looking for a foothold in the future. The Wilson years and *Swinging London* had loosened the chains of class, though accent, manners and an entrenched education system remained enforcers. Americans were held in unspoken contempt for their revolution and the debt owed to them for their contribution in winning the war against Hitler. The English were too proud ever to accept themselves as part of a greater Europe. In this climate it was acceptable to indulge and encourage ex-colonials, especially if they made you rich.

Brian and I might have been intimidated by our situation had we time to notice. Instead, Brian flung his bare feet over the faded velvet of the Palace Theatre seats and contemplated details of the vast steel and glass ramp he designed to define the playing space, the comings and goings of an elegant colonnade of floating pillars and the electronic news board urgently flashing details of place and time—*Jerusalem: Sunday*.

New York lighting whiz Jules Fisher created visual marvels, including a nuclear cloud swathing a Jesus seemingly crucified midair, and I simply got on with the show. Always on the lookout for creative input from surprising sources, Rufus Collins, recently departed from the controversial Living Theatre, created the free-form choreography. The cast were encouraged to be vocally and dramatically intense, and there were a few divas-to-be in the choral ranks: a future Evita, Elaine Page; *Rocky Horror*'s Richard O'Brien; and the brilliant Paul Jabara, a memorably asinine King Herod. The musical direction of the proudly cockney Antony Bowles was sympathetic, and the simple ritual at work in the staging was derived from my recent experience of Japanese theatre.

There were hiccups: some ill-considered costumes that needed last-minute replacement, and the elevation of an understudy Mary Magdalene in the form of a vocally and physically impressive Dana Gillespie. Tim Rice hovered as a calm, cool presence and Andrew managed to combine moments of inspired insight with a few anxiety attacks. Before long, it had opened, everyone was happy, and we were toasting each other across a floodlit swimming pool at the first-night party in the grounds of Robert Stigwood's mock-tudor mansion at Barnes, where, in the company of The Bee Gees, Brian Thomson finally got to meet his falsetto hero, Robin Gibb.

As it is sung from beginning to end, *Jesus Christ Superstar* is technically an opera. While the suggestion might horrify classicists, *Superstar* could be said to be one of the most popular operas of the twentieth century. As opposed to other standout musical-theatre shows I directed, where the productions were influenced by the personalities of the cast and could alter dramatically with every role change, *Superstar* felt more like an opera production. You could change the cast, but, assuming they understood the role and hit the spot and the note, the many changes over its long run made little impact on the overall performance.

By now, my musical productions were beginning to accumulate across the world, with *Hair* and *Superstar* both on tour in Australia, the Tokyo and Boston stagings of *Hair*, and *Superstar* in the West End. Professionally, this was satisfying. On the other hand, it became increasingly unsettling to turn up at a theatre to see a production I had created which now featured cast members I had never rehearsed and, in many cases, hadn't even met. It was to continue for some years, however, and the presence of Richard O'Brien in the *Superstar* chorus was evidence that a hidden card was yet to be played in this musical poker game of three-card stud.

When I revisited London in 1981 and saw workmen finally pulling down the signs outside the Palace Theatre, I let out a long sigh of relief. Then I focused my camera and recorded the event. It was somehow reassuring to know that even *the kingdom of heaven* didn't last forever.

WARNING
THEATRE EXIT
SUPERSTAR
NOW IN ITS
9TH YEAR
"Is still one of
the best shows
in London"
"Second visit reinforces
admiration for
confident, exhilarating
musical score by
Tim Rice and
Andrew Lloyd Webber"
TIM R
GABRIELLA FALK
ANDREW L
Musical Director
ANTHONY BOWL
directed by
SHARMAN

SLOANE SQUARE

It was a few days after *Jesus Christ Superstar* had opened, and I was walking past the Royal Court Theatre humming Dusty Springfield's *I Just Don't Know What to Do with Myself.*

One truth about directing is that up until opening night you're captain of the ship and crucial to every decision, but once the boat has docked, the opening night passed, the champagne corks popped, you're irrelevant. The director represents the audience during the long rehearsal process, but once the real audience arrives, you become, at best, a functionary. The sense of loss can be sudden and palpable; you're simply cut adrift.

It was in this post-euphoric haze that I found myself in a London I barely knew, contemplating how best to enjoy my time in this cultural metropolis. For me, enjoyment meant work. I looked up at the Royal Court Theatre sign floating over Sloane Square and thought:

This will do. And marched inside.

Finding myself upstairs in a maze of cupboard-like offices, I asked someone, who turned out to be the theatre manager Anne Jenkins, if I could speak to the artistic director.

When would you like an appointment? Anne curtly enquired.

Now.

In England this is not the way things are done. Not anywhere, really, but especially not in England. You don't just bowl in. There are protocols: agents and phone calls and appointments and waiting. But I was a young man in a hurry, and the mention of *Superstar*, which was new and currently the talk of the town, opened doors.

Oscar Lewenstein was an elderly Jewish impresario and I was a brash young Australian director; so we grinned and understood each other straightaway. Oscar had been a producer with Woodfall Films and involved with the Royal Court since its inception. Within moments of our meeting, this silvery, short, distinguished man with a mischievous smile was keen to have me direct at the Court. As the downstairs main stage was programmed for the year, a production in the more experimental upstairs studio space was the best option. As a contrast to big stage musicals, this was a return to my roots and I was open to the prospect. In lickety-split time, I was introduced to the Theatre Upstairs team of Nicholas Wright and Harriet Cruikshank and plays were being discussed. I soon found myself back in Sloane Square staring up at the Royal Court Theatre with the prospect of a new home for my work, a pile of scripts under my arm and, for the first time since I had arrived in London, a sense of belonging that I found hard to explain.

The scripts were good, but didn't engage my imagination. I was pondering this dilemma over a drink a few days later with an expat musician friend from Sydney. He was just back from Spain and casually offered the phone number of an American drummer he had met there and who he thought wrote plays. The drummer from Spain turned out to be Sam Shepard. We were soon meeting and trading opinions on music and theatre. Sam was like a cool jazz musician and had a tiny tattoo on his hand in the shape of a crescent moon. It caught my eye over our initial handshake. I later learnt the *hawk moon*, as it was known, was residue from his time with Patti Smith, poet, singer and muse to the young playwright in his earlier, wilder New York days. It was a work from this era that Sam proposed for me to direct. *The Unseen Hand* turned out to be a small gem of a play; it instantly captured my imagination and the production was underway.

Brian Thomson was soon busy supervising the carrying of tiny boxes of grass up the many steps to the Theatre Upstairs. He carpeted the floor in grass and organised a sprinkler system to maintain it. This was an early example of applying the principles of installation art to stage design. A surprised audience would soon find themselves seated on the grass and facing an old wrecked Cadillac convertible; behind it, in the shadows, a stripped-back honky-tonk piano. Brian sprayed the car in bright red graffiti:

AZUSA—*Everything from A to Z in the USA.*

Sam Shepard was briefly resident in London with his then wife, O-lan. A quiet observer, he spent much of the rehearsal time consulting the greyhound form. He wrote, raced his greyhound, kept to himself and always seemed laid back, like the Humphrey Bogart character in the film *Casablanca*. His steely eyes and appealingly haunted look echoed those of another Sam—the young Samuel Beckett. He seemed genuinely pleased to see his play in simpatico hands. We would collaborate again at the Royal Court on his more ambitious work, now a classic: *The Tooth of Crime*. This later play involved a totally unmotivated contest between rival gangster-rockers. It would unleash a few decibels and shake the rafters in the Downstairs Theatre; but, for now, we were upstairs on Brian's grassy knoll.

I spent a lot of time by the piano, enjoying musical chat with the cool, calm and recently collected Richard Hartley. Richard was a musician and composer I'd met on *Superstar*. A tall, handsome teddy bear of a man, with a rock musician's eye for very attractive model girlfriends, he became one of my closest friends and collaborators in London. The link was, as ever, through music; Richard shared many of my classical to pop enthusiasms and offered valuable counsel. The director can be an isolated and single-minded person through the production process, and Richard joined Brian Thomson as a colleague whose advice and wisdom I often sought and acted upon. He proved a generous friend and a stimulating and intelligent collaborator.

Our cast was led by Warren Clark, hot from droog duties in Kubrick's *A Clockwork Orange*. Warren played Blue Morphan, the lead character—an old-timer having an alien encounter with Richard O'Brien, whom I'd rescued from the chorus of *Superstar* to play Willie, the Space Freak. Richard had the painted hand of the play's title embossed on his skull. Canadian actor Christopher Malcolm—soon to be Brad Majors in *Rocky Horror*—spent a lot of rehearsal time practising how to light a cheroot like Lee Van Cleef in *A Fistful of Dollars*. Everyone brought their own pop cultural references to our rehearsals.

Sam's play was a science fiction fantasy with a rock-and-roll heart. It had been a chance mention of my earlier film *Shirley Thomson Versus the Aliens* that prompted Sam to propose it. *The Unseen Hand* was set in an alien Californian landscape with wonderful aria-like explosions of language, each crafted like extended jazz riffs by the ex-drummer turned playwright. In performance, these proved to be the bravura highlights of the show, which proved popular with the London public.

I loved the tiny venue and the atmosphere at the Royal Court and, as I had suspected, I felt right at home. The fact that budgets and salaries were low was balanced by the sheer joy in the endeavour. Even nights spent shivering in Sloane Square after the theatre was evacuated during IRA bomb scares, a common occurrence at the time, failed to dent my enthusiasm. I felt a great sense of camaraderie with the band of outsiders assembled for this production. I wanted all this to somehow continue. But how?

Before the question was asked, it was answered.

One night after rehearsals, Richard O'Brien took out his guitar and sang *Science Feature / Double Feature*, from a musical he was writing: *They Came from Denton High*. Great song—terrible title for a musical, I thought. After *Superstar*, a lot of musicals came my way, many of them predictably biblical.

I hope it's not religious, I quipped.

Richard smiled; but the laugh was on us. Renamed *The Rocky Horror Show*, it turned out to be the first musical to inspire its very own cult. That story is yet to come, but let's pause here … there's a history to all this. A history that began with an English director called Tony Richardson.

Tony was tall, thin, acerbic, with an oddly languorous high-pitched accent: often imitated. He had shaken English complacency with ground-breaking and often anti-establishment productions at the Royal Court Theatre and Woodfall Films: John Osborne's *Look Back in Anger*, Shelagh Delaney's *A Taste of Honey*, *Tom Jones*, which made a star of Albert Finney, *The Loneliness of the Long Distance Runner* and *The Charge of the Light Brigade*; all fine films. Tony came to Australia to film *Ned Kelly* starring Mick Jagger. He saw *Hair* and arranged to meet me. His flattering verdict on the production was intoned with a very high inflection:

It was simp-ly ma-a-arvellous!

Influenced by the films of Jean-Luc Godard, I assumed *Ned Kelly* would feature Mick Jagger as a street-smart rebel rock star and also as the bushranger in some wild poetic take on this too-oft-told legend. I volunteered to assist Tony and, in return, I would have the chance to observe the day-to-day process of film-making. My entrance coincided with the exit of the film's co-star, the soon-to-be-brilliant chanteuse, Marianne Faithfull.

As I entered the hotel where the cast and crew were staying, Marianne was departing on a stretcher, from an overdose— not a good omen. I did observe how to make a film but soon realised it was a conventional period drama—another bad omen. I decided Tony was filming the Australian bush as if it were the English countryside. He disagreed, but I grew disillusioned and departed the project.

Tony respected my rebellious attitude. Indeed, he had probably flattered and hired me to better observe it. Personally, we got on well and I learnt much from him. We kept in touch and before he left Australia he offered me use of the basement in his impressive South Kensington home in Egerton Crescent on my next stay in London, an offer I gratefully accepted.

Through Tony's generosity I met the Royal Court family: director Bill Gaskill, who became a good friend, Australian producer Helen Montague, who became both friend and one of those angels who appear at difficult moments with helpful advice, and film-maker Lindsay Anderson.

My stay at Egerton Crescent was brief and eventful. Half of London seemed to pass through that house. Tony had been married to actress Vanessa Redgrave and they had two daughters, Natasha and Joely, who became fine actresses. He had left Vanessa for Jeanne Moreau, though after the split, he remained fiercely loyal to Vanessa. He also managed a few discreet gay flings, though in those *don't ask, don't tell* days, I was unaware of this. That is, until I returned late one night to my basement and heard what sounded like a party. I wandered upstairs and was startled to discover dancer Rudolf Nureyev and writer Christopher Isherwood arm-wrestling on the coffee table. Celebrity games! Nureyev won, to the evident delight of both parties. Tony motioned me in, and I stepped out of the shadow of the doorway, all fringed suede and long hair, to join the circle around the coffee table. There was a flash of interest from an eager young dancer, seemingly attached to Nureyev, who whispered. *Is he a hustler?* Tony swiftly intervened: *Jim is a theatre director from Australia.* All interest vanished.

The Egerton Crescent house was eventually sold by Tony to producer and friend Michael White. As Michael produced *Rocky Horror*, my association with this impressive house continued, ending a decade later at an extraordinary dinner party thrown by Michael and Lyndall Hobbs, his vivacious Australian partner, for the then editor of the *Times*. It was a night meant to impress, a tensely formal affair that kept unravelling in interesting ways.

Firstly, Lyndall made the tactical error of reminding a high-spirited guest, Chop, who was bored and pushing the envelope, to watch his manners. Chop—a young New Zealand actor who was reputed to have made his way to London via the Philippines as a Diana Ross impersonator—bristled:

I don't need to be taught manners by an ex–weather girl from Melbourne!

Chop and partner were discreetly asked to leave.

Then Michael's ex-wife made an unscheduled Edward Albee–like, drunken crash-and-burn appearance. She burst in to announce that our host would destroy us all, as he had her. Michael was the sweetest soul in England and wouldn't hurt a fly, but the dinner was in tatters and we all fled into the night. It was a fitting farewell to the house and the spirit of Tony Richardson, the lord of misrule.

Tony had moved to Los Angeles, buying ex–porn star Linda Lovelace's old house above the Chateau Marmont. Here he entertained and very occasionally made films. Like a lot of his English compatriots in LA, I felt his great talent disappeared somewhere in the mid-Atlantic and took this as a warning of the consequences of severing your roots. On a stopover in 1980, shortly after filming Patrick White's *The Night the Prowler*, I renewed my acquaintance with Tony and found myself guest at one of his Hollywood parties. I again met Christopher Isherwood and, soon after, visited the Santa Monica home he shared with partner, painter Don Bacardi. In some Hollywood circles they were known as *Bacardi and Coke*.

Christopher was aware of my Patrick White association and was eager for details of PW's life. I was equally fascinated to be staring at the impressive view of the Pacific Ocean from the same picture window where many famous European émigré artists had once congregated: Brecht, Lang, Dietrich, Garbo. *What did they do in exile?* I enquired. After all, these were my heroes.

Complain! he proffered. *Whine! Whine! Whine!*

I always visited Tony in Los Angeles and was never disappointed. He was generous to a fault, interested in everyone and everything and relished wicked social games and mischief. A stopover might find the arthritic Katherine Hepburn being encouraged to help Tony clean the pool, supervised by the elderly George Cukor. Evenings might involve parties with English expatriate artists and the smart end of Hollywood.

David Hockney was one English friend of Tony's who hadn't surrendered his edge to Californian sunshine. I mentioned a painting of his that had inspired a scene in my Patrick White film.

Oh that! growled Hockney. *I burnt it!*

Tony died in LA of AIDS in 1991, surrounded by Vanessa and his daughters. He is much missed by those whose lives he briefly touched, as he did mine, and by many others he influenced in more substantial ways.

So ... it was neither by fate nor by accident that I came to be staring up at the Royal Court sign in Sloane Square, though chance did play its hand. Nor was it surprising that Oscar Lewenstein, who produced several films with Tony Richardson, agreed to see me on the spur of the moment. Nor would the productions that followed—Richard O'Brien's *Rocky Horror Show*, David Williamson's *The Removalists*, Sam Shepard's *The Tooth of Crime*—during this brief, enjoyable and highly creative period at the Royal Court be completely out of the blue.

Thanks to Tony Richardson, Sloane Square had seen it all before.

The Tooth of Crime, Royal Court Theatre: Mike Pratt and Diane Langton as Hoss and Becky

PIRANHAS IN PIMLICO

Time and mortality are the sources of the greatest drama, in life and art. The rest is soap opera. You learn that. I was reminded of this truism when I took my friend Gustavo along to see his first production of *Hamlet*. The Royal Court version starred a grief-stricken Jonathan Pryce and was directed by Richard Eyre. It broke most of the rules and, cut to the bone, it ran for two hours. They ripped through it like a Hitchcock thriller. *To be or not to be?* That was the only question in this version. Mortality, simply expressed. It was swift and it was breath-taking. Gustavo hadn't expected to enjoy the outing but it proved the perfect introduction to Shakespeare and a testament to the power of theatre. He left exhilarated, claiming it was the most exciting thing he had ever seen.

Gustavo was the son of a family of diplomats from Venezuela. When we first met, in 1973, he was in his early twenties and studying photography and film in London. He was also sowing wild oats in the company of some friends from Caracas: Gonzalo and Pedro. They did the party circuit together through their London years—that is, until Pedro was hit by a truck, emerging from a dance club at dawn after one too many mandrax. For Pedro, it was not to be. I originally met this group of Latin expats through Stephen Maclean, who had taken up with Gonzalo. I ran into them in the street. They were inspecting a house up for rental and I tagged along. I was instantly attracted to Gustavo and we found ourselves dawdling in the basement while the others explored the attic.

It began with a kiss, as it often does: tender or wild; fleshy, earthy, tactile; a meeting of minds. In that anonymous basement, it was passionate and brief. We headed to my tiny Pimlico flat, just behind the Royal Court Theatre. Gustavo was travelling overseas the next day.

I started receiving postcards, photos and romantic greet-ings in fluoro Texta. From Barcelona, Madrid, Miami, Caracas. It was sweet and heady stuff. When Gustavo returned to London, he moved in. He was passionate, rebellious and sharply intelligent. I felt I had something to learn and someone

Gustavo

to hold. In a city foreign to us both we discovered a fragile security.

After several brief and unsatisfying flings this would be my second attempt at a relationship. The first had been with Stephen Maclean. That lasted three choppy years and segued into a friendship which segued into my chance meeting with Gustavo. Sometimes things work out. Maybe this time around I would be able to balance work and pleasure.

Aii! It's a punishment from the gods! was how Gustavo greeted each misfortune, from a lost toothbrush to drug deaths. *Cheaper than free!* was another favourite expression, often referring to low-life friends. He was a livewire: smart and funny.

The arrival of Latin culture in my life added a welcome layer of sensuality to the Celtic, Aussie, Japanese austerity that preceded it. *The Girl from Ipanema*, *Concierto de Aranjuez* and *Nights in the Gardens of Spain* were booming from the stereo, though it was Lou Reed's *Transformer* and Velvet Underground retro tracks that provided the soundtrack to our time together.

My friends had mixed reactions to Gustavo: some were enthusiastic, others cautious, and one christened him *Gestapo*. If the relationship was going to work, Gustavo was determined to be central in my affections, not an accessory. He was jealous of the intensity of my working relationships, especially with Brian Thomson. He correctly intuited that these were his only real competition. A dinner Brian hosted for Gustavo and me was to be a first and last attempt at social camaraderie. It began with Gustavo noting a Vasarely poster on the wall:

My mother owned the original but she thought it so vulgar she gave it to the maid.

Gustavo came from a sophisticated background and this story might have been true, but the dinner never recovered. Gustavo could be a devil and was prone to passionate outbursts at fashionable restaurants if arguments didn't go his way. He brought Latin anarchy, sensuality, chaos and pleasure into my workaholic life and I loved him for it.

It was the time of *Rocky Horror*, and Gustavo contributed, in all sorts of intangible ways, to this period. He became friends with Nell Campbell, and when I was busy working they'd go clubbing or hit the party trail, which I avoided like the plague. His other admirer was Vivienne Westwood, and he spent time at the hip clothes shops Vivienne ran with her then partner Malcolm McLaren: firstly, *Sex* and later, *Seditionaries*. Vivienne would dress Gustavo and he would arrive home in bondage chic and ripped T-shirts. He became the prototype for what was later worn by The Sex Pistols. In a fashion sense, Gustavo was one of the original punks.

The relationship lasted several years and peaked during the intensity of *Rocky Horror* filming. After that, a mutual restlessness set in. My workaholic ways and his relentless partying fuelled arguments, and tensions erupted and dissolved in a pattern of rejection and affection. The death of Pedro signalled the beginning of the end of the London sojourn for the Latino friends, and I was slowly unravelling at the Royal Court in the final days of mounting Sam Shepard's *The Tooth of Crime*. My obsessive rigour and back-to-back production schedule had again taken their toll, and by the time we reached stage rehearsals my eyes were blurred and I could barely see the stage for exhaustion. Even the usually unfazed Sam Shepard was concerned. I took in a breath of air and a dose of daylight outside in Sloane Square and bumped into a famous expat who had been an infrequent but kindly and supportive presence during my London years, Barry Humphries. He took one look at me:

Oh dear. Pause. *There's a time when people should go home, you know.*

It was not long before I took Barry's sage advice. Destiny intervened in the form of Patrick White and I would return to London only as a tourist. The same would apply to Gustavo. Every time I was back in London and he'd returned from Miami, we would meet up and rediscover our feelings for each other. This went on for years. Gustavo travelled with me to New York for *Rocky Horror* on Broadway and briefly aligned himself with the Warhol entourage.

Good evening, Mr Warhol. My name is Gustavo!

A few years later, on one of my London sojourns, and long after I had re-established myself in Australia, we decided on the spur of the moment to spend a week at a retreat in Marseilles at a secluded motel on the harbour and opposite Château d'If, the famous prison of the Count of Monte Cristo. Two devils on the Bay of Angels. Away from my work pressures and alone together, all the intervening years of to-ing and fro-ing vanished and we had a great time.

During our Marseilles stay we met up with Patrick White who was travelling in France with Manoly Lascaris. Unknown to me, Patrick was researching his next novel. We had arranged to dine at what Patrick described as *the best fish restaurant in the world*. Patrick was more than a little fascinated by Gustavo and enquired what he wanted from the menu. Gustavo, seated in *the best fish restaurant in the world*, didn't disappoint. He sighed: *Aiii!* and ordered *steak*.

Aspects of this eventful meal would later wend their way into Patrick's writing, transformed from the fun we all eventually had that memorable night into the dinner from hell in *The Twyborn Affair*.

Gustavo reciprocated Patrick's hospitality by confiding his amazement that a winner of the Nobel Prize and a man of justified achievement could be so humble when my expat Aussie friends in London were so full of themselves. Very little impressed Gustavo, but Patrick certainly did. The feeling was obviously mutual. As we left the restaurant Patrick turned to me and urgently enquired:

Where did you find him?

In fact it would be the very next day that I would lose him. The Bay of Angels reunion was pleasant but the dinner with Patrick had reminded me of my work back in Australia, and the relationship wasn't sufficient to keep me in Europe. Our intended reunion proved to be the relationship's bittersweet swan song. Prior to departure we went to Nice, and, surrounded by the pomp and splendour of the ridiculously over-decorated foyer of the Hotel Negresco, we found ourselves stranded under chandeliers and circled by a party of Japanese cultural tourists.

In this suitably operatic setting, we had the necessary argument that such endings either encourage or require. I became frosty, and our row was followed by us both staring into the middle distance on an icily silent flight back to Heathrow. For better or worse, in the emotional battle between my work and relationships, duty always prevailed. In an uncanny echo of the plot of *The Twyborn Affair*, the dinner with Patrick White had tipped the scales in favour of Australia; the Mediterranean reunion was over.

Things thawed out back in London, and before Gustavo departed for Miami we managed a rapprochement that briefly rekindled the embers of our once passionate affair. A little later, I authorised sale of the Pimlico flat and returned permanently to Australia.

My parting gift from Gustavo was typically sweet and ironic —a tiny stuffed piranha. I always smile when it catches my eye. It brings back fond memories of Gustavo and reminds me of a song from a Disney movie: *Never Smile at a Crocodile*. Decades later, on an Elizabeth Bay rooftop, Stephen Maclean would wryly observe, during a smiling reverie on our days in London:

You haven't really lived until you've been taken to the cleaners by a Latin lover.

It was a great line, but who took whom to the cleaners was a moot point. In truth, nobody did. But for the geographical distance between us, I'm sure it would have transformed, as did other relationships, into a long-standing friendship. Gustavo holds a special place in my affections for the joy he brought into my life. He offered me a brief insight into genuine passion, and the ghost of our time together holds a forever place in my work.

MONDAY TO FRIDAY
9am TO 8pm
430 KINGS ROAD
TELEPHONE 351-0764
MALCOLM McLAREN
VIVIENNE WESTWOOD
SEDITIONARIES

MALCOLM McLAREN
VIVIENNE WESTWOOD
SEDITIONARIES

ON THE AISLE

Theatre directors prefer an aisle seat. It's a tradition born of previews or opening nights when you might have to suddenly dash backstage to deal with an emergency. Aisle seats are habit-forming and they become a preference. They also offer the advantage of a speedy unobtrusive exit, should things get sticky. I've been on the aisle through countless productions and, like any audience member, I always take my seat in the expectation of pleasure, enlightenment or inspiration.

My qualifier for enjoying good theatre is simple. I want to emerge changed from the person who parked their expectations on velvet, vinyl or upturned egg crate. Transformation is the expectation. On the lightest level, you leave with a glow or a renewed delight in life. Better still, you have your complacency overturned and you see the world with fresh eyes. The best productions often have a sense of ambush about them. You arrive with expectations that are then confounded and you're sent reeling into the foyer, where you're surrounded by excited murmurs of how great *it* was.

I've often wondered what this mysterious *it* is. No one can define *it*. My feeling is that *it* has to do with rhythm, or pulse: the invisible element that instantly binds an audience. It's the same interaction that allows us to decide whether we'll enjoy a film as soon as the titles appear on the screen. How does this happen? Through science, skill, words, images, a little magic, but, above all, through rhythm. From Shakespeare, with his iambic pentameter, to Pinter, the sense is in the words but the meaning is conveyed through rhythm. Understanding and conveying the internal music of a work is at the heart of the director's art and all great theatre. From the aisle seat, that's *it*. The hidden pulse of a work is what I aim to communicate as a director and what I hope to experience as an audience.

Seditionaries: Gustavo and Nell

LATE-NIGHT MOVIE SHOW

My film education was limited to what I observed from others, notably Tony Richardson, a lot of reading and a passion for film-going that started as a kid when I attended Saturday serials at my local cinema. It developed as I saw many of Douglas Sirk's Hollywood melodramas as a teenager, often in the company of my mother. My later, solo outings explored darker realms as I became a fan of films by Alfred Hitchcock and brilliant Spanish surrealist Luis Bunuel.

The best cinema education came from a regular dose of classic films that I enjoyed during the era of the late-night movie. This enthusiasm peaked during my London years. My late-night appetite was insatiable and my favourite venue was the nearby Paris Pullman in South Kensington. Here, inspiring German silents by FW Murnau and Fritz Lang would jostle beside hilarious porn operas like Russ Meyer's *Beyond the Valley of the Dolls*.

Two rarely screened late-night movies especially caught my eye.

One was *Peeping Tom* by Michael Powell, who made *The Red Shoes*. I was alerted to this rarely seen gem by Australian actress Nell Campbell. It was the film that allegedly ended Powell's career, such was the critical storm that followed its initial release.

As a thriller, *Peeping Tom* takes a very dark and subtle idea—a notion also present in many of Hitchock's films—and makes it explicit. *Peeping Tom* suggests that filming is an act of sexual violation. The protagonist carries a camera that kills, literally, through a blade in the lens. Film-making is presented as eroticised murder. No wonder critics were upset; what would that make them—accessories? It's one of the scariest films I've seen and one of the most perversely brilliant.

The other eye-catcher was equally obscure and personally very influential. This I saw on the advice of Melbourne artist and film-maker Phillipe Mora, who took me to a rare screening of George Franju's *Judex*, a playful masterpiece of French surrealism. *Judex* was a 1960s remake of the classic French serial from the silent cinema, based on French comic-book anti-hero—and hero to the surrealists—*Fantomas*.

Judex is a nocturnal masked avenger, who doubles as a bourgeois secretary to a wealthy banker by day. This gives him access to the banker's cronies and his unscrupulous dealings. By night, in cape and mask, he enacts a terrible retribution. A remarkable scene involves the mysterious arrival of Judex at a masked ball thrown by the banker for his wealthy clients. Judex is glimpsed in the shadows as he collects a dead bird from the steps outside. The camera stays with the masked avenger's black satin cloak and gloved hand, gripping the white bird, as he proceeds through a ballroom of wealthy revellers and places the dead bird at the banker's feet. The clock strikes midnight and the banker dies.

This surreal melodrama is littered with unlikely subplots, including an amazing frenetic dance sequence in a seedy café. All of it is lovingly filmed to evoke the naïve techniques of early serials. Beards are false, dialogue stilted; shadows fall the wrong way as masked characters scale impossible walls; scene divisions are announced by Saturday serial–style optical cuts and dissolves. Once you're in on the joke, the playful surrealism and the attention to detail are sources of constant delight.

It was a revelation that a film so magical, naïve yet sophisticated, surreal yet entertaining, existed. I had never seen anything like it, and there is no other film quite like it. There is, however, one film that was greatly influenced by it: *The Rocky Horror Picture Show.*

THE HAUNTED CINEMA

We bring you all the way to London, and what do you do? Pitch a tent!

An amused Wendy Dickson was checking out the haunted cinema set that Brian Thomson had created for *The Rocky Horror Show* in the Theatre Upstairs of London's Royal Court. The attic-like theatre was swathed in billowing blue demolition-site canvas and wreathed with cobwebs. A celebrated production designer herself, Wendy had once taught me at NIDA, and she wasn't shy of reminding me of my showground past.

Wendy wasn't the only visitor to the Theatre Upstairs around preview time for this soon-to-premiere musical in the summer of 1973. What had been a few weeks of enjoyable rehearsal and inventive fun in a small studio theatre was already attracting attention. Rocks stars, well-known artists and various London fashionista were elbowing their way in, offering a taste of what was ahead. An enthusiastic Barry Humphries saw the first preview.

Do you think I've gone too far? I enquired.

In an echo of his own theatrical ethos, Barry proposed:

Go further! Take the audience to the edge.

I didn't need much encouragement. Brian had pitched the tent and I was revelling in the anarchic sideshow atmosphere we were conjuring up. It was in stark contrast to the grey earnestness that dominated the theatrical landscape of the time. Maybe this was what the Australian contingent was offering 1970s London: a burst of colour, a brashness and a cartoon sensibility that stretched from *Oz* magazine to Edna Everage. Even Joan Sutherland's legendary redheaded Lucia di Lammermoor offered a crazy kind of cartoon glamour. There was an audacious vaudeville element at play, one that would fuel Australian stage and cinema, from Bruce Beresford's Barry McKenzie films through to popular successes like *Muriel's Wedding*, *Priscilla, Queen of the Desert*, *Strictly Ballroom* and *Moulin Rouge*.

Rock-and-roll had stolen the earthy vulgarity that theatre had discarded in the pursuit of taste. The make-up, costumes and general excess of 1970s glam-rock were inspired by a borrowed, ostentatious theatricality. With *Rocky Horror* we were reclaiming it. We were also picking up where Weimar cabaret, brutally interrupted by Hitler, had left off. There was a definite link between the visceral anarchy of this German tradition and 1970s theatre and art. Germany had also given rise to the haunted screen through early silent films like FW Murnau's *Nosferatu*, which introduced the world's thinnest vampire, Max Shrek. The director in me would stare at the wiry author of *Rocky Horror*, Richard O'Brien, and conjure Murnau's classic vampire creation; though Richard's own frame of reference was more likely the more populist Carry On comedies and Hammer Horror films.

Late-night movies had created an international youth subculture, and from my earlier film *Shirley Thompson Versus the Aliens* through to Sam Shepard's *The Unseen Hand* I was drawn to it. On the magical night when Richard first strummed his guitarand sang *Science Fiction / Double Feature* I had recognised a kindred spirit. While the original script was quirky and thin, I knew the territory and, against the advice of some who were concerned about the dubious prospects awaiting such a sketchy venture, I eagerly embraced Richard's pop collage of colourful characters and tuneful songs that I enthusiastically proposed calling *The Rocky Horror Show*.

I'm just a sweet transvestite ...

How far should I go?

Tim Curry echoed my enquiry to Barry Humphries. It was the question on everyone's mind.

Just stop short of throwing Fantales to the kiddies.

Tim understood; we had many such coded conversations. While audiences around the world would soon marvel, swoon or quail at this sexually rampant Frankenstein, Tim and I knew that the character's origins were located in something much more innocent—the ancient carnival tradition of misrule epitomised by the panto dame.

Drag had been with me since childhood. It continued, years later, at the Purple Onion in Sydney. Australia has a rich drag tradition, Edna Everage being only the tip of the iceberg; it goes back to convicts throwing on a frock in the days of rum, sodomy and the lash.

I had experienced superbly designed shows at La Grande Eugène in Paris in the late 1960s on my first trip there, in the company of an incredibly tall, pencil-thin Swedish model called Aya, the girlfriend of one of the performers. Aya was the first person I ever met with cropped hennaed hair. When I pointed out how much I enjoyed her company, she merely shrugged.

I'm just the only person you know in Paris.

It was my introduction to cool honesty.

I'd witnessed the startling, San Francisco hippy-acid drag of The Cockettes in *Pearls over Shanghai* at the downtown Anderson Theatre in New York. At Sydney's Capriccio's I was fascinated by the trannies' gangster boyfriends and recalled a prison documentary where one effusive cock-in-a-frock calmly explained: *They're gangsters by day, but girls by night!*

Something of all of this clicked with *Rocky Horror*'s inspired costume designer Sue Blane, a graduate of the impressive drag-and-design heaven that was the famous Glasgow Citizen's Theatre Harriet Cruikshank, who had managed both the Citz, as it was known, and now the Theatre Upstairs, had introduced us, with a wicked gleam in her eye. Harriet knew Sue and I would revel in creating this unusual take on the Frankenstein theme. We did, usually over one or three of the many bottles of wine that brightened what became a long and fruitful friendship. Our well-lubricated dinners encouraged even greater excesses in our collaboration.

I've seen only two people play the transvestite Frankenstein to perfection: Tim Curry, who created the role, and Reg Livermore, in Sydney. Reg was a tough cookie, Bette Davis style. Tim was on the sweeter side of Frank's bittersweet equation. He developed the character through his South Kensington accent and his walk, courtesy of Sue Blane's extra-high heels. Like Dorothy's ruby slippers in *The Wizard of Oz*, the sequinned stilettos held some magic for this character.

Tim's performance was fearless. He was the man every woman wanted to be, and the woman every man wanted to be—

or secretly wanted. A remarkable and inventive actor and singer with the swagger of a rock star, he'd played in everything from *Hair* to Britten's *A Midsummer Night's Dream*. Tim sang *Rip It Up* at his audition, with his sexy-bluesy baritone, and nailed the role. He was one of the smartest, and one of the most enjoyable and creative actors I've had the pleasure to work with. Offstage, Tim could be either lively or scholarly. He displayed a remarkable knowledge of, and enthusiasm for, the novels of Patrick White. Given the show we were working on, a surprising amount of time was devoted to literary chat. While I'm unapologetic about releasing Tim's inner demons, I understood the ambivalence this reserved and intelligent actor would ultimately feel about being over-identified with his role in *Rocky Horror*.

When Richard O'Brien conceived Frank, I'm sure he had in mind a lovely dress, an elegant staircase and possibly himself. It didn't quite turn out that way. Instead, the show celebrated an edgy, gothic-punk aesthetic. Richard played the role of the embittered servant Riff Raff with relish and to perfection. The fact that I'd cast the author as the star's butler created a few tensions between Richard and Tim, which I admit to exploiting to good end in the film version—a subtlety evident to close viewers of the movie.

In fact, the onstage characters of Frank and his trio of servants—played by Richard, the eternally exotic and mysterious Patricia Quinn and the Aussie tap-dancing bombshell Little Nell, later to become New York club hostess Nell Campbell—developed a close link during the production. They bonded as a crazy sort of family and time-warped their way into the audiences' hearts. When it came time for the film version, I couldn't bear the idea of making it without them. I was offered a bigger budget and a generous shooting schedule if I switched to a range of eager, available, and bankable rock stars, but I happily settled for a B-picture budget and the home-movie approach, with a cast I loved and who instinctively understood the unique performance style that they had originated and made their own.

The same applied to production designers Brian Thomson and his partner-in-crime Sue Blane. Another vital contributor to the success of *Rocky Horror*, on stage and screen, was Richard Hartley, who took Richard O'Brien's simple, catchy and lyrically brilliant melodies and developed them into a memorable musical score. The production unit were the key creative players, and we became like a team of mad inventors. Richard, Brian and Sue helped to shape the original production and, from Farfisa organs through pink laboratories to torn fishnet stockings and stiletto heels, they added immeasurably to the film version.

Let's do the time warp again ...

The dance craze that would later sweep the world was created on a living-room rug by Richard O'Brien and his then wife Kimi Wong in response to my request for a dance for the servants to enhance both their roles and their first encounter with Brad and Janet. He sang and, unforgettably, danced it for me like a wafer-thin whirling dervish in an empty rehearsal room one morning before the cast arrived. My unlikely reference for this suggestion had been a scene in Jean-Luc Godard's film *Bande à part* where two gangsters and Godard's wife, Anna Karina, dance the Madison in a late-night café. There were many such suggestions flying around the *Rocky Horror* rehearsal room and, combined with the energy emerging from otherwise sophisticated people kicking up their heels—always an entertaining sight—it proved to be one of the most chaotic, stimulating and enjoyable periods of my working life.

I relished being catalyst to this carnival of chaos. The alchemy slowly took effect and I became more determined that this tiny jewel of a sideshow, which early doubters dismissed as being unworthy of serious attention, would reveal its rock-and-roll heart. However, I had little idea of the success that it would ultimately achieve. *Rocky Horror* was many things to many people; it was a product of its time inspired by Richard's wickedly warped imagination, the talented and often clashing personalities involved, and the crucible of its conception, the Royal Court Theatre.

The Court seemed to thrive on its own contradictions. With its defiantly leftist political ethos, it promoted an edgy and

macho working-class view of the world. This was often realised by Oxford graduates, many of them gay, all of them pretty
tough-minded. There was a lively bar, much contentious argument, and an amusing role reversal at play, with middle-class
artists striving to be working class and vice versa. Despite
or because of its contradictions, the Court was an inspiring
place to work. Whether it was presenting Samuel Beckett,
Edward Bond or Richard O'Brien, its openness to new ideas
and its dedication to new writing meant it was, and remains,
a shining model of creative theatre. My experience of working
at this essentially writer's theatre would stay with me forever
and profoundly influence much of what was ahead.

While we were practising *The Time Warp* upstairs, and being
scheduled into late-night performances so that our amplified
guitars wouldn't disturb downstairs patrons, Edward Bond's *The
Sea*, starring Coral Brown and superbly directed by Bill Gaskill,
was about to premiere on the main stage. As I sped up the many
stairs to my daily rehearsal, I passed a door that opened onto
the downstairs theatre balcony. On one occasion, a fantastic
voice caused me to stop and peer in. It was the grand dame
Coral Brown applying her swooping vocal skills to a magnificent speech by a character called Mrs Raffi, the self-appointed
dowager monarch of a small fishing village. Coral got to the
end of the speech, there was a pause, then Bill Gaskill's voice
floated up from the stalls:

Oh Coral, you … Oh, it doesn't matter…You'll never get it!

Coral's face hardened; she turned upstage and muttered:

Oh yes I fucking will!

Coral turned back and unleashed a rendition of the very same
speech that might have blistered the paint on the theatre walls.
Completely stunned, I discreetly shut the balcony door and
continued on up the stairs to my own rehearsal.

Witnessing that moment had a great effect on me. Most actors
faced with a director saying *You'll never get it!* would storm off
to the bar and complain to their colleagues about what a pig the
director was, and how he obviously hated actors. This was not
the Coral Brown approach. Faced with a challenge she rose to

it—just as Bill Gaskill knew she would. I realised I had observed a modern take on the oft-quoted directorial remark from the late Tyrone Guthrie after a long day's rehearsal:

Amaze me in the morning!

Observing this encounter hardened my resolve as a director, and I watched everything with steelier eyes. Our rehearsal atmosphere had been playful, but if our show was to realise its potential, it needed higher stakes and greater performance bravura. I became much more demanding, especially of Tim Curry, whose every effort, no matter how brilliant, was greeted with a blank stare that implied:

Is that the best you can do?

After our last rehearsal prior to opening night, Tim confided:

I'm getting anxious and you're not helping, you know.

Unmoved, I replied, *Aren't I?*

No, you're being a bastard!

If only the character you're playing was an even bigger bastard!

I saw the same dangerous glint in Tim's eyes that I'd witnessed in Coral Brown's.

We both laughed. *See you tonight, Tim. Good luck!*

That night, Tim was magnificent. Critics raved. The show never looked back.

While I might have encouraged delusions of superstardom in order to achieve the performance megalomania required to break through the barriers of English reserve, it did produce results. This cast of great talents and true eccentrics created some astonishing performance energy, and I was in thrall to all of them. Something of our shared affection and the sheer mad joy we all had in the show's creation translated to the audience and contributed to the initial success. The cast simply had a great time and therefore so did the audience.

This was in contrast to the equally effective but much flashier Los Angeles version at the fashionable Roxy on Sunset Strip. The dynamic rock club version starred Tim Curry and a young LA cast, and opened to an A-list audience of Hollywood movie and rock stars. Many in the cast found themselves in the spotlight for the very first time. They virtually elbowed their way to the front of the stage to compete for attention. It was Hollywood ambition on speed. I was alarmed and felt for Tim, who was a serious actor and not used to such antics. I needn't have worried. Tim remained upstage, exactly as we had rehearsed, and slowly the audience focused on him. Realising their error, the rest of the cast began to edge their way back upstage and resume the rehearsed production. It turned into a terrific night, but one which revealed a stark contrast between sophisticated theatre artists and a more superficial culture of fame and gratification.

Rocky Horror had come a long way from its humble beginnings at the Theatre Upstairs. We were lucky with all our producers. The simpatico Michael White in London transferred the show from the Royal Court into the converted cinema of the Chelsea Classic on the Kings Road. This upscaled yet still intimate version, with a long flowing ramp for Frank's spectacular entrance, further established the show and set it on its path to long-running success. Actress Britt Ekland saw the Chelsea Classic version and recommended it to her then partner, rock impresario Lou Adler. He had the vision to re-configure it at the Roxy, his intimate LA rock club. After its success in London, Sydney and, most of all, LA, and through Lou's Hollywood connections, the film was set up. Shot in London, its line producer, the ever-thoughtful and simpatico John Goldstone, completed the triumvirate.

Our producers were alert to what made the show special and only miscalculated once, in New York, where instead of respecting *Rocky Horror*'s street savvy and choosing an intimate venue they converted a legendary Broadway theatre, the Belasco, into a vast cabaret. The show had previously played only in smaller, studio theatres, converted cinemas and rock clubs. The mainstream critics made it clear they preferred its grittier intimate context and the Belasco version closed after a brief run.

As chance would have it, this paved the way for the success of the movie. New York, which had been deprived of the show, became the site for the first late-night screenings of the film and the birthplace of the cult movie phenomenon of audience participation. Dressing up as your favourite character and talking back to the screen became de rigueur; water pistols squirted, confetti flew; and the fun began.

The late-night double-feature picture show. I wanna go!

Late-night cult screenings couldn't have been further from our minds as we stood shivering in an English winter at Bray Studios, shooting *The Rocky Horror Picture Show*.

The 20th Century Fox film was set up and nurtured by producer Lou Adler. It was made on a Fox executive's lunch money and shot on a tight schedule. My decision to stay with many of the original cast and add American actors only for Brad, Janet and Eddie did affect the film on its initial release. There were no known movie star names to attract an audience. However, the decision contributed mightily to the film's longevity as everyone I cast, including the singer Meatloaf, who had played Eddie onstage in LA, and the then unknown Barry Bostwick as Brad Majors and the wonderful Susan Sarandon as Janet Weiss, understood the style.

Everyone assumes *Rocky Horror* is just pantomime camp, but it's subtler than the cliché suggests. The secret isn't in the outrageousness but in the fact that Richard O'Brien created a skilful comedy of manners—a tradition as old as eighteenth-century Restoration plays or Mozart and Da Ponte operas. This is often overlooked in revivals, and the results can be grotesque. The cult audience engaged with the cast and the characters but also with the style in which it was played. Casting, down to the last hand-picked Transylvanian, was a key element in the film's success. Many of our cross-cultural Transylvanians were partners, friends and extended family of the cast and the creative team. I often think of *The Rocky Horror Picture Show* as one big home movie.

A filmic structure was already in place as the show was modelled on a B-picture format from the outset. During rehearsals, I'd asked Richard to add the opening wedding scene that established Brad and Janet. This was partly to introduce the characters who would take us on their journey but it was also to delay Frank's appearance until around fifteen minutes—the traditional entrance timing for a Hollywood star turn.

Rocky Horror celebrates movie references and my contribution to the screenplay was to propose a dark underbelly version of *The Wizard of Oz*. I encouraged Richard Hartley to speed up the Transylvanian voices on *The Time Warp* so they would resemble the Munchkins singing *We're Out of the Woods*. Other ideas that echoed the Judy Garland classic, such as beginning in black and white and progressing to colour on Frank's appearance, were jettisoned for technical reasons, but many remain. The small-town church congregation being Transylvanians in disguise, or vice versa, has its roots in Shakespeare's *A Midsummer Night's Dream*, where the real world inhabits a parallel universe with the fairy kingdom.

Brian Thomson's brilliant design embodies a thousand film and art references that multiple-viewing audiences enjoy picking up on. His work on the film is incredibly detailed, bold and inspired. The seductive title sequence has Pat Quinn's luscious lips syncing with Richard O'Brien's falsetto, establishing a disorienting sense of ambivalence and androgyny. The floating lips were inspired by many things: a Man Ray image of lips floating in the sky, which I'd glimpsed on Brian's studio wall, a play by Samuel Beckett that I saw at the Court, in which only a mouth appears, the opening credits of Alfred Hitchcock's *Vertigo* and, above all, my desire to celebrate incestuous twins Riff Raff and Magenta, played by Richard and Patricia, and to see them eternally morphed together in image and song.

Sue Blane again created the incredible costumes; she knew exactly how to frame a face with the perfect collar and how to create a great silhouette, something I emphasised in my shooting approach by choosing frontal angles and echoing the composition of pop-inspired paintings. Above all, Sue knew how to make everyone look and feel rock-star sexy. Sue was recently honoured with an MBE; I privately hoped it was in acknowledgment of her innate skill in understanding the right gap to leave between stockings and crotch when arranging fetishist underwear. Sue's costumes were both a turn-on and a triumph. Susan Sarandon, as Janet, was momentarily perplexed by her character's nocturnal cabaret turn in stilettos and underwear, until she decided that down-home Janet was fantasising herself as Ann Margret in a Las Vegas floorshow.

We shot at Bray Studios in homage to Hammer Horror. The temperatures were freezing and the steam coming from the actors' mouths was real. My closest collaborators beyond the cast and production team were the cinematographer and editor.

I invited Peter Suschitzky to shoot the film after seeing his work for Jacques Demy on a French version of the fairytale *The Pied Piper*. At a time when cinematic realism held sway, I wanted images reflecting the world of myth and fable. Peter was quiet, ever-supportive, and he understood and shared my interest in European cinema from Murnau to Franju.

There was a moment on the set, as I was calmly grouping Tim Curry's transvestite Frank and his sexy servants into a family portrait around a throne-like chair, when Wally Veevers, the veteran special-effects genius who had worked on Kubrick's *2001*, confided that he'd not seen anything like it on a London sound stage since the days of Josef von Sternberg, a Hollywood film-maker famous for fusing his cinematic mise en scène into an erotic depth charge, often in the service of Marlene Dietrich. If I was reviving that long-forgotten aesthetic, I couldn't have been happier.

The editor was Graeme Clifford, who went on to direct *Francis* with Jessica Lange and Sam Shepard. Another brash, gifted Australian, Graeme had worked on Robert Altman's wonderful early films and was famous for having kicked a Moviola editing machine through a skyscraper window at Hollywood's Century City. A perfect pedigree. Graeme was the only editor I've ever worked with who signalled his intended cutting points with karate chops.

We mostly shot in sequence. In the early scenes, Susan Sarandon and Barry Bostwick had not yet relaxed into the dialogue style—their lines are like cartoon balloons in Roy

Lichtenstein paintings—and my direction was as stilted as their delivery. By the next scene, in the broken-down car, we'd all hit our stride and they brilliantly nailed the heightened-but-real delivery. Once inside the castle, Brad and Janet's ordinariness contrasts with the wild eccentricity of Riff Raff and Magenta. The servants' fetishism in these early scenes owes something to Erich von Stroheim in *Sunset Boulevard*, including the famously deleted scene where von Stroheim lovingly irons Gloria Swanson's underwear.

Much of the pleasure of *Rocky Horror* is in its deliberate and loving echoes of favourite cinema moments: King Kong and Fay Wray on Brian's sweetly cut-out 2D RKO tower; David Toguri's Busby Berkeley–like choreography for *The Time Warp* and Richard O'Brien's Nosferatu–like appearance at a window. Each echo and cross-reference was considered, and they are endless. In that sense, *Rocky Horror* is a film fetishist's wet dream. The nuptial setting for Frank and Rocky prompted Tim Curry —emerging bleary-eyed from his daily four-hour make-up session—to enquire, with a chortle:

What's this? The Pasolini sequence?

Frank's two creations, Rocky and the rough-trade rocker Eddie, required special thought. Rocky was more cameo than title role. The problem of finding a great body and voice was tricky in the days before gym culture—a culture that *Rocky Horror* might have inadvertently encouraged. Onstage, it was less important than the charismatic rock-star element, captured so well by Raynor Bourton in the original and Kim Milford in Los Angeles. For the film, the muscularity had to survive close-ups, and the strikingly handsome body-builder and fashion model Peter Hinwood seemed perfect casting. The sequence involving the birth of Rocky became a personal testament to James Whale, the originator of the Frankenstein films. We were able to do what Whale and earlier generations couldn't— reveal that the creator loves his creation and vice versa.

The scene where Brad and Janet are introduced by Frank to his newly minted Dionysus is a perfect example of the comedy of manners in Richard's writing. How does a small-town girl greet an illustrious transvestite scientist? Does she shake hands, or curtsey? It's played to perfection by the flirtatiously shrewd Susan Sarandon. Likewise, Janet's seduction of wide-eyed Rocky, involving jump cuts, ripped petticoats, sex-with-the-neighbours fantasies and her understated rendition of Richard's brilliant ode to the eternal itch *Touch-a Touch-a Touch Me*. It was no surprise to me that Susan and Tim became both onset friends and good-natured competitors. More than Rocky or any other character, it's Janet Weiss that develops through her exposure to Frank and the haunted house. The series of jump cuts as Janet runs through the *If Only ...* list of her life is my favourite sequence in the film, probably because it is the most cinematic. The camera is an amoral beast and it loved Susan Sarandon. Through the viewfinder, it was obvious she would enjoy a great screen career.

Meatloaf had already played Eddie at the Roxy; he'd worked with Tim and the rest of our creative team, and was an obvious choice for the cameo rocker. Despite his intimidating heft and powerhouse tenor voice, he was one of the sweetest people in the *Rocky Horror* family. I met him through Jim Steinman, an unusual American composer of German and American-Indian origin, who had written a musical he wanted me to stage called *The Dream Engine*. An inverted Peter Pan myth, it had gangs of highly sexed lost boys flying through the sky singing *Bat Out of Hell*. I arranged for Jim to preview his musical for Lou Adler in the foyer of the Chateau Marmont when we were in Los Angeles. Jim's fingers unforgettably bled on the keyboard, like Chopin's, as he pounded out his amazing score. The JM Barrie estate finally refused to allow the Peter Pan story to be transformed into a William Burroughs fantasy, so Jim's great score became the basis of Meatloaf's hit album *Bat Out of Hell*.

Eddie is axed and later eaten in an eerie cannibalistic dinner scene. I devised this scene the night before we shot it with the aim of raising the dramatic stakes, and we improvised on the shoot. I managed to create the necessarily unpleasant mood onset by ripping poor axe-murdered Eddie's teddy bear from the props man's hands and stabbing it with the penknife, many times, to the evident distaste of those who witnessed it. This tense day of food, song and cannibalism was witnessed by a few Fox executives who had decided to visit the set. They quickly fled, appalled.

As we began shooting the final scenes we ran out of time, money and patience. The creaky old barn of a film studio was icy and the actors were shivering in their underwear. I was able to encourage further excess from the freezing cast on the simple principle that *the wilder it was, the sooner it would be over*. By the time we got to the underwater erotics preceding *Wild and Untamed Thing*, we all felt unhinged and snap-frozen. Before long, Tim had turned over the death card in *I'm Going Home* and Brad, Janet and Jonathan Adam's Henry Kissinger–like Dr Everett Scott had been spat out of the haunted house and crawled through the debris, smog and decay of *Super Heroes* in the brief time left to shoot the final sequence. This original ending was thought too downbeat and was cut by the studio. Happily, it's been restored at the insistence of fans. Thanks, fans! The film doesn't make sense without it. In the final scene, the narrator, played by the late magnificent Charles Gray, spins an illuminated globe of the world and, again by chance, it stops on Australia. Or is it New Zealand? Or China? Certainly, there was a Pacific Rim influence on this film.

ABOVE: Tim Curry poolside in LA

OPPOSITE, CLOCKWISE FROM TOP LEFT: Tim Curry after his final performance in Chelsea; Richard Hartley recording *Rocky Horror* with Richard O'Brien; Richard O'Brien after his final Riff Raff in Chelsea; *Rocky Horror* designers: Brian Thomson and Sue Blane.

If only we were among friends or sane persons ...

Brad and Janet, the small-town couple who wander into the haunted house on that memorable night of clouds—*heavy, black and pendulous*—are the innocent heart of *Rocky Horror*. I assumed Brad and Janet's adventures somehow echoed Richard O'Brien's experience of growing up in conservative New Zealand, then journeying into the haunted house of European culture and the madness of hippy London—a journey I understood and to a degree shared. Maybe that was the invisible thread linking our sensibilities and informing our rare and productive collaboration.

In a sense, *Hair* and *Rocky Horror* book-end the hippy era. *This is the dawning of the Age of Aquarius* began it. *Frank N Furter, it's all over* was its requiem. We had lived through the *don't dream it, be it* period and its all too brief *jump to the left*, and were now about to witness a very firm *step to the right* and a return to conservatism in the endless time warp of global politics. Prophetic lyrics, those.

It was great when it all began ...

As I stood in the drizzling rain on a June night in 1973, a small audience of around sixty huddled in a tiny studio hovering above the Royal Court in Sloane Square. It was ten o'clock as I made my way up the familiar stairs and squeezed into the cramped dressing room to offer final thoughts and good wishes. Backstage excitement ran high as glitter was applied to faces and fishnet stockings were slid over unlikely legs.

Our guest of honour, Vincent Price, the legendary star of countless horror movies, had been invited to give the show its Hammer Horror seal of approval. He was among the last to enter, accompanied by his stately companion Coral Brown, fresh from a great performance downstairs. There was a frisson from the crowd as this famous couple was silently escorted to their seats by phantom ushers wearing eerie featureless masks.

Vincent, Coral and the rest of the audience that night found themselves in creaky old cinema seats circled by cobwebbed ramps eye-height to a stiletto heel and facing red velvet curtains that would soon open to reveal a blank cinema screen with a rock band concealed behind its gauzy surface.

The ushers shed their masks. One of them, author Richard O'Brien as Riff Raff, slammed shut the entrance door to the tiny theatre. The audience jumped at the sound. There was an alarming sense of being suddenly trapped in a haunted cinema. Before they had time to relax, I signalled musical director Richard Hartley, who gave the downbeat for the cymbal crash that began the show.

At that precise moment, thunder and lightning erupted all over London. It was an electrical storm, a tempest. Incredible synchronicity. I knew something special was about to happen. And it did. In the words of the show's narrator:

It was a night out they would remember for a very long time.

At the Royal Court *Rocky Horror* was a small miracle. As it moved down the Kings Road from one soon-to-be-demolished cinema to another, it picked up speed. When I think of the show, it's that first transfer—the Chelsea Classic version—that most comes to mind; the staging that sealed its long-running success. In Los Angeles at Lou Adler's Roxy Theatre it was wild, with coked-up movie stars in the audience; in Sydney, Harry M Miller's production offered a brilliant cast, the best since the original. In New York it missed onstage but created a cult at the cinema. An amazing ride from a few strummed chords, a modest script outline and a pitched tent in Sloane Square.

Over thirty years later *The Rocky Horror Show* still plays in theatres, cinemas and, via DVD, in homes across the globe. A musical that began its life by turning a tiny fringe venue into a haunted cinema now turns cinemas and living rooms into live theatres. Fans dress up as their favourite characters and sing, dance and party along with the screen. As a liberating celebration of excess and retribution, it has become the rite-of-passage movie for all time.

Decades after *Rocky Horror*, I was rehearsing Shakespeare's *The Tempest* and a weird sense of déjà vu came over me. Where had I seen this before? I wondered. A reclusive scientist, young lovers, crazy servants ... I recalled Richard's enthusiasm for *Forbidden Planet*, which he saw as a kid in New Zealand. A penny dropped. *Forbidden Planet* was a 1950s sci-fi reinvention of *The Tempest*. So perhaps what we were once playing at the Chelsea Classic was a classic after all. If not, it surely is now.

WEIMAR ON THE HARBOUR

As *Rocky Horror* settled into its seven-year run in the converted cinemas of Chelsea, I found myself sitting quietly in the stalls of the Drama Theatre of the Sydney Opera House with my one-time babysitter, Gloria Dawn. It was the spring of 1973, the paint was barely dry on the walls and we were discussing cats.

Gloria played Mrs Peachum in my production of Bertolt Brecht and Kurt Weill's *Die Dreigroschenoper*. The production was *The Threepenny Opera* with an Aussie accent, my contribution to the opening season of the Sydney Opera House. It was a privilege to be part of the unveiling of this great building, though our venue lacked the resources of the larger halls.

The Drama Theatre was originally intended as a cinema, hence its rectangular widescreen stage. All this was changed when Danish architect Jørn Utzon departed the project. The influential ABC, which controlled the nation's symphony orchestras, lobbied for the main hall, originally conceived and designed for opera, to be reconfigured as a concert hall. The argument of the day was that there were greater audiences for concerts than opera. The ABC view prevailed. In the subsequent reshuffle, opera lost out and drama was relegated to a converted cinema in the basement.

The result was an exterior that takes your breath away and a prosaic and often impractical interior. Having grown up in Sydney at a time when the Opera House was under construction—like a giant, beautiful, living organism rising slowly from the harbour—the dismissal of Utzon was widely viewed in the arts community as a triumph of short-sighted pragmatism over artistic vision.

Like the ghost of Hamlet's father, the spectre of what might have been still haunts this Elsinore of Bennelong Point. Imagine if, instead of being sent packing, Utzon had been invited to design other buildings in the city? The result might have compared with that other great harbour city, Barcelona—defined by the architecture of Antonio Gaudi. It was not to be, and the great Danish architect would never return to Australia.

Gloria's cat had been run over; she was late for rehearsal and in a state. This wonderful vaudevillian had always prided herself on her professionalism, though she carried the stigma of having *trod the boards* as opposed to *working legit*. The Sydney Opera House was about as *legit* as you could get, which is precisely why I chose to direct this guttersnipe of a musical and relocate it around the harbour in the 1930s, when razor gangs and brothels thrived. Pirate Jenny's famous death ship of sails and cannon might have disgorged its phantom crew at the nearby quay. The fact that *The Threepenny Opera* concludes with a royal messenger offering a false happy ending and that the queen would be visiting Australia to open the Opera House had implications that were noted only by a few.

As Gloria was from the old school, a cup of tea did the trick. Her dead cat wasn't forgotten, but calm was restored and the rehearsal resumed. It felt odd directing my ex-babysitter; our early encounters had been among sawdust and tents and here we were in one of the finest arts venues in the world, discussing cats! But the old trouper knew how to play Brecht. Theatre folk were astonished when a guest director from Brecht's own Berliner Ensemble had overlooked many a highly regarded actress and cast Gloria Dawn in a Melbourne production of *Mother Courage*. It's easily understood. Brecht's ideas were derived from Weimar cabaret, and vaudevillians make the same direct connection with their audience. They're comfortable about slipping in and out of character and their down-to-earth, working-class manner signals that this is no actor but a real person stepping up and doing a turn. Gloria would knit and chat in the wings, then put down her knitting, quietly excuse herself and nonchalantly walk onstage; she'd rip the roof off singing *What Keeps a Man Alive* and return to her knitting and conversation as if nothing had happened. It sounds easy, but it requires a fully lived life, offstage and on, to achieve.

The Drama Theatre was a hive of activity as the opening approached, as was the whole building. I gather the unofficial opening of the building occurred during the production week for Prokofiev's *War and Peace* in the Opera Theatre, when one of the whores from our production managed a *quickie* with a Russian general from *War and Peace* in one of the boxes of the Opera Theatre. It's an entertaining thought that still amuses me during occasional longueurs in operas at that venue. I often wonder—which box?

All the events and productions that opened the Sydney Opera House—plays, operas, concerts—were considered and of substance, but the real excitement was the building itself. I felt I'd grown up with it, as if the city had come of age and the culture expanded along with the building blocks, cement pours and the emergence of its glistening sails. For all the compromises, the building brought with it a sense of optimism and hope. In time, it would become the icon of Sydney and, culturally, it announced a shift from the halls and makeshift venues it replaced. It tasted of the future and offered a sense of infinite possibilities, encouraging the idea that something progressive was in the air. I sensed this and wanted to contribute, be part of it.

The Threepenny Opera offered me the undeniable pleasure of hearing the laughter and applause of an Australian audience again. I'd missed it: the emotional communication you derive from an audience whose history, understanding and accent you share. In London, I had directed mostly international musicals, or American and Australian plays; interestingly, nothing specifically English. My first instinct in approaching *The Threepenny Opera* was to give it an Australian context, and it was during this visit that the seeds of my return home were sown.

Part of the pleasure of this production was the quality of the cast. Standards had risen in the time I'd been away. Robin Ramsay played a vicious, charming Macheath; Pamela Stephenson was the sexy, ambitious Polly Peachum; Kate Fitzpatrick a steely Pirate Jenny. Gloria, Arthur Dignam and Drew Forsythe led a cast of ne'er-do-wells in a gutsy performance that would have held sway on any stage in the world.

When the applause faded at the end of *The Threepenny Opera*, I would soon find myself on another plane being sped to another hotel then into another limo to rehearse another cast in another city in another country. But these homecoming thoughts would gnaw at me. For the moment I was back on the international circuit. But ideas, like seeds ... grow.

BERLIN

I'm just the waterboy. The real game's not over here … but my heart is overflowing anyway …

Lyrics from Lou Reed's mighty album *Berlin* were on my mind as I walked home on a wet night from the Royal Court Theatre where my production of Sam Shepard's *The Tooth of Crime* was playing. I had been a fan of Lou's since his early Velvet Underground days, and the fact that his latest album had received a lotof critical flak only enhanced it to my mind. I thought it was a masterpiece and had considered a stage version. I'd mentioned the idea to Mick Rock, a friend and the official photographer to the glam-rock era. That was why the phone in my Pimlico apartment rang around midnight …

It's Mick … I'm here with Lou and he saw Sam's play and would like to meet … he's flying out in the morning … can you drop by Blake's Hotel …?

It was too late. I was exhausted. Wait a minute. Lou was the only person I'd ever been a fan of. I remembered the night with Lillian Roxon at Andy Warhol's Factory all those years ago.

OK. I'll be right over.

It lasted until dawn. It wasn't in the bar. It was in the room. Pretty small room, too. Bed. Table. The usual. Mick Rock was slumped on the bed. We sat at the table. Some Warhol paraphernalia was in place. A cassette to diarise the conversation. But those Factory days already seemed long gone. Lou had cropped his hair and dyed it blond and was about to release *Sally Can't Dance*. He played a demo to us. The title said it all. Lou was still smarting from the reviews of *Berlin*. Thirty years later it would be recognised as a classic and Lou would perform it all over the world. But that was hard to imagine at the time of its release. The album had cost a fortune to produce. RCA had promoted it as *a movie for the mind*. The producer had succumbed to a nervous breakdown. It was to be the *Sergeant Pepper's of the '70s*. It wasn't. *Berlin* was reviewed as dark, depressing, morally bankrupt and a failure.

I play it all the time, Lou.

Flicker of a smile; then, deadpan:
Did well in Sweden.
Lou and I spoke of a stage version.
You could narrate.
I was the protagonist.
Oh.
Andy thought it might make a ballet—with Nureyev.
The Tooth of Crime came up.
Sam's the Edward Albee of the Underground.
We weren't getting anywhere. It was 3 a.m. and Mick had dozed off. There was a bottle of scotch and two room service wine glasses and a lot of cigarette smoke. It was hardly King of The Velvet Underground terrain. The level in the scotch bottle descended as the hours ticked by. Lou would make as if the conversation was over. I would make to leave. He'd bring up something else. I'd stay. All through the night. I got it. A test of perseverance. How much do you care? If you hang in then something might happen. It did. Lou slowly turned from his image into himself.

Where'd you get those glasses?
I had orange wraparound glasses—all one thin sheet of plastic.
Twenty-four-hour chemist.
Let's go.
A car was summoned. Mick was left asleep on the bed. We cruised all-night chemists until we found one with the glasses. Lou put on the glasses. We drove back. Outside Blake's Hotel we parted. It was very tender. All that rock-and-roll armour to hide such a sensitive soul. He'd taken himself and everyone else to the edge but he'd made sure his own footfall was firm and steady.

It was dawn. I walked home feeling very light.

And I made up a little story about a buffalo.

With Lou Reed, Blake's Hotel

THE BUFFALO

And so the curious buffalo galloped to the edge of the cliff, as he wished to see the view below. Once there, he stopped and stared. The rest of the herd followed, blindly and unthinkingly, and they cascaded over the cliff in a flurry of howling and baying and they landed below, a concertina of flailing flesh and cracking bones. Puzzled, the curious buffalo looked down at the dazed herd, shook his head, and said: *I didn't tell you to jump.*

KINGS ROAD

Sam Shepard didn't really want to see *Rocky Horror*. I'd directed his plays, so I guess he felt obliged. It wasn't cool with serious writers. Tennessee Williams had come to the Chelsea Classic opening and we had chatted for hours, but not about the show. He was mainly pushing for me to do his plays, explaining that the English couldn't do them but Australians probably could because we were more *visceral*. Maybe he was making a pass. Does that sound like a pass? I guess it does.

I was pacing outside the theatre, waiting for Sam, when a familiar figure loomed. It was ... no, surely not ... yes, from all those years ago at the Chateau Marmont. It was James Rado, the author of *Hair*. We did quick catch-ups and he went inside. Then I turned and ran into Andrew Lloyd Webber buying a ticket at the box office. I intervened and organised complimentary seats. Andrew was pleased but a little embarrassed to be seen there.

Don't worry, I said. *They tell me David Bowie's been many times but he comes in disguise. At least you came as yourself!*

Andrew laughed. Beneath his sometimes prickly exterior there beat the heart of a true enthusiast. I wondered what he'd make of the show.

It's one of those nights, I thought.

Sam surprised himself by liking the show. He thought it could have been darker, and gave an unexpected and startling rendition of the foot-stamp and heel-grind he felt Frank could use. It was Bette Davis style. Sam would have liked Reg Livermore in the Sydney production. Australians are more visceral. Tennessee was right.

After the show, I took Sam to meet Richard O'Brien and Tim Curry. Sam was polite but seemed a bit distracted. He was amazed when I told him James Rado was in the audience. Sam was living in London in retreat from New York; the underground scene there had overwhelmed him. He was planning a return, however, and the mention of James Rado triggered a few memories.

As Sam and I emerged from backstage, we bumped into James Rado. Straight up, Sam grinned and called him *Jimmy*.

They had this sudden rush of enthusiasm that Americans get when they run into each other in foreign climes. There's a special thing to it.

I noticed Andrew heading home and waved. He smiled back and looked like he'd had a pretty good time.

Then it happened.

Crash.

Just like that. I spun around and James Rado had fallen. Hit by a swerving car.

James was OK—but shaken. Not hit just by the car but by the night and maybe the show as well. I helped him up. Settled him. Hailed a cab. I turned and noticed Sam Shepard. He was still and kind of frozen. He seemed to have turned into a character from one of his own plays. He was staring, ghostly and mumbling, and repeating:

Jimmy Rado got hit by a car. In London. Jimmy Rado got hit by ...

Are you OK, Sam?

He snapped back to Mr Cool. It was farewell time. Sam gave me a book of his stories, *Hawk Moon*, with a little inscription: *Thanks for the nifty production.*

James Rado I would not see again.

Andrew went on to create *The Phantom of the Opera*.

Sam returned to the States. He took up with Jessica Lange and wrote a Pulitzer Prize–winning play: *Buried Child*.

I returned to Australia.

It was one of those nights.

IN 1979 ...

A revolution in Iran returned Ayatollah Khomeini from exile in Paris and heralded the birth of an Islamic state. The Shah of Iran fled to the United States. Iran created a hostage drama that ended President Jimmy Carter's reign and set the scene for Ronald Reagan's election as president. Margaret Thatcher became the first woman prime minister of Great Britain, and the western world took *a step to the right* ...

The Clash released *London Calling* and Stephen Sondheim created *Sweeney Todd*. There was nuclear fallout at Three Mile Island. Sony introduced the Walkman. Snow fell in the Sahara Desert. Zimbabwe was renamed Rhodesia. Vietnamese troops occupied Cambodia, and the Khmer Rouge and Pol Pot were ousted. Muhammed Ali retired. Mother Teresa won the Nobel Prize.

Norman Foster's towering Hong Kong and Shanghai Bank opened its doors. Deng Xiao Ping introduced the open-door policy in China, and families were limited to one child. The Soviet Union signed a Nuclear Proliferation Treaty and invaded Afghanistan. Punk rocker Sid Vicious murdered his girlfriend Nancy Spungeon in New York's Chelsea Hotel and subsequently OD'd.

Andrew Logan ushered in the 1980s with his *Alternative Miss World Party* on New Year's Eve in a Thames warehouse, with special guest *Divine*.

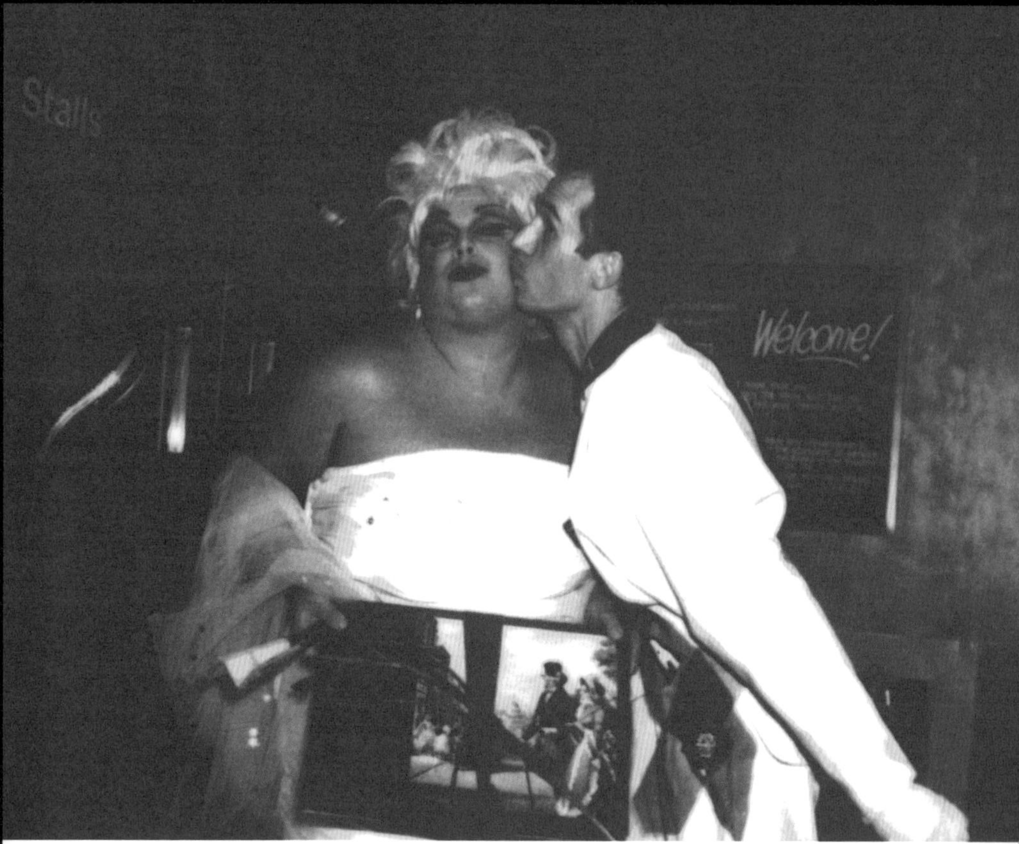
Stalls
Welcome!

WORLD'S END

The cloud-capped towers of Andrew Logan's Alternative Miss World pageant-parties were a London legend, a view that was shared by his good friend Derek Jarman, who had just made a film of Shakespeare's *The Tempest*.

Andrew and Derek were two for the road in 1979. Well, three, counting the painter Duggie Fields, who helped out with the decorations. They were part of a small coterie of London artists valiantly trying to keep the lovely eccentric heart of the city alive.

With the election of Thatcher and the approach of a new decade, Andrew's 1979 party had special significance. England was about to become a more efficient, more self-interested and much less pleasant place to live. I'd settled in Sydney but had returned to London to work with Brian Thomson on designs for our forthcoming Adelaide Festival production of Benjamin Britten's *Death in Venice*. I accepted an invitation to spend New Year's Eve in Andrew's now familiar Thames studio-warehouse.

I sensed an air of apprehension, almost craziness, as 1980 approached, even among practised revellers like Boy George, a singer who would thrive in the fashion-conscious decade ahead. The crowded warehouse was draped in calico, and over-sized, bejewelled mirrored sculptures were suspended overhead. The centrepiece was a brightly coloured child's plastic swimming pool with rubber duckies.

Divine, the guest of honour, was the flamboyant star of John Waters' wild and wonderful movies. I had known *Divine* in New York as a shy, bald, plump actor called Glen Milne; a very sweet guy. *Divine* was his alter ego, a Mrs Hyde to his demure Dr Jekyll. Years before, I had attended a premiere screening of John Waters' film *Pink Flamingos* in New York, where *Divine* ran down the aisles throwing dead fish at the audience.

As midnight chimed, Vivienne Westwood, the anti-fashion designer who oddly resembled Margaret Thatcher, though definitely on the other side of the political fence, grabbed her former protégé, the pale and very Irish ex–Sex Pistol Johnny

Andrew Logan and guest, *Divine*

Rotten, and pushed him, fully clothed, into the tiny pool, triumphantly announcing:

It's now 1980 and you're MrYesterday!

The wind-down from the glitter and punk culture of 1970s London had been a long time coming, and seeing Johnny Rotten, drenched, in a kids' pool, grinning ludicrously and surrounded by bobbing rubber duckies, was evidence of its final decline. The tipping point had been reached a year earlier and, by chance, I'd had a ringside seat.

I was meeting with Richard O'Brien in *Asterix*, a pancake and coffee franchise named after the well-known French cartoon character, at the end of Chelsea's Kings Road in a strip known as World's End. It was an appropriate place name for Richard's and my discussion about our collaboration on a musical film that would emerge a few years later. *Shock Treatment* would be set in a desperate future, where the only currency was fame and the media-dominated population had become slaves to the banal values of reality television.

We sat at the window table, chatting, eating and staring out towards Malcolm McClaren and Vivienne Westwood's fashionable clothes store, situated across the road. Malcolm had shifted from the rag trade into pop management, furthering punk by creating The Sex Pistols. Richard and I had known them both since they began their radical exploits at a little shop further down the Kings Road, originally called *Too Fast to Live—Too Young to Die* before they transformed it into the catchier *Sex*. Vivienne would cut quite a figure, often reclining on Astro Turf, dressed in a pink latex catsuit, reading Wilhelm Reich.

Their rebellious young clientele would have been surprised to discover that their heroes were ex-schoolteachers who met on a Nuclear Disarmament march. I got to know Vivienne when she became fast friends with my Venezuelan companion Gustavo, a model for her proto-punk outfits. Vivienne was the designer and Malcolm the spruiker for the punk movement. Their smart new store across from us was a stylish establishment called *Seditionaries*, with pearl-frosted windows like a dentist's surgery and a discreet brass nameplate by the door.

Every Saturday, working-class punks, with their safety-pinned noses and rent-a-punk bondage outfits, would train in from the East End and take over the fashionable Kings Road. At the same time, working-class soccer fans would be heading down to the nearby Chelsea Stadium. The resulting clashes inevitably ended up in a tribal brawl. All the locals knew the rules, even the police: everyone either entered the fray or kept well away.

In the previous week, Malcolm had effectively disbanded The Sex Pistols by sacking Johnny Rotten at the end of a disastrous American tour. The fans felt betrayed and were outraged. They advanced on Malcolm's headquarters: *Seditionaries*.

In a scene worthy of the French revolution, they started hurling stones, bricks and each other at the pearl-frosted windows. The air was rent by the sound of smashing glass and the screams and the *yee-yaw-yee-yaw* of police and ambulance sirens speeding to clean up the consequences and arrest the perpetrators. The sense of violence fuelling the mob was impossible to ignore.

Richard turned to me, shook his head and wryly observed:

I think Frankenstein's monster has just turned.

It was one of Richard's and my last purely social encounters, and the chaos outside brought back memories of our shared connection to the three rock musicals that helped define an era—our first nervous meetings in the cafés of Chelsea and Fulham, as we excitedly transformed Richard's musical gem from an improbable idea to a possible production and ultimately into an international success. So much had happened and been shared. Now we were no longer players but witnesses, seated safely behind glass, eating pancakes.

Looking at Richard, I was reminded of the skull-like ghost of Crow, the ruthless, nihilistic character he'd played in Sam Shepard's punching bag of a rock-and-roll gangster show *The Tooth of Crime*. The uncompromising anarchy of that character had inspired Malcolm McClaren in his creation of Johnny Rotten and The Sex Pistols.

Sam had been influenced in writing *The Tooth of Crime* by the young Bert Brecht's *In the Jungle of Cities*, another take on the Faust legend. I was reminded of the last line of that play as

I stared at the violence outside. At the pancakes. At Richard. And sensed that something special had ended.

The chaos is spent. And that was the best time.

As rocks crashed through the windows of *Seditionaries*, I was mentally preparing to say goodbye to international adventures, cut some slack and …

Original *Rocky Horror Show* poster by Michael English

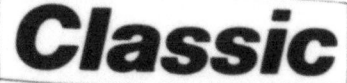

THE ROCKY HORROR SHOW

ALIVE ON STAGE

Music Book & Lyrics by RICHARD O'BRIEN
Director JIM SHARMAN
Designer BRIAN THOMPSON   Costumes SUE BLANE
Lighting GERRY JENKINSON   Musical Arrangements RICHARD 'RITZ' HARTLEY
The Theatre Upstairs Production presented by MICHAEL WHITE

ALL SEATS BOOKABLE

Classic   CINEMA **CHELSEA**
148 KINGS ROAD SW3
BOX OFFICE 352 4388

3

Sarsaparilla

rick White

Vivisector

Penguin Moder

Patrick W

The Vivise

uffield loves only what he paints. The

SEASON AT SARSAPARILLA

Three erudite provocateurs had jolted the Australia I returned to in 1975 out of its complacency. Progressive Labor Prime Minister Gough Whitlam was one, brilliant conservative satirist Barry Humphries another. I admired them both. The third man was writer Patrick White. We would meet and collaborate for over a decade, and our friendship would last until his passing. Nobel laureate, ex–army officer and sometime *Tiresius of the suburbs*, Patrick created a distinctive Australian voice, and his faith in what he called *perpetual becoming* offered another way of seeing the world.

Ring-ring: Tokyo, 8 a.m., Sunday, 30 September 1990
I awoke to the *whirr* and *click* of a bedside fax machine in my rented apartment in Sendagaya. I reached for my glasses to read a simple message from Brian Thomson in Sydney.

Dear Jim,
Sad news.
Patrick passed away this morning.
Love, Brian.

Half-naked, half-awake, staring, a little dazed, at the grey shimmer of an autumn morning, I recalled my last meeting with Patrick at his Martin Road home, opposite Sydney's Centennial Park. On that occasion the spacious rooms, which once tinkled with the laughter of guests, had taken on the antiseptic air of a private hospital. The mischievous gleam in the old warrior's eyes had dimmed and been replaced by an unhappy complicity of illness, rheumy pallor and untypical doubt.

JS: *You must be enjoying the fruits of old age.*
PW: *What are they?*
JS: Pause. *Wisdom?*
PW: *I knew more when I was eighteen.*

I stood blinking at this recollection, slightly shaken, before proceeding to a shower and a shave. There was no sentimentality about Patrick White, and I was determined that there would be little from the sorcerer's apprentice. Patrick's death was hardly unexpected, and he had led a fulfilling and productive life.

The Vivisector at Bondi

I quickly faxed a grateful reply to Brian, requesting my condolences be communicated to Patrick's partner and muse, Manoly Lascaris.

It was Sunday, I reminded myself. I'd arranged to meet two friends, Georgina Pope and Dennis Watkins, for breakfast at a neighbouring German bakery. Dennis was the librettist on a new opera about the creation of the Sydney Opera House: *The Eighth Wonder*. This was his first visit to Tokyo. After the early-morning news, I was looking forward to their company and was suddenly hungry for freshly baked pastries. Georgina had arranged tickets for me to accompany Dennis to a matinee at the nearby National Nō Theatre.

On hearing the news from Sydney, there were downcast eyes and respectful silences across the breakfast coffee, and suggestions of rainchecks. Either through denial or determination, I wouldn't hear of it. I didn't want Dennis to miss out on a unique travel experience and I knew the meditative nature of Nō, with its ceremonial ghosts and timeless pace, would offer a reflective atmosphere where my memories could swirl and flow in private reverie. And so they did. Within moments of the performance beginning, a resonant chime reminded me of a recurring motif in my relationship with Patrick … the telephone.

Ring-ring: I was feeding fish from a little wooden bridge over a carp pond in my rented Paddington house. On my return to Australia, I had spent some transitional weeks in the impersonal surroundings of the space-age Gazebo Hotel before accepting the offer to move into this converted inner-city stable with its faux Japanese garden. I was filling in time tending to the carp while nervously awaiting my first phone call from Patrick White. I had no idea what to expect or what it might herald.

Invited by Ken Southgate from the Old Tote Theatre management to direct a new production, I'd suggested reviving *The Season at Sarsaparilla*. The choice was greeted with surprise, but it was part of my determination to reconnect with Australia and challenge myself as a director. Management understood, but shook their heads. Patrick White had publicly proclaimed his disillusionment with theatre and had vetoed any attempt to revive his plays for over a decade.

Nonetheless, tentative enquiries were made and now the phone was ringing.

I tossed the remaining fish food into the pond, wiped my hands and picked up the receiver, wondering what to expect. A low-modulated voice uttered the opening gambit:

This is Patrick White . . . Pause *. . . I understand you want to disturb the dust.*

I explained the reasons behind my proposed revival of his play.

PW: *Well . . . we should meet.*

JS: *Sure . . . When?*

PW: Pause. *In half an hour?*

I briefly panicked . . . *What if he quizzes me about all those books of his that I haven't read?* I had been prepared for the voice-of-God effect down the line, but was thrown by this sudden switch to showbiz urgency.

JS: *I was thinking . . . next week.*

A time was made. I hung up, wandered to the bookcase and started browsing one of his books. *Voss* had been my introduction to Patrick White as a teenage reader. I was impressed, overwhelmed, exhilarated even, but reading *Voss* had been a struggle. In London, I'd returned to it with greater insight. There are some things to savour early in life: rock-and-roll, dance parties and political extremism, for example. Other things require more maturity, like Mahler symphonies, political reality and the writings of Patrick White. I stared at the first lines.

There is a man here, miss, asking for your uncle, said Rose.
And stood breathing.

Our first encounter had been a decade earlier, when I was twenty. It was as curious as it was spontaneous and took place in Edels midtown music store, an important stopover in my city walks since student days. I was flipping through the new releases rack when Peter Sainthill, the shop manager, brushed past: *There goes your fan club.*

I looked up to see the back of a tall, distinguished-looking man in a bulky sweater heading out the door. Puzzled, I turned to Peter, who whispered: *Patrick White.*

During my early NIDA tenure, I had staged a revue, *Terror Australis*—a spirited attack on many Australian sacred cows. The then critic of the *Sydney Morning Herald*, HG Kippax, had joined an audience officially invited to a black-tie opening. On arrival, they had to crawl through a sheep run to enter the theatre, only to be greeted by a cast mimicking sheep and *baa-baa*-ing their way through the current national anthem *God Save the Queen.* It was confronting satire on the colonial roots of conformity and racism from a cast led by Helen Morse and a pre–Norman Gunston Garry McDonald. The tone of the *SMH* review was angry, derisory and dismissive. Harry Kippax's outrage was fine by me; it matched that of the show. A few days later, a letter appeared in the paper questioning the review and supporting the production. Its author was now heading down King Street. In a flush of youthful excitement, I charged onto the street with a cry of *Mr White! Mr White!* Ignoring age and reputation, I bashed him on the back. The startled author spun around, saucer eyes staring:

JS: *Thanks, Mr White, for your great letter.*
PW: *Well* ... Pause ... *Thanks for the great show.*
Awkwardness. Gratitude. Departures.
That was it ... until a decade later, when the phone rang.
Well, not quite.

Beyond seeing Patrick's early controversial plays *The Ham Funeral* and *The Season at Sarsaparilla* as an eager teenager, there had been one other sighting. I had attended a concert of electronic music by German composer Karlheinz Stockhausen at the University of New South Wales. It was during my hippy days and I had dropped a tab of acid, thinking it would enhance the experience. It didn't, but I survived the night and the electronic music. Across the interval foyer, I was fascinated to glimpse Patrick White talking to the music critics Kurt and Maria Prerauer, my *Don Giovanni* supporters. I later discovered the Prerauers had translated the German version of Patrick's

Riders in the Chariot. Fortunately, in my stoned state, I didn't resort to backslapping introductions, but I was fascinated by the intensity of Patrick's gaze as his eyes scanned that crowd like a one-man X-ray machine.

That was my sum total of Patrick White encounters. Yet here I was, knocking on the door of his Centennial Park home and wanting to revive his dormant theatrical career.

Our first meeting went well, with no literary quizzes and a little awe on both sides. There was much theatrical chitchat and discussion of my return to Australia, which struck a familiar chord with the writer. To my surprise, and possibly his, we were underway.

Ring-ring: Once the calls started, they never stopped. Usually around 8.45 a.m.

PW: *Good morning. I've been thinking … Yairs, definitely Kate Fitzpatrick as Nola Boyle. That Peter Whitford's a marvellous actor. Is he a thought for Mr Pogson?*

JS: *Perfect … and Max Cullen and Bill Hunter as Ernie and Digger.*

PW: *Yairs … very good.*

Max and Bill were superb and guaranteed an earthy depth to *Sarsaparilla*. Patrick became fascinated by Max's voice. It would inspire several characters in his writing. Patrick rarely took on whole aspects of a person, rather a characteristic. So-and-so's eyes or such-and-such's voice would conspire in the crucible of his dreams and imagination with an incident from way back when, or something he'd read in the morning paper, to create a fictional character. I sensed Robyn Nevin would be great as Girlie Pogson, recalling *gin rummy on the mosquito-proof veranda* and relishing the comic conformity of Sarsaparilla, brilliantly captured in Girlie's mantra: *I like a hat to look different, so long as it's what the others are wearing.*

JS: *Robyn Nevin for Girlie Pogson?*

PW: Pause. *Do Kate and Robyn get on?*

JS: *Well …*

PW: Chuckle. *That could work.*

I had released Patrick's backstage genie. It had been dormant too long. He wanted showbiz; I wanted art house—we each had needs and something to offer. Now in his sixties, Patrick had written most of his great novels, and his early plays and short stories. He'd been honoured with the Nobel Prize for *The Eye of the Storm* and had reached a point of renown and stasis. He needed something or someone to enter his life to disrupt and inspire him. As I sat in his sunlit study at Martin Road, I felt like Puck in *A Midsummer Night's Dream*, sent to *sweep the dust behind the door*.

For my part, Patrick was the mentor I had been seeking: a challenging guide to new horizons. I didn't exactly understand where this was leading, but it felt right and I trusted my instincts. I knew that if I stayed on the rock musical merry-go-round I would be repeating myself and, at around thirty, this was my greatest fear. A careerist will always repeat what the public expects of them; it's a professionally understandable choice. But it wasn't what drove me. I certainly embraced success when it came my way and I'd been lucky on that score, but I was dismissive of it, as I searched, or blundered, my way towards the next challenge. I was an explorer, not a builder; more terrorist than warrior. Hit or miss, I would move on, more interested in journeys than destinations. I knew Patrick would offer insight into the psychology of character, as well as historical connection with my own country and a new way of seeing the world. This was what I needed; craved, even. I eagerly embraced the collaboration.

Sarsaparilla turned out to be the hit of the season. Wendy Dickson's design spread the three kitchens of heaven, earth and hell across the letterbox stage of the Sydney Opera House like three vivisection slabs. The production was stark, bright, Brechtian; it was rigorously faithful to the text and acted with clarity by a remarkably fine cast. As the dialogue flicked and sprayed from household to household, from animation to stillness, the rhythmic and musical skills of director and actors were put to the test and not found wanting. On a simpler level, the production subscribed to Patrick's curiously old-fashioned showbiz dictum: *I like a good laugh and a cry*.

An audience that had been startled by the original production a decade earlier could now, through the window of time,
comfortably embrace this spiky kaleidoscope of a play; they
were less confronted by the uncomfortable truths it offered
about their former selves. So much so that Patrick muttered,
in an aside, as he was heading up the aisle after another stamp-
ing ovation: *I might write something about them next time.*

Big Toys, the play he wrote for Kate Fitzpatrick, Max Cullen
and Arthur Dignam, was yet to come. For the moment, I was
happy enough that my decision to return to Australia and challenge expectations—my own and others'—was beginning to
bear fruit.

In the week prior to the final performances of *Sarsaparilla*,
another visit to Edels held a further surprise. Looking up
from the new releases rack I sighted a familiar, if now slightly
diminished, figure flipping through the string quartets. It was
HG Kippax, who had recently given up reviewing theatre. In
many ways, Harry represented the old guard my generation had
overtaken. His response to my own work had been measured
and often hostile, but he had been a strong and vocal supporter
of Patrick's writing in the days before it was fashionable. I was
surprised by his gloomy, downcast manner and wondered if
Sarsaparilla might be the remedy. Harry seemed oddly moved
by my interest and cautiously accepted an invitation.

As the cast prepared backstage for the final matinee performance, I came across a bewildered Kate Fitzpatrick. She
was costumed and ready to play Nola, but her fellow actors
from the Boyle household were missing. What to do? I urgently
consulted our stage manager, Ian Tasker. The prospect of can-
cellation was in the air when two sheepishly hung-over actors
stepped into view. Their unshaven faces and blurry explanations
of a night on the town with drinking mate and ex-con turned
playwright Jim McNeil didn't bode well. I was fuming, but
there was nothing to be done, except glare and hope for the
best. Patrick was attending, and I'd seen Harry Kippax take his
seat, so, wishing everyone well but fearing the worst, I trudged
into the auditorium.

From the audience's perspective the performance was probably fine, but I was in a terse mood and aware that Kate was feeding lines and repositioning to keep her household on the rails. It certainly brought out the best in her; electric bolts seemed to emanate from the character of Nola Boyle, and each line seemed to challenge her fellow actors, normally so brilliant, to dare to forget their responses. Nola's reverie *I could eat the roses!* had never been rendered so passionately. At interval, I was too tense to go backstage. Instead, I stalked the harbour promenade and chain-smoked my way through the break. Returning to my seat, I ran into an unexpectedly gleeful Patrick. He had spent the interval backstage catching up with the actors and on all the dirt: *Oceans of Irish catholic guilt and remorse back there!*

Everything improved in the second act except my mood. The performance received an ovation, but I headed outside to cool down before going backstage to offer a few less generous observations of my own. A beaming Harry Kippax suddenly materialised, like a ghost dancing in the sunshine.

It was inspiring! he enthused.

It was bloody awful! I muttered.

No. No! gushed the usually taciturn ex-critic. *It's restored my faith in theatre.*

At this point Patrick emerged. Harry Kippax, almost beside himself, rushed towards him, arms flailing. *Patrick. Patrick! I've been meaning to contact you. I can't tell you how terrible my life has been. Seeing this has completely revived my spirits.*

Patrick looked startled, guarded, almost horrified ... *Pleased to hear it.*

I could see the drawbridge of his emotional castle closing fast, denying further access. One thing I'd observed from working with him was his utter abhorrence of self-pity.

Harry plunged mindlessly on. *But Patrick ... You, above all people, would understand. I've lost my faith ... in myself ... in everything!*

Patrick briefly became the man I'd read about.

Well, there's a harbour ... why don't you jump in it!

And was gone.

Shocking, but maybe that was what he needed to hear.

A few weeks later, Harry Kippax resumed his role as Sydney's most influential theatre critic, with a notably jaundiced view of his ex-friend Patrick White's future dramatic output.

And that was only the matinee.

Ring-ring: *Well … What did you think of my speech?*
Patrick had just spoken at an anti-nuclear town hall rally, echoing Mag Bosanquet, the central character in his new play *Big Toys*. I attended, but in the crowd I ran into a young drama graduate I had recently met and was strongly attracted to. He and I were at the rally for the same reason—Patrick's speech. James Waites had writing ambitions, and so it was our shared interest in Patrick that brought us together. Assuming it would be ages before the keynote address, we adjourned to the nearby Apache coffee shop. Enjoying each other's company, the coffee and the 1950s retro décor, we sauntered back to the rally late, only to discover we'd missed Patrick's speech. We ended up at my new Bondi apartment and subsequently lived together for several years.

Patrick was aghast that the director of his latest theatrical offering had missed the speech he had been building up to for weeks—there had been many phone calls on the subject—but when I brazenly conceded the reason, there was a long pause followed by a burst of forgiving laughter down the line.

Struck it lucky, eh? Well … that's all right. Chuckle. *I thought you were a nun!*
Patrick White is often represented as a scowling curmudgeon, yet I found him to be exactly the opposite. He was simply one of the funniest and most generous people I've known, and the most human of writers. While Patrick could turn frosty at pretentious society antics, especially when they involved artists, he had all the time in the world for the postman, the shopkeeper, the neighbour's problems, people on buses, the tramp in the park. One of our happiest encounters was over a rare beer at the Hotel Bondi, amid Maori pool players and kids running around in towels and thongs. Patrick viewed ordinariness with

a reverence others save for sacred sites. His perceptive gaze was always seeking the extraordinary behind the ordinary. The war had taught him to mistrust appearances, but he always embraced life's possibilities and potential. Patrick only became disillusioned and bitter when he saw spiritual aspirations sacrificed to political expediency, lazy seductive comfort and mindless pragmatism. He was an advocate of all that was life-affirming and a scourge to what he saw as life-denying. He was also a great judge of character. When others would over-praise this or that person, Patrick would demur, or sometimes violently disagree. Time and events often conspired to confirm the accuracy of his judgment. It's a quality Patrick shared with my grandfather, who, in many surprising ways, he resembled. Maybe it's a country-bred necessity to dispassionately size up a person on sight. Despite his urban sophistication, Patrick was a country boy at heart. *Paddy* White, the wealthy landowner's son from Belltrees, in the Hunter Valley, was never too far away from the writer who rose with the light and cast a custodial glance over the parkland estate. His hillside home loomed like a country manor over his beloved Centennial Park, and it was fitting he came to rest there, his ashes scattered over an unlikely lake.

Patrick's landowning background made him a rarity among Australian writers as it granted him unique access into the workings of power in society. His insights and spilling of the beans, especially the machinations of the greedy and their enthusiastic cheer squad, meant Patrick was often regarded as a class traitor by powerful friends and relatives. Whether in the sprawling Mahler symphony of *Riders in the Chariot*—his finest novel, I always thought—the cello concerto of *The Eye of the Storm*, with Elizabeth Hunter as its soloist, or a Mozart trio, like his play *Big Toys*, he knew and revealed how power and history colluded in Australian society, and to exactly what end.

Patrick's friendships were many and widespread, encompassing everyone from old-money society hostesses to union leaders like the influential Jack Mundey. These would come and go, depending on what he was writing at the time. When friends were dumped, seemingly on a whim, their *Ouch!* was loud and public. This vocal chorus of disaffected friends always suggested to me a misunderstanding of his artist's instinct, which was to view everyone as components of the legendary characters in those mighty books. I would see him puzzle over former friends attempting to renew old ties, as if he were thinking: *What are you still doing here? I've written your book.*

Our friendship survived two decades. It was intense, during collaboration, and more casual once our work was fulfilled. Others were not so lucky, or they simply misread the rules of engagement.

Ring-ring: *I'd like to invite you and Kate to dinner …*
The invitations were rare but the dinners were riveting. Patrick used his daily phone calls to audition dialogue and ideas, and his dinners also contributed to the working process, though his guests were mostly unaware of this fact.

Patrick's plays are littered with offstage lines from the kitchen, and many of these were given a trial run as he sweated over a troublesome dish. Around the time of *Big Toys*, Kate Fitzpatrick and I were invited to one special dinner to provide diversion while he was busy in the kitchen. At a time when a slew of public figures had been stricken with cancer, we found ourselves in the company of lawyers, politicians and their wives. For some reason they burst into impromptu song, and a chirpy chorus of *Do you know the way to San Jose …* was cut short by the sudden appearance of their host, his face hovering like a mischievous devil over a curtain of steam from a platter of cooked rabbit, and bellowing *Terrible about the cancer deaths!*

I understood Martin Road dinners as a mixture of theatre and reconnaissance. Patrick had spent his war service in Egypt, working in surveillance for British Intelligence. At university, he had been a contemporary of the Cambridge spies. When I read John Banville's marvellous, veiled portrait of Anthony Blunt, *The Untouchable*, I felt a strong echo of Patrick White. He was always collecting intelligence. Whether he was on the phone to his network of callers, or peering over a neighbour's fence, or consulting with Manoly about what was said when he left the room after he'd deliberately raised a contentious matter over dinner, everything he did served the work. Patrick's was a life sacrificed to those great novels.

Once, he had a collection of his books sent from the United States. This was after I had casually admired the simpler design of the US editions. They were a gift. Heaving the heavy box onto a coffee table, he misjudged, and the books tumbled out, onto the rug. There was a terrible pause as we both stared at his life's work, scattered across the floor, then long, loud, raucous laughter at the ridiculousness of the situation. No wonder that, in death, he gave away everything in his desire to be reduced to a shelf of books and a sprinkling of ashes on a lake. Like Voss' companion Le Mesurier:

Now that I am nothing, I am. And love is the simplest of all tongues.

In the church of *perpetual becoming* the novels were parables, Patrick was celebrant and Manoly acolyte. My role was either licensed fool to Patrick's Lear or a stray swallow who found ultimate pleasure in the service of the Happy Prince.

Ring-ring: *I've had a call from the opera company.*
It was my agent on the line. The Patrick White revival had consequences. I hadn't heard from the opera world since the heady days of *Don Giovanni*. The national company had recently embraced the bel canto enthusiasms of Richard Bonynge and Joan Sutherland, and had staged many a romantic pageant to showcase them. These popular productions were as vocally sumptuous as they were dramatically thin, so we had little need of each other. Change was on the way, however, following the arrival of Peter Hemmings from Scottish Opera. He had recently been appointed general manager, and his very different view was that opera should be presented as music-theatre. Peter was acutely aware that our national opera company had no original works in its repertoire and his plan was to commission Richard Meale to create an opera from Patrick's novel *Voss*. He felt my involvement would assist negotiations and help to bring his bold idea to fruition.

Voss was a touchy subject with Patrick as there had been several failed attempts to film it. I met with Peter, who impressed me, but, like others who ruffled local feathers with artistically challenging proposals, he would become another sacrifice on the altar of pragmatism—in his case, bel canto supremacy. Peter's great legacy was the commissioning of *Voss*. I admired his initiative and offered my assistance, proposing poet and writer David Malouf as librettist. I agreed to discuss it with Patrick and to direct the opera when it was ready for production. New operas take time. Peter proposed three years; *Voss* took seven.

I often think these great works have a life of their own. If so, *Voss* didn't want to be a film, but seemed happy enough to become an opera. Patrick would have preferred something original and contemporary, and he swiftly embarked on a new libretto to that end. When *Births, Deaths and Lotteries* didn't exactly fly, he very reluctantly agreed to *Voss*. Patrick knew Richard Meale's music, and David Malouf's involvement proved decisive. David was one of a select band of writers Patrick trusted and admired. He had an eye for writing talent; I recall him accurately predicting longevity for English novelist Ian McEwan on the slender evidence of a book of short stories.

David's libretto was far better than any screenplay of *Voss* I had read. He instinctively understood that the central dilemma in translating the novel into another form was the mysterious communion between Voss, the explorer in the desert, and his muse and spiritual companion in the city, Laura Trevelyan. Opera can dissolve time and space. All that this complex contact required was a vocal harmony and a stroll across the stage and you had it: *flesh and flesh together*. David's lyrics inspired the composer, and the translation of *Voss* to the opera stage was underway.

Ring-ring: *Well … did they milk the theme?*
The day before this phone call, we had been in a recording studio putting final touches to my film of Patrick's short story *The Night the Prowler*. I'd invited him to the recording session for soundtrack music, supervised by the composer, Cameron Allan.

From the control room we listened to a string orchestra play the accompaniment to the film's final images. The central character, Felicity Bannister, played by another of Patrick White's favourite actresses, Kerry Walker, fudges details of a reputed prowler attack as a means of liberating herself from her claustrophobic parents, superbly played by Ruth Cracknell and John Frawley. Felicity, clad in leather, like an animal, journeys into nature via a neighbouring park, where she finds a dying tramp. His ambitions have been reduced to necessities: *No rats and an easy pee.*

Confronted with the old man's death and her own isolation, and framed by dawn light creeping through the shutters of a derelict house—created by the film's production designer, Luciana Arrighi, to echo both the Bannister family home and Felicity's state of mind—she arrives at a bleak, truthful, oddly liberating understanding of life's depths and realities.

The string orchestra was syncing to a picture image on the studio screen. The music completed, Patrick smiled and made to leave. I suggested a retake and started giving the composer an overcomplicated explanation of what was missing. As Patrick headed out the door, Cameron hit the microphone button that linked to the musicians and crisply translated: *Again. And milk the theme!*

My rough but ready low-budget film of *The Night the Prowler* managed something that had eluded the much-touted film of *Voss*, in that it survived the hurdles of financing and made it to the screen. This was thanks mostly to producer Tony Buckley and the New South Wales Film and Television Office, encouraged by executive Michael Thornhill, who had produced an earlier low-budget film of mine, *Summer of Secrets*. Neither film found a wide audience, but *The Night the Prowler*, by far the better of the two, acquired a large following among film buffs. Audiences prefer their films cut and dried, comedy or drama. *The Night the Prowler* was both, and the transition from one to the other wasn't always a smooth ride.

A very Australian understanding of tragi-comedy was the strongest element connecting Patrick's writing and my realisation of it, whether onstage or onscreen. What Mozart and

Da Ponte called serious comedy, or *dramma giocoso*. This aspect contributed to *Big Toys* and what proved to be our finest and most popular collaboration, the stage revival of *A Cheery Soul*. The production initiated the newly constituted Sydney Theatre Company at the Drama Theatre of the Sydney Opera House in the summer of 1979.

Ring-ring: *What time does that bloody dress rehearsal start?*
I'd told Patrick several times, but the calls kept coming. He was nervous. *A Cheery Soul* had had a chequered history. Its initial Melbourne production in 1963 had been a flop. *A Cheery Soul is a dreary soul* was the word on it. The public and critical rejection of this play had rankled with Patrick and was the source of his alienation from the theatre.

I considered *A Cheery Soul* to be Patrick's best writing for the stage. He'd achieved what only a very few Australian dramatists have: embodying all the ideas of the play in a barnstorming protagonist, who thrills and engages audiences, inspires actors and drives the narrative. Miss Docker is Patrick's only stage creation who matches the might of such iconic characters in his novels as Voss and Laura, Hurtle Duffield, Elizabeth Hunter and Eddie Twyborn, all of whom have taken their rightful place in our literary landscape.

I proposed a revival to the Old Tote, with Ruth Cracknell in the title role. My onetime supporter and local Chekhov specialist, Professor Robert Quentin, became my adversary in this matter. He was no fan of White's plays, especially this one. The season was ultimately cancelled. It was then scheduled as the third production of the short-lived Paris Theatre venture. Despite extraordinary efforts by administrator Elizabeth Knight, the resources couldn't be stretched to a third production, and Patrick's play was again cancelled. It seemed that *A Cheery Soul* was somehow cursed and destined never to be revived.

If these works do have a life of their own, maybe this one was biding its time while awaiting the right circumstances. Productions can fall into place with ease, but the process of overcoming hurdles can often lead to even greater outcomes; and so it was here. John Clark and Elizabeth Butcher, then running NIDA, were appointed to plan the interim season that would establish the Sydney Theatre Company. They invited me to open it with *A Cheery Soul* under the Paris Theatre banner.

My attention focused on casting the indomitable Miss Docker. I decided this eccentric protagonist needed to be more than the comic charity worker described. My approach was less realistic, more vaudeville—King Lear in clown-face. This interpretation required the energies of an actor not so close in age or temperament to the character, but gifted with the imagination, energy and technique necessary to sustain a three-act bravura performance. One such actor had been involved in the Paris Theatre Company and had already demonstrated an impressive feel for incarnating White's tragi-comic characters. Thus I cast Robyn Nevin as the ubiquitous ex-orphan turned charitable vampire—*You're not one of those who're afraid to prune!*—Miss Docker, the scourge of Sarsaparilla.

My insights into this play were myriad, but a crucial one went back to my NIDA student days when, as a young director, I was sent to take weekend workshops with the Castle Hill Players. This suburb was Patrick's previous stomping ground and the model for *Sarsaparilla*. In Castle Hill, I was taken up by the wonderful Voysey family, friends of Patrick from his *Riders in the Chariot* days, and Myrtle Dunlop, the leading lady and diva of the Castle Hill Players. Manoly Lascaris had once confided that, being Greek, he'd avoided Myrtle Dunlop's *Medea*, but the local butcher had reported: *The play wasn't up to much, but Myrtle was fantastic!* Through exposure to Myrtle, the generous Voyseys and other local characters, I had a pretty good idea of the background to *A Cheery Soul*.

By now, I was confident about directing Patrick's work and no longer felt the reverence that had informed earlier revivals and sometimes constrained my approach. On this production I was also reunited with my design colleague Brian Thomson, recently returned from London. Brian's non-literal, visual approach informed the staging, as did the experience of our time at the Royal Court, where the style had been influenced by the minimal oriental aesthetics of Brecht's Berliner Ensemble. If my musical-theatre productions had been notable for their exuberant air of carnival, *A Cheery Soul* revealed a sparer, more sophisticated approach, which influenced much that came after it.

Having conscientiously involved Patrick on every aspect of our collaborations to date, I asked that he didn't attend rehearsals for this play and I declined to consult with him on the production. Patrick initially baulked, especially at my plan to use a small ensemble cast and ignore gender in the distribution of roles—a novel idea at the time. I held firm and he reluctantly agreed. I was privately planning this long-awaited revival as a personal gift to him.

A Cheery Soul, as written, has a literary idea informing it; the play was originally adapted from a short story. The militantly charitable and abrasively comedic Miss Docker moves through the houses, churches, shops, schools and old people's homes of Sarsaparilla until, like Shakespeare's Lear, she confronts her own isolation via a tramp and a dog on the blasted heath of a windy suburban street. Patrick's stage directions require this world to begin naturalistically and slowly abstract to echo the character's growing isolation. This idea is fine in a story, trickier to realise onstage. After much thought, Brian and I did exactly the opposite. Beginning at endgame, we started with nothing.

All the inhabitants of Sarsaparilla were revealed on a starkly lit empty stage, with only a grand piano and a low, rectangular playing rostrum. A small, rodent-like figure in clown-face turned and grinned hideously at the audience, as chords chimed from the piano. This was the audience's chilling introduction to Robyn Nevin's Miss Docker. A little sign saying *Kitchen at the Custances* flew in, and a low, billowing silk curtain swept across the vast width of the letterbox Drama Theatre stage to provide a background. The play was up and away. The cast remained onstage throughout, stepping in and out of character as required, while the attention-seeking kidult Miss Docker let rip centre stage.

As the powerful opening image of Sarsaparilla revealed its silhouette at the dress rehearsal, a loud gasp echoed from behind me. It was Patrick, and I knew our theatrical audacity had found a receptive audience. Later, he confided that he'd never felt so excited in a theatre ... *since the opening of Oklahoma!* The play flowed effortlessly; Nevin's Miss Docker, supported by an inspired ensemble cast, was frightening, hilarious, vulnerable and magnificent in turn. Robyn revealed an astonishing ability to mask malice and resentment in a cloak of vaudevillian glee. All memory of dismissive reviews was consigned to the dustbin. The play opened a few nights later to audiences that stamped and roared their approval. For Patrick, if there was such a thing as theatrical redemption ... this was it. *A Cheery Soul*, once dismissed, despised and discarded, was revealed for what it is —a classic of the Australian stage.

In the foyer on the opening night, I was warmly embraced by my nemesis on this project, Robert Quentin, who reversed his earlier judgment and declared the play *greater than Chekhov.* This encounter meant a lot because, along with my early mentor, Robin Lovejoy, Robert would soon pass on.

The establishment of the Sydney Theatre Company meant that a generation of practitioners could observe their pioneering work bearing fruit and Australian theatre slowly coming of age.

Ring-ring: *You're not still working with those traitors, are you?* It was 6 a.m. and the voice sounded drunk, hung-over or mad. In fact, Patrick was none of these; he was merely making sure anyone who meddled with *Voss* knew exactly what it had cost him to write. The traitors, on this occasion, were composer Richard Meale and librettist David Malouf, whom Patrick had entrusted to translate his novel into an opera, currently in rehearsal. This was not Patrick in extremis speaking, however, but Voss. Writers often vie with directors as life's unsung method actors, and it was the megalomaniac explorer on the line.

Yes, we're having a great time, I replied, very much the cheery soul.

The old bully recognised the tone in my voice that let him know I wasn't taking the bait. Not all of our phone calls were cosy and gossipy. I had learnt from Patrick exactly when to announce *Someone at the door!*—and slam down the receiver.

There was a shadow side to Patrick's generosity, but I was rarely its recipient. *Voss* had become a thorn in his authorial side; he had a love-hate relationship with it. As his most popular novel, it was also his albatross. *Voss* contained characters who held the secrets of his best and worst side: the powerful, obsessive, megalomaniac explorer and the humbler, loving Laura Trevelyan; a portrait of faith personified. My advocacy of the opera provoked his displeasure more than any other collaboration. This was partly because he wasn't involved, which made him feel old and sidelined, though when he finally deigned to attend a rehearsal, his sometime cavils, complaints and antagonism, the hurdles he placed in its way, which I interpreted as his means of upping the ante, dissolved into tears of gratitude for the work and, especially, its creators. Patrick's abrasion masked an essentially romantic, idealistic nature. He could be an artistic snob—*A person's got to have standards!*—but, at heart, he was very vulnerable and kind. Designer Wendy Dickson's comparison of him to the Wizard of Oz rang true to me: a gruff voice through a loudspeaker, until the curtain pulls back to reveal a sweet soul with a microphone, acting tough.

Patrick was a great giver of gifts. Among a pile of books and several paintings that came my way, I especially enjoyed a copy of Alma Mahler's biography *And the Bridge Is Love*. It was for my fortieth birthday, and it arrived with the inscription: *Expect you'll enjoy this load of old kitsch as much as I did!* Volumes of Strindberg and Lorca followed—*I think these should be yours!*—and a revealing inscription accompanied his last work, *Memoirs of Many in One*. Here, he confronted old age and senility as tragi-farce. His final novella was a knees-up, in the manner of Verdi signing off with *Falstaff*. Patrick's accompanying scrawl read:

A few more scenes from the preposterous farce.

Voss production team, left to right: Stuart Challender (conductor), Jim Sharman (director), Chrissie Koltai (choreographer), Brian Thomson (stage designer), Luciana Arrighi (costume designer) and David Malouf (librettist)

Ring-ring: *I hear it went very well!*

Voss became the first Australian opera to take its place in the repertoire of the national company, premiering at the 1986 Adelaide Festival and, with small revisions, playing Sydney and Melbourne. It was revived, recorded and telecast with an original cast that included Geoffrey Chard in the title role and Marilyn Richardson as Laura Trevelyan. Patrick had seen a rehearsal but had not attended the premiere in Adelaide, waiting instead for the Sydney opening. Nonetheless, he was eagerly on the phone the morning after the festival performance. It had been a night of anticipation from cast and audience alike. I had filled the tense hours before the performance in the company of our inspirational conductor, Stuart Challender. After coffee and idle chat, we wandered into the casino adjacent to the Festival Theatre. Strangers to gambling, we bet on something and won. Stuart was encouraged to play on but I suggested we shouldn't tempt fate. The lucky streak fortunately extended to the performance. In fact, as the expedition set off at the end of the first act, an unsubtly stirring moment, the audience responded with an ovation. Good as this scene was, I felt the response was recognition that a need had been met: the desire to see our own stories and history re-imagined onstage. The musically stronger and more complex second act was equally well received. Following the hushed conclusion of Richard Meale's Mahler-inspired setting of Laura Trevelyan's final words—*The air will tell us*—there was an outpouring of audience gratitude.

It was the culmination of years of work for the creators: David Malouf, the librettist, and, especially, Richard Meale, who had had to dig deep and discover a lyrical complement to his atonal musical style in order to compose the opera. Stuart Challender provided confidence and support for Richard, and working with his young assistants, David Stanhope and Simone Young, Stuart's conducting and musical direction were superb.

My own preparation for *Voss* had involved time in Adelaide researching the writings of anthropologist Theodor Strehlow, from his work with the Arrernte tribe at Hermannsburg in Central Australia. I embarked on a solo expedition, starting on the Ghan train from Adelaide, stopping at Alice Springs, where I stayed at the Yulara Sheraton, a luxury billabong in the middle of the desert. Then up to Darwin—still a frontier town where in local pubs topless dancers performed behind chicken wire to protect them from being pelted with tinnies. I spent my days in Darwin with a sympathetic German librarian, looking over the original journals of the explorer Ludwig Leichhardt, whose ill-fated expedition had partly inspired *Voss*. I visited Kakadu and flew over the moon-crater landscape of Arnhem Land and across to Broome, home of white-sand beaches, legends from early pearling days and flourishing tourist resorts.

None of this was strictly necessary, but it illuminated the production. Brian Thomson's setting offered a duality between the endless landscape of Voss and the domesticity of Sydney society. With Voss and Laura ever present in each other's worlds, the audience was free to read the expedition on many levels; it could even be seen as if imagined by the survivor, Laura. Luciana Arrighi's detailed, realistic costumes were in stark relief to the surrounding abstraction. The production focused on the metaphysics of the journey, the internal and external exploration of character, rather than romanticised outback imagery. Stuart Challender often observed that I was putting the book back into the opera.

The *Voss* premiere marked the first season planned by my colleague Moffatt Oxenbould, who had stepped out of the shadows to assume artistic direction of the opera company. Moffatt's appointment, followed by that of Donald McDonald as general manager, heralded a reawakening of opera as a popular form. *Voss* was followed by new operatic commissions and a stream of enlivening and challenging productions by young Australian directors: Neil Armfield impressed with Janacek and Britten; Baz Luhrmann created a memorable Paris for *La Bohème*; and Barrie Kosky inspired with Wagner and Berg. Sadly, Stuart Challender's early death robbed Australian music of a strong advocate and its most inspired interpreter. *Voss* was only a very small stone in the operatic pond, but its ripples spread and contributed to a more original and confident future.

At the post-performance reception for *Voss*, a young journalist enquired if, after the epic novel and now this long-awaited opera, Patrick White's conclusions were similar to those of Bob Dylan's 1960s anthem: *The answer is blowin' in the wind.* I put this to Patrick during our subsequent phone chat and, after a chuckle and a silence:

As a matter of fact ... Yairs, it is.

Voss, in 1986, was my last collaboration on a work by Patrick White. There had been other new plays, including *Netherwood*, Patrick's take on Australian identity, gender and the underclass: a tragi-comedy that ended in a Jacobean bloodbath. I directed *Netherwood* for Adelaide's Lighthouse Company but, over time, I passed the baton of staging Patrick's work to my younger colleague Neil Armfield, inviting him to premiere *Signal Driver*, which I had commissioned for the 1982 Adelaide Festival. I saw less of Patrick during these years, but memorably came upon him in the Adelaide Railway Station during rehearsals for *Signal Driver*. I was in bustling festival director mode and was surprised to encounter him incognito among itinerants on a train station bench, munching his lunch. He looked up, wearily:

I'm just an old man eating a pie ... leave me be.

Patrick was full of such surprises. Another encounter was my brief visit to St Vincent's Hospital, when he was recuperating from a minor operation. There were several hospital stays during his last years, and he usually preferred the public wards; during one stay he was particularly pleased by a visit from Midnight Oil rock star and conservationist Peter Garrett, which had encouraged greater attentiveness from the nurses. On the occasion of my visit, Patrick had been transferred to a private room on the top floor of what he described as the *Jesus Hilton*. Dashing in unexpectedly at the end of a day, I discovered him gazing at a television set. This was ironic, as he refused to have one in his own home, and his choice of program was even more so: *Neighbours.*

Well ... this is what they all watch, isn't it?

Neil Armfield subsequently revived *The Ham Funeral* and *A Night on Bald Mountain* in outstanding productions, as well as

The Season at Sarsaparilla and *A Cheery Soul*, and he premiered
Patrick's final play, *Shepherd on the Rocks*. Between us, we kept
Patrick's theatrical flame burning bright for two decades. The
flame has flickered since, but not gone out. It merely awaits
other hands to plunge into the ashes. *The Burning Piano*, a two-
hour dramatised documentary I made for ABC Television with
authoritative interviews by Patrick's biographer, David Marr,
served as a final eulogy and a cultural record of those closest
to Patrick. David's interview with Barry Humphries, who was
in hilarious, irreverent, bravura form, along with readings by
many of Patrick's favourite actors, including Geoffrey Rush
and Judy Davis, contributed to an audacious memento. Among
its highlights is a revelatory reading of Theodora Goodman
from *The Aunt's Story* by Judy Davis that makes you marvel at
the collision of talent on display. While filming this sequence,
I realised these two great artists were temperamentally very
close. *The Burning Piano* is a telling portrait of a complex man
and it remains a personal favourite among my film work.

Tokyo: Sunday, 30 September 1990
After the Nō performance, Dennis Watkins and I stepped out
from the theatre into one of those sudden downpours that afflict
Tokyo from time to time, prompting a frenzy of undulating
umbrellas and scampering legs. We dashed for cover and found
ourselves in the tiny Watari Gallery, designed by Italian architect
Mario Botta and something of a Tokyo landmark. Inspired by
the architecture and the events of the day, we spoke about *The
Eighth Wonder*, Dennis and Alan John's proposed opera about
that Elsinore of Bennelong Point, the Sydney Opera House.
Jørn Utzon and Patrick White shared a special place in my
imagination as Australian visionaries, and *The Eighth Wonder*
would ultimately succeed *Voss* in the Opera Australia repertoire.

It was around midnight when I was finally alone with my
thoughts and I found myself again staring at Brian's message
in my hand. I put on a CD of Kurt Weill music, *Berlin im Licht*.
My mind wound back a few years to a phone call to Patrick
after I had heard news of the deaths of two French writers on

the same day: Jean Genet and Simone de Beauvoir. Patrick had once been dismissive of Genet: *A few diamonds among the shit!* However, a couple of lines from Genet that I once quoted had stopped him in his tracks: *The crimes of which a people are ashamed constitute a country's real history* and *The family is the original criminal cell.* I had noticed a copy of *Our Lady of the Flowers* on his desk during the writing of the finest of his later works, *The Twyborn Affair.* Patrick's final gift to me was a copy of Genet's almost biblical diary of his time spent among the Palestinians: *Prisoner of Love.*

News of the deaths of these writers had prompted a solemn, thoughtful pause from Patrick, followed by a long sigh and a chillingly accurate prediction: *Well ... pause ... she'll get a state funeral and he'll never be heard of again.* A week later, there was a state funeral for Simone de Beauvoir. Genet was quietly buried by a few close friends in an anonymous grave in Morocco.

A pure soprano voice, haunting in an early Kurt Weill aria, *Die Still Stadt—The Silent City—*soared from the window of my apartment, and seemed to evaporate in the Tokyo night. I sat quietly, listening intently, feeling strangely dizzy, the sound drifting and dissolving as effortlessly as ashes on a lake.

OPPOSITE: Kate Fitzpatrick and Patrick White at Le Café
OVERLEAF: Robyn Nevin in *A Cheery Soul*

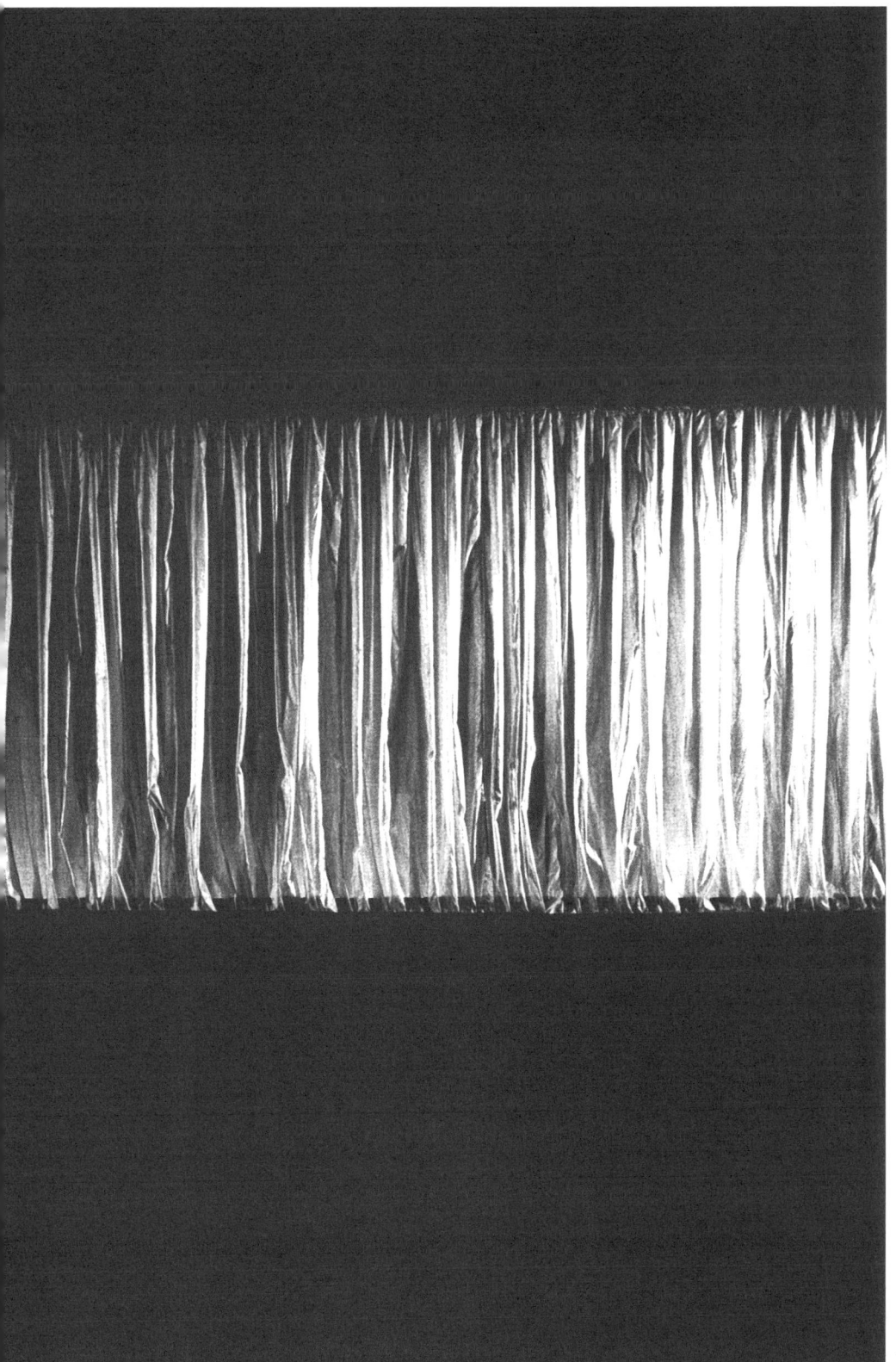

MADANG HARBOUR

I somehow associate James Waites with tropical gardens. We had one tucked away in the courtyard of the federation house we shared through the late 1970s in Sydney's inner west. In this house, James sketched out a few early bottom-drawer novels, one of them exceptionally well written; he gardened and cooked wonderful meals, while I got on with the business of staging Patrick White's plays. It was a calm, tender, productive time. For me, it was a respite from an often chaotic life. We were both living under the spell cast by the lush vegetation. There was something exotic and tropical about James as well. He was tall, thin, fragile, like a strelitzia.

James grew up in colonial Niugini. After independence was declared, he returned with his family to attend high school in Australia. With writing ambitions and a strong passion for theatre, he studied drama at the University of New South Wales. Unlike my earlier relationships, there was an age gap; I was in my thirties and James his twenties. The most fraternal and compatible of my relationships, from the outset our friendship and shared interests set the agenda along with a dry, profoundly Australian humour.

Our initial time was spent in my apartment in Bondi. This modest purchase was the first sign that I intended to stay in Australia, although I made several return trips to London during this time. Bondi Beach was then neither a desirable nor an expensive location, and my tiny apartment was perched on top of an unlikely cliff, in an uninteresting liver-brick block at Ben Buckler on the northern promontory. The living space was narrow and rectangular, like a caravan, but it opened onto a vast balcony with magnificent views of the city, the boomerang sands of Bondi and a breathtaking panorama of electrical storms over the Pacific Ocean.

The Hotel Astra, now history but then a Bondi landmark, stood on the opposite promontory. It was there that James' father had died, having slid from a bar stool with a dollar still clutched in his hand, after ordering his last beer. Dispossessed ex-colonial administrators from Niugini had a hard time readjusting to suburban Australia. However, it was not the ghost of colonialism past but the desire for a more spacious house where we could live separate lives together that prompted the move from the apartment with an outlook to the more interior house with its seductive tropical garden.

Since my return I had reconnected with old friends like my once housemate Michael Ramsden, who was now a painter and married to fashion designer Jenny Kee, through whom I met the Flamingo Park team of Fran Moore and Linda Jackson. Fran and Michael would become especially close friends. New friends included future record and film producer Martin Fabinyi and the composer Cameron Allan, who together founded Regular Records, an underground label that nurtured and promoted Australian talent, the cinematographer Gale Tattersall and his then partner Diana Kearns, the producer and writer combo of Margaret Fink and Bill Harding, and the documentary film-maker and journalist John Moyle. These, and several others, made up the guest list for the only party ever held at the Bondi apartment. Patrick and Manoly were special guests, along with composer Richard Meale. Patrick and Richard hadn't seen each other for many years, and it was at this gathering, amid savouries, balcony views and drinks, that prospects for the opera of *Voss* were advanced. Not all my friends and contemporaries appreciated my new-found enthusiasm for Patrick White. Some deemed it obsessive. Others saw a conflict looming between the professional relationship with Patrick and the personal one with James, though it was James who actively encouraged and shared my commitment to Patrick and his work. Many friends preferred my rock musical persona. Now over thirty, it was a skin I was happy to shed.

My commitment to this was tested when I was invited to direct the London premiere of the new musical *Evita*. The dates clashed with my planned revival of *Sarsaparilla*. To most it seemed obvious—return to London and direct *Evita*. My decision to pursue *Sarsaparilla*, which surprised many, wasn't a reflection on the musical, which I admired, but was part of a determination to commit myself to Australia and a new and different way forward. All change involves some sacrifice, and my international experience had created a desire to put my knowledge to work in my own backyard.

In the reaction to this decision in arts circles and even among sophisticated Australians, there was a preference for successful artists to work overseas rather than at home. In this thinking— much encouraged by journalists, whose voices are loud and whose ranks include the most ambitious of non-achievers—lie the seeds of a cultural insecurity that prefers its arts endorsed by established cultures. This is why, with some notable except- ions, Australia celebrates a repro culture, and true originality is often greeted with caution verging on suspicion. I like to think this attitude has changed, but having seen others return from international careers only to face the same dilemma, I wonder. This cultural insecurity also explains why the obvious is often over-praised while true originality can languish in the shadows. For me, the decision was perfectly straightforward, and the subsequent success of *Sarsaparilla* opened the door to future collaborations that helped widen the perspective of Australian theatre.

My relationship with James became closer. The house offered space and stability. His writing and my productions flourished; it was an incredibly happy time. Realising that we also needed some adventures together, James and I planned a holiday to Niugini, so he could revisit his old haunts and share with me some of his own history.

In Port Moresby we stayed with an old friend of James' who lived with the local policeman. James' mother and sisters had returned to Australia, but his brother had married a Niuginian and worked in Moresby as a marine biologist. After James reacquainted himself with friends and family, we flew to the remote northern coastal town of Madang. On a beautiful harbour flowing into the Bismarck Sea, it consisted of two villages, a Saturday market, the Tropical milk bar and cinema—run by two cheerful lesbians from Cairns—a Burns Philp office, a motel on the promontory, where we ate, and a thatched hut hotel, where we stayed.

James had accompanied me on a previous London jaunt. That was his visit to my world, as it revolved around my friends and theatres, galleries, restaurants familiar to me. In Niugini I was offered a glimpse into his world, and it was in stark contrast to European culture. To be stripped of familiar comforts and cultural certainties and be exposed to simple village life was an eye-opener.

We strolled around the town and its idyllic harbour with pleasure and ease. The days when western tourists would be sheltered by security wire from rascal gangs armed with machetes were yet to come. The Tropical cinema still had segregated seating, or maybe the locals were simply used to sitting on the side aisles. The motel restaurant where we dined most nights was run by an imperious French woman whose colonial manner, evening gowns from another era and *chop-chop* hand clap approach to the staff suggested news of independence was yet to reach her pearl-encrusted ears. James and I were reminded of the Princess de Lascabanes from Patrick's novel *The Eye of the Storm*, who took comfort from every emotional crisis by reading Stendhal.

A visit to the Saturday market revealed that the villagers were being introduced to modernity via a black-and-white television monitor. They crouched and crowded around a wire cage, staring in giggling wonder at video images of Abba performing *Dancing Queen*—programmed on repeat.

Niugini revealed another side of James, a wilder, more exuberant and athletic personality that responded to his tropical surroundings with relish, as if revisiting his childhood sense of freedom and adventure. His days were spent swimming and walking and running, while I played the tourist in the chair with the book. Twilights on the harbour were magical. As I stared at moonlight over an azure sea, I couldn't help but feel a sense of déjà vu at the similarities to my earlier sojourn on the Bay of Angels in Marseilles.

Returning to Sydney, there was enjoyable rewriting of holiday history over dinners, where I would claim I had loved every minute of it, and James would reply that I hadn't stopped complaining from the moment I arrived. Neither was quite true. During this time, a change began to come over James. The freedom that had been revealed in Niugini seemed inhibited by his return to the city; the jungle had been replaced by a suburban garden and restlessness entered the equation. Illness set in and after I'd assisted him through one particularly long bout, his sister was diagnosed with cancer. We stood vigil over her swift decline, along with James' distressed family, before she was shifted to morphine after her spine collapsed; the end came shortly after. All this affected James deeply; the writing stopped and his social life outside the house increased. Our relationship had already turned into a friendship, which we were both happy enough with, but that transformed into shared tenancy, which created a divide and tensions. What had been outbursts of exhilaration in Niugini became frustrations in the city. They were rare incidents, but a stone thrown at a bus that passed him by at a local stop nearly landed him in trouble and suggested a greater malaise. He developed other relationships and, as it seemed impossible to revive the original spark, he left to pursue his own walk on the wild side. Alone in the house that had so many happy memories, I felt like a pea in a saucepan; even the garden was bereft of its guardian angel.

My time with James was one of the most productive of my working life, possibly because it was the most stable. It encompassed the key Patrick White years, and his spirit presided over that period. If there was a peak in our time together it was the night of a surprise party we organised for Patrick's sixty-seventh birthday. The place was filled with light and balloons; the garden glowed; there was the warmth and company of friends and colleagues. Patrick and Manoly arrived for what they had assumed would be a quiet dinner. Their shock at the assembled feast and the sudden cries of *Surprise!* accompanied by the laughter of children added to the joy. As food, wine and gossip flowed and birthday candles were blown out there was a rare sense of serious artists at play.

As we later cleared the debris, I doubt if either of us realised the night was a prelude to the decline and that separation would follow. James needed what I had seen revealed in him in Niugini, and he pursued it with a mixture of destructive and creative glee. The destructive side found him at the bottom of a cliff, bones shattered, after a stroll with a new carefree partner and a fall. I heard about this when I was in London and was devastated. The creative side always won out with James, and he was restored to health and matured by this traumatic experience. He then rediscovered his original passion for the theatre and established himself as an arts writer and theatre critic.

I read his reviews and would sometimes be delighted by their insight and wit. At other times, I would wince and shudder at barbed attacks that seemed gratuitous and reminded me of that stone thrown at a passing bus. However, his passion for theatre remained as strong and articulate as it was when we first met; it was real and true. We kept fitfully in touch, keeping an eye out for each other, as old friends do.

It was a sad time for me, and understanding it made the situation somehow worse. There had been a deal of competition for both our friendships among our small social circle, and our own relationship had been eroded as a consequence. An element of taking things for granted on my part contributed to our separation. As usual, work had taken preference, and I had to conclude that while I was good at beginning partnerships, the skill and attention required to maintain them were not in my repertoire.

My energies went back into my work and travel. I was invited to direct my first opera in a decade, Benjamin Britten's *Death in Venice* for the State Opera of South Australia at the 1980 Adelaide Festival. Following *A Cheery Soul*, it marked a progression in my stage design collaboration with Brian Thomson and Luciana Arrighi, who had designed *The Night the Prowler*. Luci's costumes created elegant silhouettes that evoked a holidaying prewar European society on the brink of collapse. Brian's magic black box and silken seas, lit by Rory Dempster's chiaroscuro of soft white light, offered an unending labyrinth that provided just the right landscape for Aschenbach's obsessive, trance-like and solitary journey to death. The contrast of abrasion and sensuality made for an insight into an extraordinary world. With Robert Gard as Aschenbach, himself dealing with the strain and sadness of his wife's dying from cancer, rehearsals for *Death in Venice* proved to be an emotional period. The opera also became one of my most deeply felt productions, and prompted the recently deceased Benjamin Britten's biographer, Donald Mitchell, to shake his head and confide: *If only Ben had lived to see this.*

Over time, James and I fell into a strange ritual of meeting each year for dinner on the halfway date between our two birthdays. Pisceans. Two fish swimming in opposite directions. Sometimes, we even recall the past. For me, it represents the best and worst of times: personally challenging and artistically rewarding. Our time together remains a fond and complex memory.

FOLLOWING PAGES: *Death in Venice*, Adelaide Festival. Ian Wilkinson (left) as Tadzio and Robert Gard (right) as Aschenbach.

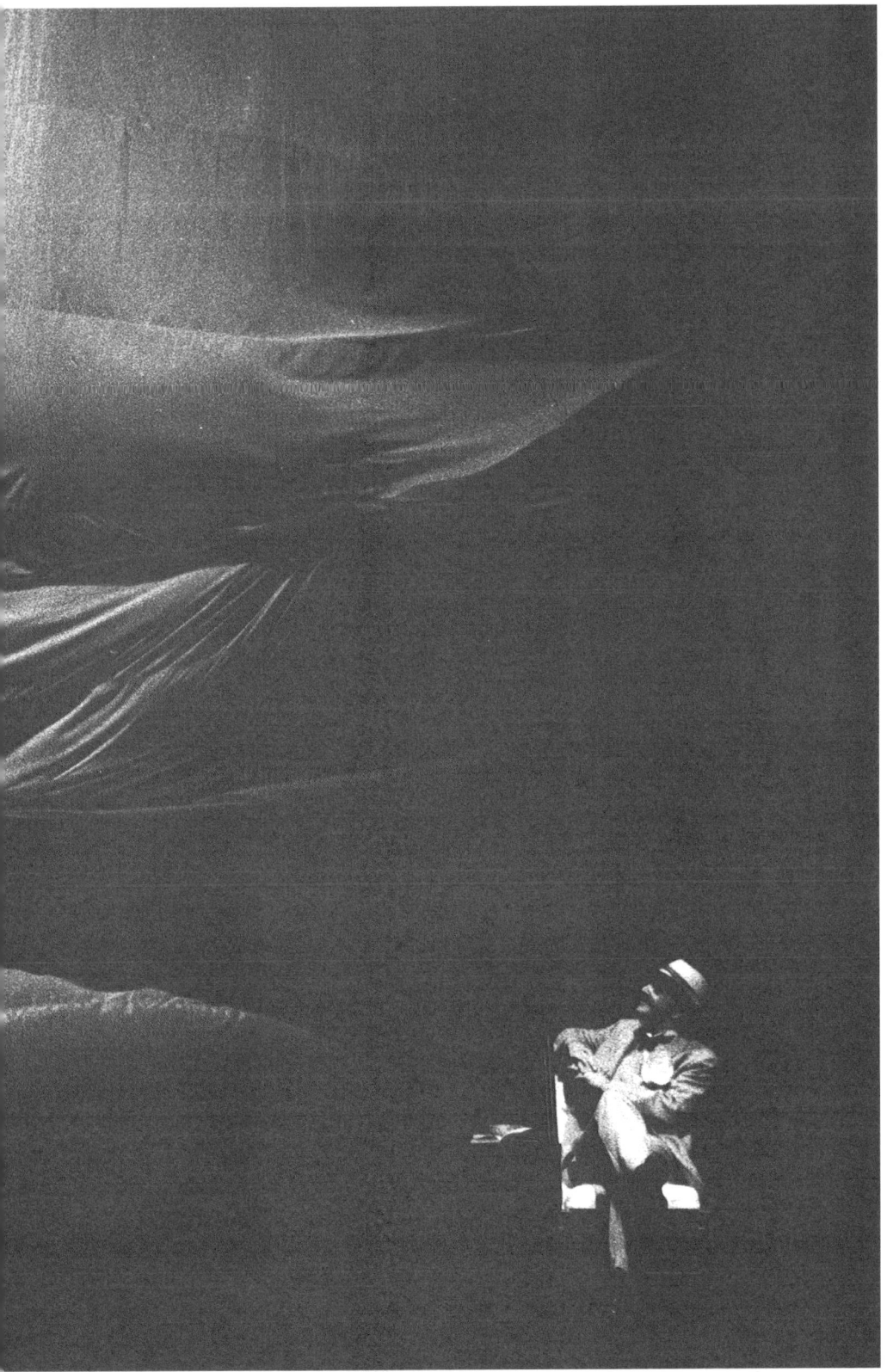

LOCAL KNOWLEDGE

My itinerant lifestyle had distanced me from my parents. After my return to Australia I saw them more frequently. My father, who had spent decades on the road amid the toughness and occasional glamour of the showgrounds, had breathed a sigh of relief when the travelling sideshow finally folded its tent and entered the realm of folk legend. Television had crept into the living rooms of country Australia, and sideshow entertainment began to look quaint and old-fashioned. New government rules and regulations contributed to making boxing displays a less attractive option. Fashions had also changed, and what was once admired as working-class grit was now seen as exploitation. The rigour of life on the road had lost its sexy poster-colour appeal and revealed itself as sheer hard work. After sixty years of *Who'll Take a Glove?*—the slogan first uttered by my grandfather in 1911—my father finally swept the sawdust from the sweat-and-blood-soaked canvas for the last time. Acknowledgment of his and his father's pioneering efforts would come much later, in 2003, when then New South Wales Premier Bob Carr presented him with an award from the Royal Agricultural Society, officially recognising Jimmy Sharman as a showground legend. It made him a proud and happy man in his old age.

He spent some of the intervening years on the Gold Coast, where, in partnership with the O'Neill family, he ran dodgem cars in the Grundy Entertainment Centre. It was a living, but, as he would shake his head and rue: *It's not the same.* There were enjoyable compensations: Gary O'Neill took him to Italy and Japan to import the dodgem cars, his first and only time out of Australia. Young Greg O'Neill worked with him, and my father became part of Greg's extended family, a sort of surrogate dad, which he enjoyed. His own son was off being successful, somewhere. My mother joined him, but they soon tired of life on the Gold Coast, home to so many retired show folk. They returned to Randwick, where Dad stayed active and sociable by playing bowls at the nearby club; he was chuffed when the members named a green after him. He would often venture off on his own to towns he knew from the show circuit to renew

Dad with dodgems, Surfers Paradise, 1984

past acquaintances and retell tales, tall or true; his old travel-ling habits were hard to shake.

He and my mother spent a few months of each year in Surfers Paradise and I occasionally visited them there, where I would offer a receptive ear to his oft-repeated tales of life on the road, while my mother continued to keep abreast of my exploits through her meticulously kept newspaper clippings. Dad seemed to cope better with what amounted to semi-retirement. My mother was less at ease. Their marriage was predicated on rituals of solitude, space and separation, and this had given way to everyday company. On one trip back to Australia I visited her at St Vincent's Hospital; she had been admitted after some form of nervous collapse. With rest and care she recovered, but I felt something had dimmed in her eyes, though she was lively enough in my company and that of her older sister, Annabella, and her immediate family.

My father had a relentlessly optimistic streak, born of dealing with travel and rugged experience, and this helped him cope with whatever life threw at him. Nonetheless, on one surprise visit to Surfers Paradise, I was en route to their apartment and passed the local RSL, where, through an open door, I glimpsed the solitary silhouette of a man on a bar stool with a middy of beer, a blank stare and a television blaring above. I was so shocked when I realised it was my father, I just kept walking.

He lived into his nineties and it was in his later years that the great divide between us slowly closed. We spoke then of the solitude in our family. *Everyone's gotta run their own race* was his sage advice. It was a hard tradition, learnt from his own upbring-ing and branded by his own father's distance and silence. How-ever, in our silences, warmth and affection grew over time and I began to listen more closely to his tales and learn from them: of him, of his history, and the rules of itinerant life.

Itinerants trust local knowledge. That was something learnt from my father, who learnt it on the road. I often applied it as I moved from production to production, city to city and country to country. Local knowledge was at the heart of a tale my father took special pleasure in recounting. It concerned a one-legged Aboriginal, some ants and a flash flood at Moree, in northern New South Wales.

It had been a busy show day and everyone in the troupe was looking forward to a night off. The plan was to pack and then to travel the next morning. My father was about to set out on his twilight showground refresher stroll when he noticed a one-legged Aboriginal, propped up by a tree near the tent. He'd been there all day. Dad recalled him from previous years, always in the same spot. They nodded, by way of greeting.

Hey, Jimmy ... the man signalled.

My father joined him under the tree.

There's gonna be a big blow. You better get moving tonight.

My father demurred. *I can't do that, mate. The blokes are looking forward to a night on the town. If I tell 'em to pack up, they'll scalp me!*

The elder confided ... *When the ants start climbing the fence posts on Mrs Murphy's farm, that means there's a big storm brewin'. It's gonna flood ... I'm tellin' ya!*

Mrs Murphy's farm. Chuckle. *Yeah?*

Yeah!

My father thanked the old-timer for his warning. Whether from character assessment, superstition or some deeper instinct, my father trusted the man's judgment, and he advised the other showies to pack up and skedaddle. They smiled indulgently at this tale of ants and fence posts, and stayed put. Undeterred, he instructed the troupe to pull down the tent and load the truck. The men were furious, cheated of a chance for their tent-show trifecta. He insisted. They grumbled and packed. The truck drove through the night to the next town. A freak storm descended on Moree later that night. All the roads were flooded and *Jimmy Sharman's Boxing Troupe* was the only show to escape being flood-bound for three weeks. This story, with a few embellishments in the retelling, has entered showground folklore.

The only witness to the beginning and end of *Jimmy Sharman's Boxing Troupe* was Rud Kee. He knew my grandfather from the days when they were young sparring partners in the Riverina, and he had left the Queensland mining camps to help

Grandad manage the troupe in 1911. Rud had cooked countless camp-fire meals, applied salves to bruises and egos and mentored many of the young troupe fighters. He was a fixture outside the tent, with his battered, brown-leather ticket bag. Old Rud seemed like part of our family. He might even have been the source of my later curiosity about, and ease with, all things Asian. Both my parents loved him and they often visited him in retirement.

Cheong Lee, known as Rud Kee, *the man who never looked at a face, only a ticket*, took his own unique history and much of the troupe's with him when he died peacefully in his sleep, in his late eighties.

Rud Kee and Jimmy Sharman

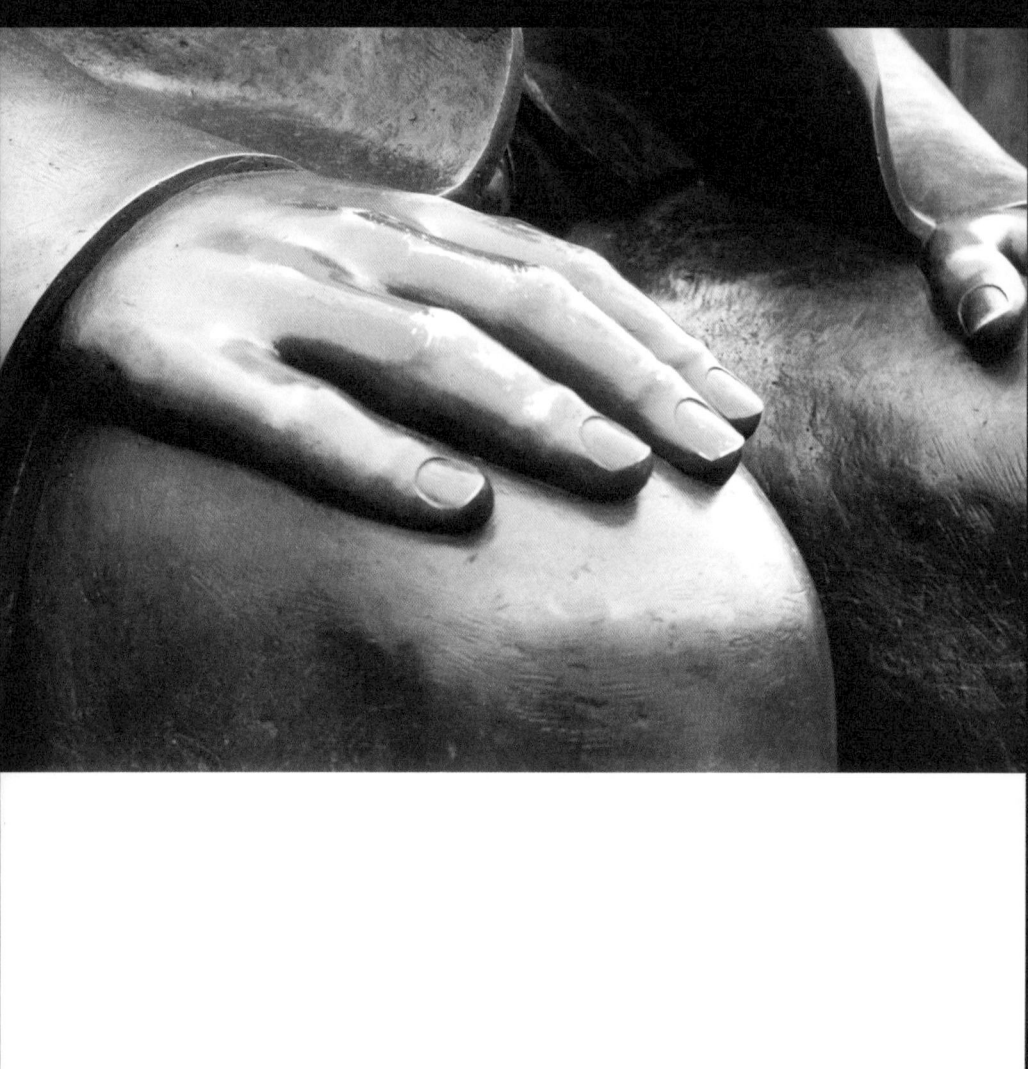

THE EIGHTIES

War, disease and assassination were rife. Attempts on the lives of US President Ronald Reagan and Pope John Paul II were followed by the assassination of Egyptian President Anwar Sadat, Indian Prime Minister Indira Gandhi and singer-songwriter John Lennon. A deadly virus spread worldwide and was diagnosed as AIDS. Britain and Argentina went to war over the Falkland Islands. Soviet President Mikhail Gorbachev introduced policies of glasnost and perestroika. At the end of the decade the Berlin Wall fell and Germany was reunified. The pro-democracy movement spread to China, and army troops massacred protesting students in Tiananmen Square. Ayatollah Khomeini transformed Iran into an Islamic state and declared the United States *the great Satan*. Iraq invaded Iran. Israel invaded Lebanon. A decade that began with a hostage drama in Iran concluded with the Iran Contra scandal—revelations that arms were supplied to Iran in return for American hostages.

I was at a news-stand in New York during the Iran stand-off. The vendor was angry, glaring at the headlines:

HE: *We should nuke 'em!*
ME: *Then they'll nuke you.*
HE: *That can't happen here.*
ME: *Those skyscrapers would melt fast!*
HE: *We've got God on our side.*

Australia's decade began under the Fraser government, followed by the Hawke Labor government. Treasurer Paul Keating floated the Australian dollar and Native title was proclaimed at Uluru, previously Ayers Rock. The bicentennial was celebrated and a new parliament house and national gallery were opened in Canberra. Australia won the America's Cup, and *Crocodile Dundee* became the most commercially successful Australian film of all time.

Culturally, the 1980s saw the emergence of the new German cinema, led by film-makers Rainer Werner Fassbinder, Werner Herzog and Wim Wenders. Artist Andy Warhol died in New York. A great twentieth-century opera was premiered: John Adams' *Nixon in China*.

Karl Marx statue: Berlin, 1989

FESTIVAL FIREWORKS

After the press conference to announce my appointment as artistic director of the 1982 Adelaide Festival of Arts, Maggie Kirkpatrick, a wry actor who had played in several of my productions, elbowed her way through the crowd of smiling well-wishers:

Well, you've joined the establishment now.

I laughed … but she was right.

I had first visited the Adelaide Festival in 1972 as a young hippy director launching the rock concert tour of *Superstar* at King's Park tennis courts. A decade later, I was thrilled, surprised and happy to be invited back as artistic director.

Adelaide was once tagged *the city of churches*, and, during the cultural boom of Don Dunstan's premiership, *the Athens of the South*. The city resembles a dustbowl Texan settlement on its perimeter and a tidy German university town at its centre. Sited along the artificially diverted River Torrens, there's a culture strip of sandstone and greystone: an art gallery, a museum, a library, a university and a trio of state theatres gathered under a white cement tent known as the festival centre—where I would work.

Adelaide is proud of its festival, its cultural credentials, its early female suffrage and its being founded by free settlers, many of them German protestants fleeing religious persecution in Europe. Descendants of these immigrant families planted the renowned vineyards in the Adelaide Hills. Food, wine, medical research, the festival and a short-lived flirtation with white goods all helped put Adelaide on the map. The city made up for its lack of founding criminality by becoming known for bizarre murders. I'd once made a flying visit in the late 1970s as a guest of Peter Crayford's Independent Film Festival. *The Night the Prowler* was scheduled to open the program, but the press conference became a no show. My embarrassed host explained that arts coverage in Adelaide ran a poor second to the latest murder, and, at that precise moment, *the body in the fridge* was being unveiled.

Martin Sharp's poster for the 1982 Adelaide Festival of Arts

My festival appointment meant moving to Adelaide in 1980, and I was to stay for four years, until the end of 1983. A curious pattern of events had led to my becoming artistic director of the largest and most prestigious arts festival in the country: the Australian equivalent of Salzburg or Edinburgh.

How it happened: After attending my 1979 production of *A Cheery Soul*, festival director Christopher Hunt offered me a play to direct in his 1980 program. He was also planning the Australian premiere of Benjamin Britten's final opera, *Death in Venice*, which interested me more. An Englishman who had recently run the Royal Opera at Covent Garden, Christopher wasn't inclined to offer the Britten to an Australian director, especially one who, at this point, was neither a safe pair of operatic hands nor a Britten specialist. But Christopher was adventurous and was intrigued by my persistence.

Usually, I chose work myself or was offered something. I had a reputation for mostly declining, which was how I maintained a degree of artistic freedom. I only accepted work that offered a challenge, and my determination meant that—win, lose or draw—I felt deeply about every production. I therefore declined the play while continuing to express enthusiasm for the opera. Fortunately, I had advocates in the form of State Opera director Ian Campbell, who was alert to my neglect by the opera establishment, and Mary Vallentine, Christopher's confidante and the festival administrator. They lobbied successfully in my favour, and Christopher finally offered me the production.

I was elated and instantly rang Patrick White to convey the good news. Unbeknown to me, Patrick was about to visit Watters Gallery to choose a painting as a gift of thanks for my revival of *A Cheery Soul*. He walked into the gallery only to be confronted by Geoffrey Proud's portrait of the youthful Tadzio from Visconti's film of *Death in Venice*. The coincidence was too great to ignore. Two decades later, Tadzio's portrait still hovers over my writing desk.

Just as the White play had led me to Adelaide, Britten's complex modern opera became a highpoint of Christopher's

1980 festival, and resulted in my being invited to direct in 1982. As the first Australian since Robert Helpmann to be invited to do so, I readily accepted. The festival offered a rare chance to open a few cultural doors, and the distant sound of bells and drums started echoing in my ears.

Events moved swiftly after my appointment and I garnered many insights from Christopher Hunt. I quickly realised that getting on with the town, the board and the media, while staying focused on artistic goals, was the name of the game. I had an outstanding team to help fulfil my transforming ambitions. Mary Vallentine administered and was sympathetic to my view, as were her assistants, Penny Chapman and Rob Brookman; they would later emerge as outstanding producers. We set about the sometimes daunting task of devising ways to present a program that aimed to be both radical and a popular success.

My boardroom manner was quiet and determined. After an initial meeting where I enthusiastically outlined my plans for high art to rub shoulders with popular culture and to make the festival more Australian, most of the traditionalists resigned. It was tabula rasa. I dealt with the press by saying nothing and getting on with the job. Adelaide being a small, gossipy town, I was circumspect in my social dealings. A boring but wise choice. The story was going to be the festival, not me. Arts journalists became intrigued as my lack of flamboyance frustrated them. There was a sense that the city expected visiting artists to be court jesters who would rattle their bells and be applauded or booed off. It was not a game I intended to play.

I began by commissioning new work. The festival would become more adventurous by actively creating culture, and the criteria for the imported part of the program was to shake up things and open a few doors to the future. This approach is now the norm for festivals, but that was far from the case at the time; it was a shift away from the cultural shopping spree paradigm.

Plays were commissioned from Patrick White—*Signal Driver*—and David Hare—*A Map of the World*—and I launched an award for young composers that resulted in the Sydney Symphony Orchestra opening the festival with *River Run* by Graeme Koehne. I scheduled preview concert scenes from the forthcoming *Voss* opera, and invited Australian director Elijah Moshinsky and Swedish soprano Elisabeth Soderstrom to join forces on the State Opera premiere of Janacek's *The Makroupolis Affair*. I was fascinated by the work of American realist painter Edward Hopper, not then well known in Australia, whose images had influenced film-makers from Alfred Hitchcock to Martin Scorsese. A retrospective was negotiated between the State Gallery and the Whitney Museum in New York. Hopper's figures stranded in often alien landscapes seemed to chime with the Sam Shepard plays I had programmed. A country and western concert featuring the music of Slim Dusty raised middle-class eyebrows and validated another previously unconsidered part of our culture.

Much of what I planned was outside the box, and I realised its presentation to the public would have to be persuasive. Fortunately, I discovered graphic artist Geoffrey Gifford in a studio above Adelaide's Hindley Street. He devised festival brochures that offered a modern take on early Australian periodicals like *Pix* and *People* magazines, and I commissioned photographer William Yang to create portraits of every visiting artist, plastering their images on banners across the city. There was no reason why festival emblems shouldn't be art, so I invited pop painter and colourist extraordinaire Martin Sharp to create a festival poster.

Adelaide director Scott Hicks, who filmed a documentary about this festival, and who went on to make the award-winning film *Shine*, mischievously suggested Martin's was the brightest poster for the darkest festival. This wasn't a view I shared. If anything, my aim was to bring highly original artists out of the shadows.

Many of these artists I encountered in some very unlikely places.

Raymond's Revue Bar is a seedy London strip club. Its Soho clientele are not usually festival directors scouting shows, but men in overcoats. Festival types are more likely to be found on the South Bank, at the Royal something or other.

Around midnight, I walked up the stairs and into an atmosphere reminiscent of Weimar Berlin. Backstage, in cramped dressing rooms reeking of stale beer, I met the anarchic spirits that made up the cast of *The Comic Strip*: compere Alexei Sayle, future stars of *The Young Ones* Rik Mayall, Nigel Planer and Adrian Edmondson, driving force Peter Richardson, and the two brilliant women who would create, among other things, *Absolutely Fabulous*, Jennifer Saunders and Dawn French.

After the Adelaide premiere of *The Comic Strip* and over a mid-festival drink, *Guardian* newspaper critic Michael Billington was to enquire, in a slightly injured tone, if this crypto-punk anarchy was what I regarded as a highlight of English culture. It was, of course, or I wouldn't have invited them. Michael was comparing their satiric antics to classics from loftier theatrical establishments. I suggested that in a few years, no one would be talking about who had done the latest Shaw or Sheridan play, but everyone would be talking about these brilliant characters. They weren't slaves to culture; they were busy creating it. I realised there was something very Australian in my irreverence. Unlike Europeans, Australians sense that our future will be brighter than our past.

The Bay of Naples glowed as William Yang and I strolled down a hill towards a twilight performance by *La Nuova Compagnia di Canto Popolare*. I wanted to see our Italian festival guests in action, and William was there to photograph the event. We were in buoyant spirits until, with a quick thump, William fell by the roadside. A grinning teenage Mafiosi, riding pillion on a Vespa, had swept William's camera from his shoulders. It was our initiation into Neapolitan ways.

William took it in good spirits. We returned to the hotel for a backup camera and encountered shrugs as we informed the management of our apparently common roadside theft. It was quickly forgotten once we joined the crowd at the outdoor performance in an ancient amphitheatre. *Nuova Compagnia* thrilled us with their modern arrangements of traditional songs: electric rhythms and wailing voices that seemed to resound from the earth itself. It was at this performance that I became determined to open up the festival to the city, rather than shrouding it in prosceniums and limiting it to big-ticket items.

Public outdoor events at the festival had previously been given low priority, an attitude informed by economies and a slightly patronising view of what the locals might enjoy. Having grown up on the showgrounds, the notion of public celebration was hardly new to me and, if my memory had receded under the weight of more sophisticated endeavours, it came back with a wallop that night in Naples. I decided to open the festival outdoors, under an avalanche of riverside fireworks, and with the festival's finest artists floating down the river on barges and performing in the park for free. This public preview proved to be the festival's salvation. Slow ticket sales had preceded the opening, and there were smirks from naysayers. Once the festival exploded in a blaze of fireworks and outdoor performances, the city embraced it. A bit of old-fashioned spruiking on my part introduced previously unknown artists who then proceeded to dazzle. Leading the pack were *Nuova Compagnia*, encouraged by a delighted local Italian population.

The next day there were queues at every box office in the city. Word had spread like wildfire, and airline flights in and out of Adelaide were swiftly filled. In an ancient amphitheatre under a Neapolitan sky, I'd been given a timely reminder of what the word *festival* really meant.

Breakfast in East Berlin meant crossing the Berlin Wall at *Checkpoint Charlie*. William Yang and I felt like extras from a cold-war spy movie. We were met by a driver and whisked to croissants and coffee with Barbara Brecht, daughter of the playwright Bertolt Brecht and director of the theatre he had made famous: *The Berliner Ensemble*.

Our first shock was the ordinariness of East Berlin. We'd been brought up on east-west propaganda and had grim expectations. It was more provincial than affluent; the shop window displays were sparse and cars were tiny Trabbies, but the city seemed friendly, pleasant and in many ways reminiscent of Adelaide.

The second surprise was our host's Californian accent. Barbara Brecht had been schooled at Hollywood High, during her father's wartime exile in Los Angeles. I had invited her husband, actor Ekkehard Schall, to give a one-man Brecht performance at the festival. It became quickly clear that our dealings were to be with Barbara, his translator and minder, though I later discovered Ekkehard spoke perfect English.

Barbara was witty and quite a performance artist in her own right; but she knew her theatrical oats despite her legendary prickly manner. I assumed it was like father, like daughter. Barbara was all ease and charm over breakfast but, once in rehearsal at the Adelaide Playhouse, she transformed into a steely titan. The accidental intrusion of a red light into her all-white Brechtian designs met with a shriek from the stalls.

The devil's pitchforks!

Scheduled as a late-night performance that began at 11 p.m., I wondered why Barbara was pacing and timing her husband's rehearsal with a stopwatch. An unexpected bellow at the sound designer explained all.

No! No! No! Turn the volume up! It'll be midnight. Wake the fuckers up!

Sure enough, at the premiere, a few devoted Brechtians were nodding off by the witching hour, and the over-amplified tirade did the trick. I saw quite a bit of Barbara during the festival, as staff were wary of dealing with her. I came to like her and sensed her difficulty in being hostage to a political system she privately questioned. Even her demands were revealing. The requests for Concorde flights and her constant surveillance of her husband suggested someone who might have been happier as a Hollywood wife.

Breakfast with Barbara was followed by a tour of Brecht's house. I was touched by a tiny veranda room from his final years, his cot-like bed overlooking a cemetery. The bookcases were lined with unopened Karl Marx at eye height, the upper shelves crammed with well-thumbed paperback thrillers. Hollywood contradictions ran in the family. We visited the Pergamon Museum before seeing a very pedestrian performance of Brecht's *Galileo* at the Berliner Ensemble, only salvaged by Ekkehard in the title role. It would take the fall of a wall and the arrival of a new director, Heiner Mueller, to re-invigorate this cold-war theatre. Brecht's theatre had become the prisoner of its own legend: just another cathedral of culture huddled around Friedrichstrasse Station.

Supper with Pina Bausch followed a performance of her three-hour memory poem *1980*. It was late at night in a large, cosy, old-fashioned restaurant in the German town of Wuppertal. At the time it was known mainly for its monorail, the Bayer Aspirin factory and choreographer Pina Bausch. Years later, another artist from Wuppertal, film-maker Tom Tykwer, would revive German cinema with *Run Lola Run*, one of my favourite films.

1980 was a ritual of loss. A memento mori for the company's original designer, Pina's recently deceased partner Rolf Borzic. It was performed and danced by the revolutionary Wuppertaler Tanztheater and played out on a vast acreage of grass, with a harpsichord to one side and a small statue of a baby deer upstage. It might have been subtitled *Who Killed Bambi?*

This stage poem reeked of love ... for him, the dancers and the gestural choreography it helped to create. The full title was *1980: A Piece by Pina Bausch*; a truer translation might have been *A Piece of Pina Bausch*.

I attended *1980* on a quiet Monday night. It had only just opened and the audience was sparse—some enthusiastic, others baffled. The worldwide success of Pina Bausch was yet to come. I had few expectations. A few rows behind me sat the gaunt figure of Pina with her sculpted features, surrounded by col- laborators, handmaidens and a tiny man with eyes like lakes. This gentle soul I would later know as Raimund Hoghe, the company dramaturg. The grouping of Pina and her colleagues brought to mind court scenes painted by Velasquez.

1980 had humour, solemnity, promenading, reminiscence and a little playfulness with underwater sprinklers. All this to an eclectic soundtrack that interwove Purcell with latin tangos and bandoneon music. The dance was ritualised and flecked with dialogue in various languages. At one point, a very familiar accent cut the air. Australian dancer Meryl Tankard entered to reminisce about having lost her sunglasses in Venice. It was my first thrilling glimpse of this great artist and future choreographer.

While never literal, it was obvious that *1980*, with its contrasts of exuberance and ritual intimacy, was based in shared personal memories of loss. International critics later compared it to Proust. Elusive to describe, it was astonishing to experience.

I discovered that Pina had been brought up in restaurants, a shy and inarticulate child checking out adult moves and behaviour. Maybe there was some unconscious connection here to showground childhoods. The theatre of Pina Bausch explored and revealed personalities—the quirks and emotions of her dancers. There was no narrative. It was like arriving at a party where you didn't know anyone. By the time you left, you knew everything—maybe too much.

Over supper after the performance, Pina held court. A bevy of other festival directors flattered her. I sensed I was in a cultural bidding war. As dates for Paris and Vienna were tossed around in various languages, I felt self-conscious, like an ill-fitted suitor in the casket scene of a Shakespearian play. The conversation turned to repertoire. Here, flattery segued into euro-smarm. The miracle we had all just witnessed onstage was forgotten as enquiries shifted to Pina's earlier, acclaimed and more conventionally balletic version of Stravinsky's *The Rite of Spring*.

Paris must have Le Sacre, *Pina … c'est magnifique!*

I had been silent through all this, and with a wry smile, Pina turned and enquired: *And what would … Adelaide … choose?*

Ignoring Pina's slightly condescending swoop on the word *Adelaide*, I replied:

What I've just seen … 1980.

Party over. The other festival directors were politely dismissed. We got stuck into the wine and the chat. Hours later, as chairs were being firmly placed on tables, we stumbled into the chill air of the Wuppertal night.

The goodnight kiss was incredibly tender and reminiscent of the Lou Reed farewell. I don't think sex is such a revelation, but you can tell a lot from a kiss.

I finally brought three Pina Bausch works to Adelaide: *1980*, in my opinion the festival highlight, *Blaubart*, or *Bluebeard's Castle*, and *Kontakthoff*, about courtship, cruising and mating rituals. It was set in a ballroom and performed in a town hall with a history of just such sweaty encounters.

Kontakthoff opened the season to acclaim, and in a Greek restaurant in Hindley Street, Pina Bausch's dancers mingled with opera divas, punk comedians, Italian troubadours and local artists. Here, I was able to introduce two artists I felt were among the greatest of the twentieth century: Pina Bausch and Patrick White. Both were smitten and shy, and I left them to it.

I sat at a table with colleague Rob Brookman and suddenly felt the full weight of bringing the festival together. It was somehow distilled by the introduction of Pina to Patrick. I burst into tears. As I was thought unemotional, cold even, Rob must have been surprised. He had the tact to study the menu.

Pina Bausch, Avignon Festival

DREAMPLAY

Methinks I see these things with parted eye, when everything seems double.

So speaks Hermia, one of the lovers in Shakespeare's *A Midsummer Night's Dream*. She has recently awoken from a drug-induced night of changing partners in the woods outside Athens. Awoken, myself, in an anonymous motel room in the Flinders Ranges by the sound of ribald laughter and then drowsily peering out the window at its source, I knew how she felt. On arrival at the isolated motel, the day staff had presented themselves as stolid country types—heavy-boned women and lanky men— slow, silent, wary. By moonlight, they were transformed into naked larrikin sprites, dancing and sexily cavorting in the floodlit motel pool. I stepped back from the window and glanced at the clock; it was 1 a.m. *Am I dreaming? Am I waking?* Kleist wrote in *The Prince of Homburg*. I knew how he felt, too.

I'd accepted an offer from a friend and Adelaide neighbour, Peter Crayford, to drive across the desert with its mirages and up into the Flinders Ranges for a few days' break. Here, taking time out from festival preparations, I would piece together my first season as artistic director of the State Theatre of South Australia, which I had renamed Lighthouse, in tribute to Adelaide's founding father Colonel William Light. I'd agreed to stay on in Adelaide for two years after the festival to take charge of the company. After observing the sex romp in the pool outside my window, I decided to open our post-festival season with *A Midsummer Night's Dream*.

Under blazing white light, up and down an indigo and gold Piranesi staircase designed by Sue Blane, Shakespeare's *Dream* introduced the ensemble company of twelve actors to their Adelaide public. They were led by Geoffrey Rush and Gillian Jones as boss fairies Oberon and Titania. Rarely has *Ill met by moonlit* bristled with such sexual tension. When these electric actors threatened to *rock the ground on which these sleepers be*, you knew they meant it. John Wood, in stubbies and asses ears, ensured it was *Bottom's dream*. The lovers swooned and railed;

PREVIOUS PAGES: The Lighthouse *Dream*

cross-gendered rustics with flip-up fairy wings enchanted. The modernism had enough Elizabethan flourish to capture the audience's imagination. The exalted expectations created by the festival looked as though they would be fulfilled at Lighthouse. And, fitfully, they were.

My logic was that a city which had demonstrated an enthusiasm for cultural adventure during the festival would embrace it for the rest of the year. But once the circus has left town, people go back to their day jobs and tastes and expectations adjust accordingly. Adelaide's audiences and local critics might have been happier chuckling over Noel Coward than being confronted by two years of Shakespeare in radical guise, a series of great, if previously unseen, European classics, and a bold repertoire of demanding new plays by festival opener Patrick White, Louis Nowra, Bill Harding and Stephen Sewell.

Of the fourteen Lighthouse productions we presented over two years, half were premieres. Each of them adventurous, large-scale Australian plays. A state theatre where writers were part of the furniture was a rarity. Most theatres keep them at a distance and, in opera, composers are preferred dead. It was my intention to have the writers in the rehearsal room on a regular basis and to let them unleash their imaginations in a bold series of epic productions firmly stamped *Made in Australia*.

Dreams are part of utopian visions. It was mine that Lighthouse might offer a beacon of hope for a brighter theatrical future. This view was shared by a dedicated troupe of actors, our general manager, Mary Vallentine, and Neil Armfield, who matured into an outstanding director during his Lighthouse years. Neil also created two highlights of that era: an engaging Aussie-holiday take on Shakespeare's *Twelfth Night* and Stephen Sewell's chronicle of political corruption *The Blind Giant is Dancing*. This production featured a performance by Geoffrey Rush that charted with forensic eloquence the journey of Allan Fitzgerald from everyman and idealist to demagogue. Neil's production shouted and whispered its way across a starkly beautiful revolving design by Stephen Curtis and signalled that a new generation of theatre artists had taken wing.

Louis Nowra was another Lighthouse dreamer. An in-house writer and close collaborator, Louis was seen as a benign or Machiavellian influence. In some circles he was known as Rasputin. We had the kind of friendship I value and find stimulating; one of shared enthusiasms and much parrying of ideas. It's a camaraderie I often find with writers, though it was common among the artists that surrounded Lighthouse.

Nowra shared with White and Sewell the skill and ambition to write epic plays where the core idea is embodied in the play's protagonist, in the tradition of Brecht and Shakespeare. Aussie egalitarianism often discourages this approach; the domestic ensemble is preferred. Lighthouse writers all had a taste for large-scale theatrical dreaming and I encouraged it. If this meant occasional risks and misfires, so be it. I had learnt at the Royal Court that loyalty to playwrights brings rewards.

The Lighthouse model was closer to the German theatre tradition than that of Broadway or the West End. The ghost of the Berliner Ensemble hovered in the wings, and the recent visit of Pina Bausch's company had left its trace. My enthusiasm for the German tradition went back to Max Reinhardt, and I was aware how much English theatre owed to surreptitious trips to Berlin for new ideas.

German cinema was also in full flight at this time, and film-makers like Rainer Werner Fassbinder and Werner Herzog impressed us all. Louis Nowra and I shared many of these enthusiasms and they influenced our various collaborations leading up to *Sunrise*, a haunting, ambitious play and our final production and the culmination of our work together for Lighthouse.

Sunrise involved the company in the dream-like rituals of an affluent clan from the Adelaide Hills, where a famous scientist, Clarrie Shelton, is celebrating his sixtieth. The fiery spectre of atomic testing at Maralinga hovers over proceedings. John Wood's tragic scientist hero created another Shakespearian-scale character in an Australian context. For all our ensemble aspirations, my strongest memories of Lighthouse are these larger-than-life characters powerfully conveyed through in-delible performances: Kerry Walker's gaunt, skinheaded *Mother*

Courage, Robert Menzies' mesmerised *Prince of Homburg*; Gillian Jones and Melita Jurisic's visceral confrontations in Lorca's *Blood Wedding*. For two years we rolled out starkly designed, powerfully acted and highly original dreams and nightmares.

Recollections of these plays and performances and the idea of a first-rate ensemble company of actors, writers, directors and designers have all contributed to the Lighthouse legend, which remains of interest today. It proposed a very different model from the workaday norm. It occurred in an era when subsidy came without strings and artistry was not held to ransom by marketing departments. To those involved, however, the legend bears little relation to the complex realities and often hostile reception of the time. I once explained our philosophy at a season launch by paraphrasing a Rolling Stones lyric: *You can't always get what you want, but sometimes—you get what you need ...*

A dream formulated in the middle of the night in a remote motel ended two years later over an Adelaide dinner hosted by my Flinders Ranges guide and film festival director, Peter Crayford. It was an occasion that might have provided fodder for a Lighthouse production. Peter was playing minder to visiting German actor Kurt Raab, who was touring Australia to promote a festival of Fassbinder films. The German director had recently died, and Kurt Raab was part of the original troupe of Fassbinder collaborators, on stage and screen. The other dinner guests included Louis Nowra, his then wife, composer Sarah de Jong, and some late arrivals—a duo of handsome lads from a local gay FM stereo radio station. They turned out to be party escorts for the guest of honour and were subsequently referred to as the stereo gays.

The dinner got off to an enjoyable start, with the best Adelaide food and wine. Kurtie, as Fassbinder had referred to him, luxuriated in the spread and the attention. It encouraged him to blow his own trumpet, and Louis was keen to cut through the self-promotion:

So Kurt, what does it feel like ... living off a corpse?

Kurtie erupted in a frenzy of rage, remorse and anger, while simultaneously claiming that only the early films in which he appeared were true Fassbinder. This was too much for me and I let rip. A lively row erupted, which our guest seemed to enjoy, peaking as the stereo gays appeared like a *deus ex machina* in time to rescue Kurtie, who struck a pose by the restaurant door and shrieked across startled Adelaide diners:

I bid good night to the writer who despises me! Long pause. *And the director who doesn't think I'm good enough!*

With this, he fled the restaurant. There were many such explosive social confrontations during the Lighthouse years; we thrived on them. Back in Sydney, a week later, I happened to catch an ABC Radio interview with the departing Kurt Raab. In true ABC style, it began with the eternal question: *What did you think of Oztralia?*

To which Kurt replied: *I hated every moment of it. It's a disgusting place.* Pause. *Except for one wonderful dinner in Adelaide ... which reminded me of old times.*

Kurt Raab died of AIDS five years later, in 1988.

If Lighthouse was *the stuff that dreams are made on ...* it was inevitable that when the dream ended everyone finally had to wake up. I returned to Sydney and freelance directing. Neil Armfield took his dreams to Belvoir Street Theatre and became the most outstanding director of his generation, keeping the tradition alive and kicking with a succession of beautifully staged premieres, including *Cloudstreet* and *Toy Symphony*. Actors and designers flourished; Geoffrey Rush won a deserved Oscar for *Shine*. Stephen Sewell created an extraordinary body of work, including a screenplay for the subtly confronting film *The Boys*. Louis Nowra wrote plays, novels and films, and successfully adapted *Capricornia* for the stage. His popular comedy *Cosi*, directly inspired by his Lighthouse years, was about lunatics putting on a play in an asylum.

Adelaide continued its flirtation with radical artists and dreamers. Meryl Tankard returned from Wuppertal and created one of the finest dance ensembles in the country before politics saw its demise. Barrie Kosky managed to balance new ideas and box office with a standout, transformative festival, and Robyn Archer followed suit. I was on the board through Robyn's two festivals but departed in protest at the political machinations surrounding the resignation of international guest director Peter Sellars. His was a radical and ambitious festival, socially as well as artistically, and he needed a tough, imaginative producer and a big budget. Ultimately, he had neither. Passion and zeal sometimes got the better of him, and he could be the architect of his own problems. However, his festival was responsible for highly original films by Rolf de Heer, Tony Ayres and Ivan Sen. I was not alone in finding him inspiring, courageous, and another in a long line of visionaries treated shabbily. His last words to me were double-edged, warm and ironic, like Peter himself: *Thanks for inviting me to your wonderful country.*

Back in Sydney, I settled into a new apartment in Potts Point, and my return to freelance directing began with a cycle of Strindberg productions. They started modestly, at NIDA, with a play that had first fascinated me as a student. My large cast included many promising young actors, one of whom I advised to take up directing. It was sound advice, as his name was Baz Luhrmann.

Strindberg's *Dreamplay* remains one of my favourite plays. The production proved a dazzling introduction to a world of dissolving realities and an examination of the human fear of the eternally unopened door which, when it is finally opened, reveals nothing.

PAGES 322–3: Kerry Walker in Lighthouse's *Mother Courage*
PAGES 324–5: Lorca's *Blood Wedding*. Gillian Jones as the Mother (foreground) and Melita Jurisic (background, right) as the Bride.
PAGES 326–7 (CLOCKWISE FROM TOP LEFT): Bill Harding's anarchic take on the three sisters after the revolution: *Silver Lining*; Shakespeare's *A Midsummer Night's Dream* by the Lighthouse Company; John Wood as Clarrie Shelton with Belinda McClory in *Sunrise*; the Lighthouse Company in Louis Nowra's *Sunrise*.

THE NINETIES

The fall of the Berlin Wall was followed by the dissolution of the Soviet Union, and the map of Eastern Europe was redrawn. Nelson Mandela was released from prison in South Africa. He led the African National Conference to power and ended apartheid. In other parts of Africa there was famine and genocide. Iraq invaded Kuwait and the United States retaliated, forcing an Iraqi retreat. India and Pakistan engaged in nuclear testing. The Asian financial crisis and civil unrest provoked General Suharto's fall from power in Indonesia. The Taliban proclaimed an Islamic republic in Afghanistan. Hong Kong was returned to China. Bill Clinton was elected president of the United States. Tony Blair became prime minister of Great Britain. Diana, Princess of Wales, was killed in a car accident in a Paris tunnel, prompting widespread grief and conspiracy theories.

In Australia, Paul Keating replaced Bob Hawke as prime minister. Keating introduced many social and cultural initiatives and promoted Australia's economic and geographical future in Asia. John Howard's Coalition government came to power and economic prosperity became the buzzword in a new era of globalisation. Mobile phones and email became forms of everyday communication.

China began a cultural renaissance as part of its process of modernisation. The new Chinese cinema was led by directors Zhang Yimou, Chen Kaige and actress Gong Li. Hong Kong director Wong Kar-wai became an art house favourite, and the Taiwanese Ang Lee achieved international recognition as one of the world's great film-makers.

Winter in Nikko, Japan

KAISEKI

Room 3518 at the Hilton in Shinjuku shook. Earthquakes are common in Tokyo. This one was just a little tremor. All tall buildings in Tokyo have structural allowance for movement between floors, and the quakes are cushioned, but my complimentary green tea still rippled in its lacquered cup, and the wooden saucer rattled. There were other quakes during my stay. Most distressing was being on an underground peak-hour train, squashed inside a carriage in the bowels of the city. The lights went out and panic set in.

How terrible to die like a sardine.

The train purred back to life. The lights flicked back on. We lurched forward. That was the scariest quake I experienced in Tokyo.

No one seems to know if these small tremors are good and release pressure to avoid a bigger quake, or whether they are a prelude to something much worse. That keeps you on your toes. A city subjected to earthquakes, fires and bombs is resilient, alert and open to change. Tremors energise you.

It was twenty years since my last visit and everything had changed. The austerity and lone violins that characterised my 1970 visit had given way to skyscrapers and conspicuous prosperity. Accommodation was at a premium, as was real estate. International restaurants and cafés were on every corner. The city had even achieved perfume-label status: *Paris, London, New York, Tokyo.* The prosperity bubble would soon burst, but Tokyo would remain one of the most desirable destinations among the great cities of the world. The only riots during this stay were among the young fashionista of Harajuku, outraged that the latest *Jean Paul Gaultier* collection hadn't arrived on time from Europe. Old Japan still existed in 1990, but it was the international theme park version that prevailed.

Georgina Pope, an Australian involved in film production in Tokyo, had invited me to launch a festival of Australian independent films, which would open with *The Night the Prowler.* I jumped at the chance to re-acquaint myself with Japan.

The Independent Film Festival revealed intrinsic differences between the two major cities of Japan. In Osaka, a port and trader's town, the questions from the film press were commercially driven: *How much did it make? How many cinemas did it play?* I enjoyed their frankness and replied in kind: *Not much. Not many.* Tokyo, with its Parisian aspirations, was a different story. The city revels in art and obscure tastes. The Seibu empire of specialist shops with names like *Wave*, *Parco* and *Saison* were filled with designer labels and, to my delight, rare CDs and literary gems in many languages. The Tokyo film press focused their questions on the film's literary origins, its thematic concerns, actors, imagery. I was more at home in Tokyo and the film was well received.

Georgina fascinated me. Another example of the smartest eyes in the room, she displayed a Jodie Foster kind of mischievous swagger. In every city there's the network person about whom everyone says: *You must look up …* Journalist and rock critic Lillian Roxon fulfilled that role for decades in New York. In Sydney, Kate Fitzpatrick played host to a string of celebrities. The men and women, though it is mostly women, who take time to enhance the visits of international guests are a special breed: a modern incarnation of those fabulous women who ran artists' salons of the past. They're generous with their time and their address books, they know all the places to go, and tables become mysteriously available in otherwise booked-out restaurants. Georgina was always up for an outing. On one occasion we went with some Japanese and European friends to a dance club in the basement of a Buddhist temple in Shinjuku. There were no monks on the floor, instead a line of all-girl Japanese bootscooters. As I was revelling in this sight, one of the Europeans in our group launched into a bitter diatribe about the growth of Asia and how Europe was the only true centre of civilisation. He stormed out and returned to Paris the next morning. Some westerners couldn't hack the Tokyo challenge; Georgina and I thrived on it.

Initially, I assumed Georgina was simply a great Tokyo networker, and she often fulfilled this role. As I got to know her better, I realised there was a more complex story. An art-school graduate from Brisbane, she had arrived in Tokyo with nothing and no one. She learnt the language and established herself in film production, and, in partnership with actor and businessman Kenji Isamura, she set up 21st City. It offered production services to film and video artists requiring local Tokyo knowledge and became popular with everyone from Sofia Coppola to Madonna.

The self-made woman is a recent phenomenon in Japan. On my early visits to Tokyo, women were still being described as *the thing of the house*. In such a culture, Georgina's achievement was considerable. As we travelled the film festival circuit together, politeness gave way to enthusiasm and we became firm friends. It was Georgina who alerted me to the story of journalist Richard Sorge, the legendary Soviet spy and Don Juan of the Ginza in wartime Japan.

Sorge brazenly operated his espionage ring, which included a member of the Japanese cabinet, out of the German embassy, right under the nose of the Nazi regime. He persuaded the Japanese cabinet to refuse Hitler's plan to invade Russia from east and west, with the strategy of splitting and defeating the Soviet army by making them fight on two fronts. The Germans invaded Russia alone and were defeated by the winter snow. By the time they approached Moscow they were exhausted and depleted. Stalin brought in his fresh troops from Siberia, knowing there was no longer a threat from Japan. Sorge had helped to turn the tide in the European war, and Stalin's victory owed much to this unlikely agent in Tokyo.

Sorge was made aware of Japanese plans to attack Pearl Harbor. He alerted Moscow, who reputedly warned their allies in Washington. Later arrested for espionage and convicted by the Japanese military government, he was executed in Sugamo Prison in 1944.

Sorge's complex tale of international intrigue had captured the imagination of many historians and novelists, and I was about to join the club. My interest in writing a screenplay based on his story engaged me for well over a year, much of it spent in

the beachside town of Kamakura, once the capital of old Japan
and now a temple town and artists' colony. It was the perfect
place to work, but I often wondered if my Sorge obsession
wasn't an excuse to further explore Japan and to arrive at a
deeper understanding. Sometimes the two seemed to go hand
in hand. This process accompanied my writing of what became
Shadow and Splendour.

Kamakura was yet another Japan. A beach to walk on, a local
Kinokuniya bookstore with a large English-language section for
research, and a six-tatami room, empty but for a futon and an
answer-phone. The house was rented by a friend of Georgina's who
was often in Tokyo at Kendo classes. A highly intelligent journalist,
he seemed in monastic retreat from his previous employ as a
broker for an Australian finance company on the Hong Kong stock
exchange. His tales of 1980s excesses, where young marketeers,
high on cocaine, worked through the night bankrupting third-
world economies by shifting wealth, via computer, for their
financial masters, gave globalisation a new meaning.

There had been many Sorge film projects over the years,
and one helmed by a foreigner was of novelty value but of limited Japanese business interest. Georgina and I made weekly
rounds of the film studios. From Toho to Shochiku, it was
thrilling to tramp the same corridors as the great Japanese
film-maker Kurosawa. We were greeted with politeness
but little interest. I eventually faced reality and adapted the
unfilmable screenplay into a stage-able play. As I was doing
so, an incident occurred that led to a remarkable encounter.

Georgina visited the Russian embassy to make research
enquiries on my behalf. With the dissolution of the Soviet
Empire underway, previously classified World War II documentation was emerging. Georgina's innocent request for a
few dates and times turned into something altogether more
substantial, as she was ushered into a sealed security room of
documents and files. A sympathetic official explained it housed
every document related to the *Sorge Incident*. He revealed that
they also paid a weekly stipend to ex-partner, Hanako Ishii,
honouring Sorge's final request.

The documents were not for outsiders' eyes, but the official discreetly passed Hanako Ishii's telephone number to Georgina. A meeting was quickly arranged for me, Georgina and our translator, Jeanette Amano. We were to meet at a phone booth near Kichi-joji train station.

We did as instructed: rang three times and hung up, then waited. This was the prearranged signal for Ishii-san to come and meet us. Old habits must have lingered from the world of espionage. As the eighty-year-old Hanako Ishii bustled down the street to meet us, still glamorous in her powder-green Issy Miyake culottes suit and recently tinted hair, she drew a cool breath and explained: *You can never be too careful.* She snuck sly glances at me as we walked to her comfortable house, but I sensed disappointment. The hairdo and designer clothes suggested Ishii-san had been anticipating reincarnation: that the old devil might be back from Sugamo Prison, at least in spirit.

After the shoes-off formalities, we sat and I took in the room. On a shelf by my elbow was a bronze head of Sorge, sculpted by Ishii-san. The walls were adorned with photographs and portraits of Sorge. From my research, I realised the cocktail cabinet that held pride of place was the 1930s original where Sorge would have made the notorious cocktails with which he plied embassy officials, generals, admirals and high-ranking politicians while teasing out their secrets. Memorabilia filled the room; Ishii-san was not living in the present. I sensed her real life had begun and ended with Richard Sorge. We had entered a private shrine to their love and his memory. As the one-hour appointment turned into a memorable day, and conversation progressed, another startling impression emerged. Hanako Ishii appeared to have become Richard Sorge.

Most of the facts involved in Ishii-san's retelling of events I knew from research. But to hear again the story of this brilliant man who had anonymously changed the course of history, and to hear it from this courageous and still beautiful woman, was a revelation. In Japanese *Ie* means *No*; it's a word rarely used in conversation and never by Japanese women, whose language

is especially formal and polite. The only tense moment in our
day came when I enquired whether Ishii-san had herself been
involved in the espionage. Suddenly, the bitter memory of years
of interrogation that must have followed Sorge's arrest welled
up in her eyes, and she hurled her reply at me, across the room,
as a spitfire might despatch machine-gun fire: *IE!*

As we took our leave, I offered Ishii-san a conciliatory gift.
I knew she had met Sorge in a Ginza record store in the 1930s,
and in the rarities racks of *Wave* I had found CDs that would
traverse time. The first was a re-release of Lili Kraus playing
Mozart piano sonatas. This I knew the sophisticated Sorge had
bought Hanako Ishii on acrylic 78-rpm discs, when they first
met—she the beautiful young musician and sculptor and he
the handsome foreign journalist. The second was a vintage,
postwar Furtwängler version of *Don Giovanni*, which I knew
would remind her of her lover and her years as his companion,
while he seduced and betrayed his way around Tokyo. Yet
despite his legendary drinking and womanising, it was Ishii-
san who tended his grave and who had created the shrine we
were visiting.

A week later, a note arrived, thanking me for the recordings,
especially *Don Giovanni* … which Hanako Ishii had … *appreciated
and enjoyed*.

Shadow and Splendour was staged in 1990, thanks to Aubrey
Mellor at the Queensland Theatre Company and the Adelaide
Festival of Arts. My fictionalised account of the Sorge story
had a wonderful cast of Japanese and Australian actors led by
a darkly intense Colin Friels as the spy and the spirited Fumi
Dan as his mistress. The play was an inevitable compromise
of the film that might have been. In this case, the journey had
been more interesting than the destination, though *Shadow
and Splendour* remains, alone among my many projects, something I might one day revisit. *Spy: Sorge*, a Japanese film by
Masahiro Shinoda, another director obsessed by this intriguing
story, appeared years later, but it plodded along with a low-
budget international cast. The wily Richard Sorge and his

secrets remain a myth that, so far, have eluded dramatisation, though aspects of his character informed Ian Fleming in the creation of the world's most fanciful spy, James Bond.

Kaiseki meals are delicate and involve many small courses. The seasonal produce is cooked from natural ingredients, reflecting Buddhist origins. The selection is based on fresh vegetables seasoned with some modern, secular and flavourful snippets of fish and fowl. Each course is elegantly presented with an everyday poetry only the Japanese understand.

Georgina and I met for Kaiseki on my last night in Tokyo. In a quiet room with shoji and tatami, in a Japanese past reconstructed atop a Shinjuku skyscraper, the meal seemed to reflect my time in Japan, past and present: a mosaic of characters and events slowly unfolding in different locations. Here we sat, Georgina and me, as I sensed we would again, in some undefined future, at another transit stop on the *Shinjuku Shuffle*.

As each course revealed itself like a Japanese screen, fold by fold, and conversation and silence interspersed, I began to retreat into the role of tourist and felt the need to photograph, to document the meal. It was a way of gradually disappearing, slowly dissolving like a stone lapped by water, yet leaving its trace. I was trying to hold on to something undefined, fragile and precious that had informed my friendship with Georgina and my time in Japan. There would be new panels in the screens that illuminated our different lives, but something profound had been learnt, shared, felt and understood here: intangible yet lasting.

OPPOSITE AND OVERLEAF: Kaiseki with Georgina

EPIPHANIES

Any fully lived life is inevitably buffeted by squalls and tempests. When you are in the middle of these seasonal shifts they can be overwhelming. Middle is the operative word here, for it's often in midlife that some form of crisis has to be confronted; a series of testing events that have to be endured like winter storms. In my own case, my professional life had tended to take precedence over the personal. In midlife, a series of events would force me to confront a few human issues. They began to emerge in my late forties and reached a climax when I hit my fifties, in the late 1990s.

Around this time, my professional choices were becoming somewhat darker. I directed a sequence of plays by Strindberg and Genet, writers who shared an alienated interest in liberation from the prison of life, either literally or metaphorically. Their protagonists often sought an escape route from their narrow prism of existence through action, politics, fantasy or spiritual release. In some instances, there was no exit. If the difference between art and entertainment is best defined by the entry of mortality into the equation—and this is a defining differential—then it was during this time that my work became consciously, or self-consciously, more artistic. It was cerebral and confronting.

Of course, all great theatre, including that of Shakespeare and Mozart, combines art and entertainment and touches on mortality in some form, but even at the lighter end of the scale, life's tempests are revealed as an inescapable part of the human condition. Suffering was also at the heart of Patrick White's work. Ordinary human suffering and the way people choose to deal with it. Patrick was very aware of the prisons we construct for ourselves and that there was a world outside these self-limiting paradigms. It was his aim, or mission, to illuminate these possibilities. His philosophy of *perpetual becoming* was spiritual in nature and favoured humility over arrogance, grace over pragmatism and love above all.

I had understood and articulated these lofty ideas in my work. I was about to confront them in my life, which was quite another matter.

The Teardrop

In the corner of my front room sits a sculpture comprising two large chunks of battered glass suspended on a single thin wire, in a black metal frame. At its base, splintered shards of glass are strewn. *The Teardrop* is a sculpture by my brother. As I approached forty, it came as a shock to discover I had one.

This revelation occurred as a chance outcome of an electrical storm that erupted over my Bondi apartment. It had been an overcast Sunday, and the sky darkened, turning purple as bruise blood; bilious yellow lightning flashed over the Pacific. Winds blew up and tiles flew from the roof of my building, letting in the downpour. I called my father for some practical advice and a tradesman's phone number. He drove to the rescue, bringing an old showground tarpaulin, which we tied to the roof with ropes in the pelting rain. It would offer temporary relief until the tiles could be replaced.

Energised by the physical effort and the unearthly atmosphere created by the storm, we settled into a drink and one of those rare conversations between father and son that touch on intimacies usually avoided. I reflected that, in my relationships, I often felt I was seeking a brother. Dad paused over a swig of beer.

Well that's funny ... because you've got one.

I was struck dumb by this lightning bolt from the family arsenal. My father sighed and poured another beer. It was going to be a long conversation, one that he'd been rehearsing, dreading, or maybe looking forward to, for half his life. His expression harboured a mixture of relief and fear. Natural forces and the intimate atmosphere had colluded and encouraged him to spill the beans.

My father was talking about Glen Perry, his other son. The brother I didn't know I had. My father's confession had been prompted by a surprise encounter at a showie's funeral. A solidly built young man in his late thirties, with a tanned, open face, had approached him.

GP: *Remember me?*

JMS: *I know the face ... but can't quite place the name?*

GP: *I'm your son.*

On the showgrounds my handsome, sporty father had been something of an *homme fatale*. This may have been one of the reasons my mother chose to confine herself to the city and focus on my upbringing. A brief encounter with an attractive equestrian rider on a horse float at Tamworth Show in 1947 had produced a son. When it became obvious that my father wasn't about to leave his wife, the child was briefly placed in an orphanage, before being rescued by my grandfather and his partner, Flo Carroll. Glen was semi-adopted and brought up by them as if he were their son, though to visitors he was often introduced as a nephew. A tacit arrangement kept the family secret, especially from my mother, for fear of jeopardising marriage and reputation, given the rigid moral conservatism of the times. Glen's childhood was happy enough, until the death of my grandfather in 1965. The teenager was then informed that the man he thought his father was his grandfather; his mother was his grandfather's mistress; the young man he stood next to at the funeral was his brother; and the man he knew as Uncle Jim was his father.

Confused, betrayed, stripped of identity, Glen became, in his words, *a ticking time bomb*. A short time after the funeral, he fled. In a curious echo of his grandfather's past, he *jumped the rattler*. Glen spent years in Queensland as a jackeroo, a job beloved of the dispossessed, in an outback situation where few questions were asked.

Returning to Sydney, he initially lived the life of a surfie, while working a variety of jobs, including hospital technician and air-brush artist patterning surfboards. Glen met up with two recent arrivals from New Zealand, who became his closest friends: brother and sister Paul and Judith Simes. Judith was a painter and, through her, Glen developed an interest in sculpture and enrolled at Sydney Art College.

He maintained contact with Flo Carroll, his surrogate mother, whom he looked after through her declining years, but he had no contact with his father. Alerted to my theatre work, Glen followed my progress through press reports. Reading that *Rocky Horror* had just opened in Sydney, he decided to make contact and left a message at the theatre stage door. It wasn't delivered. I had flown the coop after opening night and was in Los Angeles. Glen shrugged at the missed opportunity and got on with his life, graduating as an industrial arts teacher and settling into a relationship with Paul, who had opened a café, and a share house in Paddington with Paul and Judith.

After the revelation from my father during the Bondi tempest, I became briefly obsessed by the idea of my brother. I would think I'd seen him in the street, wonder if that was him in the supermarket, imagine him in the faces of others. Later conversations revealed that Glen experienced the same yearnings. As my father had no point of contact, and he hadn't pursued the matter, there was little to be done. I agreed not to raise the subject with my mother, and it wasn't spoken about for many years. One day, after a visit to my parents, my father thrust a scrap of paper with a telephone number into my hand. It was Glen's home contact.

Up to you, he added, with a curious mixture of enthusiasm and caution.

By now, I was living harbourside, in an apartment at the end of Victoria Street, Potts Point. It was renovated in a modernist style, with a black granite console housing the telephone. The crumpled scrap of paper with the phone number sat on that granite slab for some days while I pondered when or whether to ring and what to say.

I knew everything would somehow change once I made that call. There was no knowing whether the change would be for good or ill. Knowledge must out. On a Sunday, around 5 p.m., I picked up the phone and slowly dialled. A voice answered that I later identified as Glen's friend Paul. I asked to speak to Glen, and the voice offered the traditional response:

PS: *Who shall I say is calling?*

JS: *His brother.*

PS: *Oh.* Long pause. *I'll get him.*

As I tried to make out the muffled, hand-over-the-receiver type conversation that followed, I realised that I wasn't alone in wondering about uncertain prospects.

Finally, a bright voice came thundering down the line.

So the shit's finally hit the fan!

It was a brash, loud voice, reminiscent of our father's. I had to get used to saying *our father*, after forty years of *my father*—it all suddenly seemed very catholic. *We* instead of *I* was a change in perception that would take time to assimilate, for both of us.

A slightly tentative conversation followed and arrangements were made to meet over a meal. I would visit Glen at his Paddington home and we would dine within walking distance; a restaurant provided neutral territory. There was a mutual sense of frustration that we were dealing with disembodied telephone voices and not flesh and blood.

At the house, I was introduced to Paul and Judith, both of whom I instantly liked. Things were off to a promising start. Glen hardly resembled the shadow I'd imagined in dreams and supermarket aisles, though he bore an uncanny resemblance to our sporty father as a younger man. The reunion meal took place at a Thai restaurant in Kings Cross. Curiously, many of our subsequent get-togethers have also taken place in restaurants; *as you begin so shall you* …

Our first dinner proceeded as if we were both walking on eggshells. There was a shared sense of curiosity, and we were sizing each other up. I was the introvert artist, a little formal, mannered and overly considered. Glen was the extrovert school-teacher and sometime surfer, given to folksy reminiscence and gamesmanship.

This proceeded through a course of spring rolls, until it became clear, over chilli fish, that we were the only two people alive who shared our curious family history. The tide turned into an enthusiastic embrace of our chequered past. We even managed our share of fraternal resentment: Glen's for his cavalier treatment by his father; mine for having been kept in the dark. What we both instinctively understood, but never openly expressed, was the tacit acknowledgment of our mutual hurt and betrayal. Fortunately, we were mature and sensitive enough to slowly heal the emotional damage caused by time, circumstance and imposed isolation.

For the next few weeks, we couldn't see enough of each other. Dinner followed dinner as we competed in the reminiscence stakes. Then, like a gushing tap reduced to a regular stream, everything calmed and normalised. We became brothers who kept in touch on a regular basis, like old friends who had known each other all our lives. I visited Glen's graduation exhibition from Sydney Art College. As a teacher, his glass sculpture was more hobby than vocation, but it was striking and personal, especially given that there was a history of glass work being exhibited on the showgrounds in circles close to his mother. I enthusiastically purchased his only major artwork to date: *The Teardrop*.

Much followed over the years, including a getting-to-know-you Christmas trip to Tasmania. We flew to Launceston, drove south to Hobart and made our way up the coast to holiday on the idyllic Freycinet Peninsula. This proved to be a lot of fun and the necessary bonding adventure—maybe a midlife re-run of adolescence denied.

The big adventure for Glen was the reunion and rapprochement with his father and his acceptance into the family fold. My mother had been hurt by revelations of my father's extramarital affair. These were revealed to her around the time of Grandad's funeral; Glen and my mother had both lived with this shock for a similar period of time. Nonetheless, sensitivities had to be respected. I'd always been aware of something uncomfortable yet unknown gnawing at this marriage: a ghost in the machine. I put aside personal resentment and confronted my parents with my knowledge and new-found friendship with Glen.

At this time, my Australian staging of the musical *Chess* was about to open at the Theatre Royal. It was a short-lived production of an adventurous work that was destined to succeed more in concert than onstage. I invited my parents to the opening and arranged for them to sit with Glen, Paul and Judith. All night, my attention was divided between the stage and the family reunions in the foyer. The efforts began with cool introductions but, over interval, and after my father made a discretionary exit to the toilet, Judith and my mother struck up conversation. Curious, she agreed to visit Paul's Bondi café.

The ice thawed over many subsequent cappuccinos and Christina Sharman found, to her surprise, some real pleasure in discovering new young friends and a surrogate son as she approached her twilight years. Glen and my mother slowly became close and bonded further during the trials that awaited her once she entered her eighties.

My father dealt with life as it presented itself. He approached the arrival of Glen in much the same way. As Glen appeared sporty and extrovert, Dad assumed he now had a son closer to his own values than I had turned out to be. Glen was surprised by some of the initial interrogations and so was I. Faced with one non-denominational son, Dad seemed hopeful of a Roman Catholic addition. His questioning was along the lines of:

JMS: *Do you pray?*

GP: *No.*

JMS: *Do you go to church?*

GP: *No.*

The more traditional O'Neill family in Surfers Paradise would remain my father's source of Catholic family values. Glen rightly insisted on being accepted as an individual on his own terms, so he became Dad's new young mate and driving companion. Again, as old age and illness kicked in, Glen offered invaluable support. Dad's most often quoted remark about Glen was impishly funny to him, though less so to us:

JMS: *The best thing about you is that you didn't cost me a cent.*

Though oft repeated, this was far from the truth. Dad had paid for all Glen's upkeep and education throughout his Narellan years. His own strict father wasn't about to let him forget his moral lapses and responsibilities. It remained a source of tension between them and also with Grandad's partner, Flo Carroll. I arranged a meal with Glen and Flo, his surrogate mother, while Flo was still alive. When Glen briefly left the room, Flo shed a tear and confided to me that she had dreamt it would one day resolve itself and, now that it had, she could die happy.

It was all over. The return of Glen to the family fold was ultimately a source of good for everyone involved, though the complexities are something only he and I can share—something we continue to do over our many meals together.

In the days when all this was still shadowy and uncertain, I consulted two colleagues on the situation. Patrick White confined his response to a writer's musings: *I thought there was something in it, but there's too much plot.*

David Malouf, whose play *Blood Relations* I directed shortly after meeting Glen—a play which bears lipstick traces of our story—was more forthcoming:

Maybe you were your mother's revenge on your father and Glen was your father's revenge on your mother.

I raised David's tough assessment with my cousin, Shirley Germain, who was close to my family and had especially welcomed Glen's return to the fold. Shirley looked shocked, then laughed and went silent. As you do when faced with an uncomfortable truth.

On the way to one of our regular meals, Glen and I ran into a group of his former school students, now making their own way in the world. One tall and appealingly self-assured young man, of Fijian origin, separated himself from the group and privately expressed his thanks for Glen's influence on him as a young student. He confided he'd felt a bit of an outcast at school, but now had successfully integrated himself into the world and was obviously flourishing.

I want you to know, Mr Perry, you were our most loved and imitated teacher.

Glen wasn't so sure about the imitation but he liked the love.

Father and son reunion at Grandad's Narellan shack

The Gift

My mother was frail, her sight was fading and, at eighty-nine, her memory was reduced to, well, a memory. Christina MacAndleish Sharman was a resident at Milford House Nursing Home and was to die there peacefully in the summer of 2003.

During the last months of her five-year stay at Milford House, Christina addressed her visitors as either *Nurse* or *Doctor*, as these had become her most frequent visitors and her remaining touchstone with life. On previous visits, I had been welcomed as her father, brother, husband or doctor, until I set the record straight:

I'm your son. On this visit, I got in first.

So you are, she said, not completely convinced. As if she was briefly pondering what that was, might be, might have been, or even what the word meant.

Son. Sun.

She puzzled, glancing at the glow on the mildewed blind, before enquiring:

What are you doing up at this hour?

It was midday.

We clarified details of time and weather, which she accepted with gentle thanks; her memory had deserted her, but her manners remained to the end.

And where is he? meaning her husband. On cue, he entered, tottering.

At ninety, James Michael Sharman, the former sportsman and boxing troupe proprietor, still had vitality and his wits, but not his knees. They'd been replaced by troublesome surgical constructions made of titanium, a metal that set off embarrassing alarms at airport security. Dad's knees were slowly giving way.

Her smile was luminous and their mutual pleasure was obvious; they hugged. We chattered away about nothing. Sometimes a chord from the past was struck and the conversation would flow. Sometimes she would surprise us with an insight from seemingly nowhere, often precise and wise. Any conversation I proffered about the future was listened to patiently but without any real interest. After all, it no longer concerned either of them.

My mother's meal arrived, delivered by a sometimes firm but usually smiling nurse. Christina was regarded as a gentle soul and therefore compliant. Consequently, she was popular among the nursing staff at the home. However, a bolt of surprisingly temperamental lightning was known to descend on any recalcitrant nurse who overlooked her afternoon cup of tea.

My father solemnly cut his wife's food into tiny morsels. Christina ate, and he occasionally praised, *You've eaten all your pumpkin*, and chided, *but you've left the meat!* It was clear that soft foods were the preferred option. After a while, she hauled herself back into the bed. This was the signal that it was time to go.

Her glassy eyes stared at the hovering void of an over-familiar ceiling.

Silence ... kisses ... farewells.

My father and I left the genteel environment of the nursing home, where the cushioned hush was only occasionally broken by a scream or a wail, and headed out into the knee-threatening traffic and lunch at a nearby Chinese restaurant.

Here, my father had made friends with the cheerful owner, who might have encouraged a few fond memories of old Rud Kee. They would indulge in gentle repartee before Dad settled gingerly into his chair and set about polishing off half a bar-becued duck, eating much of it enthusiastically with his fingers. In a ritual role reversal, I discreetly offered napkins and anticipated spillage and, as the meal progressed, I praised and chided. And so it went, until we parted at the supermarket. He would buy a newspaper for the sports pages, and head home to the television and the football. I would stock up on fruit, vegetables and regrets.

It was a privilege to witness my parents in old age. To see a volatile and often unhappy marriage translate into a smile and a hug of mutual love and support. They were both grateful for small mercies, for the care and concern of others, but they also knew that, at the end of the road, stripped of life's vanities and cruelties, nobody understood their needs better than a fellow traveller.

The end came for my mother shortly after this visit. As she declined, my father and I were permitted a last farewell; but my mother was unapproachable, a silent, though still breathing death mask. After this, the telephone vigil, until the call came at 6.30 a.m. announcing her departure. In what I like to imagine as a final gesture of firm will and good manners, she had waited until the darkness and an unfamiliar night nurse had given way to the arrival of the sun and Jenny, her favourite nurse, on the early-morning shift. Christina had briefly opened her eyes and smiled:

Good morning, Nurse.

Before drifting back into her endless sleep.

My father was alternately shaken and practical. The funeral was a surprisingly relaxed event. With a son skilled in theatrics, the least they could expect was a good send-off, and I was happy to oblige. My mother's final instructions to me were for her ashes to be scattered on the harbour—a ritual enacted with my father on a calm and sunny Sydney summer day from the end of a pier at Watson's Bay—and for her funeral to not be *morbid*; it wasn't. Amie McKenna's spirited rendition of *The Barbara Song* from *The Threepenny Opera* made sure of that. The amusing ballad of sweet Polly Peachum's affair with the notorious gangster Mack the Knife seemed a neat take on my parents' relationship.

If the funeral was lively and the passing sad, the eight years of caring that preceded it offered something of trial and revelation. I had learnt a great deal from my parents, but I never expected either of them to arrive at the point where they offered each other, and anyone else with the eyes to see it, a simple lesson in humanity at its most exposed: a demonstration of frailty, love, tenderness and simple endurance.

This was their ultimate strength and their gift.

Wedding portrait, James and Christina Sharman

The Dip

I hadn't noticed the green light flashing amber, and all of a sudden it was red. It was bad, not bad enough for hospitalisation, but bad. Depression is a very debilitating malaise. It's sneaky, too, creeps up on you, then, one day ... bang. I called it *the dip*.

For a long time I had skated on thin ice. Along the way cracks had appeared, but a little figure skating eluded them. Aged fifty, the ice broke and I descended into a wintry abyss.

I was rehearsing Genet's *Splendid's* at the time, a play I'd first seen at the Schaubühne, in Berlin. Having once staged *The Maids* and, more recently, *The Screens*, I was fascinated by this post-humously discovered play by Genet, and decided to direct it. During my stay in Berlin, I found myself taking a polaroid in the hotel's bathroom mirror. I should have known then that taking photos in bathroom mirrors signals crisis. Nonetheless, I returned to Australia and went into rehearsals for *Splendid's* at Sydney's Belvoir Street Theatre.

At this time my mother was still alive and in her eighties. Every night, I'd return home to a procession of repetitive messages left by her on my answer phone. When we finally spoke, she had no recollection of them. This was the start of her Alzheimer's and the messages were cries for help. Knowing nothing of the disease, this took quite some time to understand and, once I did, it took even more time to resolve the situation and to find appropriate care. It was a period of intense confusion and distress.

Things began to unravel. I became increasingly agitated, scattered and disturbed, pacing even more than usual in breaks, pounding the pavement after rehearsal trying to shed a ringing sound in my ears that wouldn't go away, while combating a spiralling anxiety and deepening sense of disillusionment. I would stare at the harbour below my Potts Point apartment and seriously consider ways of disappearing into it. Finally, I was unable to continue with the production.

Others could have their depression in the privacy of their own homes but, by withdrawing from the production, mine became public knowledge; even more so when I withdrew from a second production, the opera of *The Eighth Wonder*. This was an especially difficult decision, as I'd spent years developing it with composer Alan John and librettist Dennis Watkins; the opera was fully designed and ready to rehearse. My old friend and now opera boss Moffatt Oxenbould was especially understanding and supportive during this time. Neil Armfield stepped in and filled the breach, realising *The Eighth Wonder* imaginatively and expertly. It became a great success with the public— important, in a society where new works, especially original operas, are rare opportunities and can contribute mightily to the development of the culture.

The agency that handled my professional representation was run by Hilary Linstead, whom I'd known most of my working life. Hilary was well acquainted with my condition, having seen it all before. She phoned me and proposed a psychiatrist who had helped other clients. I had a typical artist's fear of therapy—would my instinct disappear under analysis? I was both cautious and anxious. As it happened, my cousin Shirley Germain's daughter was a child psychiatrist. To my considerable gratitude, she phoned and allayed many of my fears. I signed on with Dr Bob—not his real name, which was Hungarian, but one he correctly intuited would make him user-friendly to anxious Aussies. He was a gifted therapist with a particular talent for understanding artists, and we started talking. This was incredibly valuable and allowed a lot of fears to be put to rest. The therapy lasted about nine months, after which my patience gave out, a sure sign that recovery was in sight. Dr Bob demonstrated refreshingly blunt honesty from our first meeting, which made me relax and confide.

DR: *How are you feeling?*

JS: *Isolated ... alone in the universe.*

DR: *You are. Our job is to get you feeling more comfortable with the idea.*

I later recalled this exchange in a conversation with fellow director Barrie Kosky.

BK: *He must have been a Jew.*

JS: *How can you tell?*

BK: *We know we're alone in the universe.*

Initially, I tried antidepressants as an attempt at a quick fix. In my case, these induced insomnia and made matters worse. Depression takes different forms and each requires an individual response. Dr Bob proposed cold turkey and talking therapy. As I was resistant to drugs or other artificial aids, I agreed. This made for a difficult few months, where I would find myself stationary and staring at walls for hours or, on the other side of the bipolar swing, being crazy or behaving inappropriately when I was out and about, but it gradually settled.

The recovery was slow, but it was lasting. I was very grateful for the intervention of Dr Bob. He encouraged a return to my old habit of walking, walking.

I was out of condition. Run down. Depression doesn't come just from the mind but from the body as well. I was considerably helped in my recovery by massage, then walking, then physical training; a graded return to fitness. Friends and relatives came out of the woodwork, especially those with time on their hands. My professional colleagues were mostly too busy to do more than sympathise. Anyway, my disillusionment was such that I needed to get as far away as possible from the profession I had devoted my life to, and, essentially, to get a life. This was ultimately the right step and a great source of renewal, though it didn't seem that way at the time. In fact, my situation was initially so severe that it was felt in professional circles I might never work again.

My cousin Charles Dalgleish passed on a chance remark that helped my recovery along. It was over a dinner that he and his family had kindly proffered, on hearing of my depression. Charles had visited my mother and, despite her own problems and confinement and definitely against current wisdom, she had emphatically assured him that I would get over it and ultimately return to professional work. Having seen me bounce back from near fatal asthmatic and bronchial attacks in my youth, she spoke with some authority, and this revelation of her confidence was very persuasive.

When you're in the throes of a *dip*, you can be overwhelmed by the feeling that it will never end, that you're condemned to a roundabout of highs and suicidal lows forever. You need reassurance that this is a trial to be endured and by no means a death sentence. Dr Bob was of the same view but he knew it would take time and, especially, patience, never my strong suit, to revive my spirit and restore my undermined sense of professional confidence.

His recommendation was to study Taoist poetry. Surprisingly, this proved an important early step. To be healed by poetry was a seductive idea, and a daily reading of Lao Tzu's poems brought me in contact with the central premise of Taoism: that water is stronger than rock. Put simply, over time, water dissolves rock. Realising that I had become rigid, isolated, alienated and rock-like, I started the process of shedding a lot of stoic tension—the *I'll be fine* variety—and I became more relaxed and flowing in my thinking and manner. I had become ruthlessly self-sufficient and needed to open up to others, to let the world back in. The encouragement and acceptance of friendship, old and new, played a crucial role in my recovery. Fortunately, it was on offer. Old friends provided company during daily walks around Rushcutters Bay Park. This got the body moving and the mind focusing on other people's problems, rather than my own. A close friendship with a young film editor, which had sprung from a professional encounter some years earlier, introduced an important idea into my recovery. Aline Jacques and her then partner, painter Andrew Purvis, became especially important to me during this crisis. Aline remains a close friend, and it was she who made the crucial observation that I'd lost the very sense of lightness that had first engaged her interest.

A return to lightness and nature were central to my return to stability. Aline organised a trip to Bali, which rejuvenated my spirits. My brother chimed in with coastal seaside drives, and Dennis Watkins took me on inland treks to national parks where nature asserted its priority. He introduced me to David Haertsch, an architect who had a family home on the coast. There my reconnection with nature continued and I began to develop an interest in architecture. The rebuilding was under-way. The return of lightness, friendship, nature, new friends and interests opened previously shut doors and sped my recovery.

However, these were essentially singular experiences and I needed a return to society. Close friends Mark Gaal and Brendan Blakeley offered dinner invitations and, over many meals, my social confidence was restored. Given my own faltering steps with partners, I also took the opportunity to closely observe the care that sustained their successful personal relationship. Pleasure and gregariousness and more generous perspectives on existence returned to my life: another step in the right direction. I joined the writer Louis Nowra, himself recuperating from a life-threatening pancreatic illness at this time, over morning coffee in nearby cafés. These meetings renewed my interest in writing, theatre and film. My recovery advanced step-by-step, physically, socially, professionally, but it was one particular incident that played a decisive role in the turnaround of my situation.

Hilary Linstead proposed a few days' stay at her coastal weekender at Pearl Beach, where I might relax and do some writing. In late afternoon on a summer's day, I set out, walking, walking over the rocks and around the cliffs towards the next coastal town, Patonga. It's quite a walk, but I was basking in the late-afternoon sun as I climbed, jumped and strolled across the sand and rocks, wearing little more than shorts and thongs. Patonga seemed a long way away, but I kept doggedly going until sunset announced itself. In my preoccupation, I had been walking for well over an hour. As darkness descended and the tide rose, I realised I was cut off and there was no way back over dangerous rocks in the dark. Panic set in. Here I was, a depressive, caught in the dark, with the tide rising and no exit.

I found a large slab of rock and knew there was nothing for it but to survive the night and wait for the dawn in order to return to the beach house. I covered myself with scrub branches to ward off the cold. The tide continued to rise and waves started crashing around my solitary rock; a chill breeze started to bite into exposed flesh, and teeth began chattering. I began to sing. Curiously, I chose Cole Porter: *Night and day, you are the one …*

Far from surrendering to depressive thoughts—I could have easily tossed myself into the ocean, the surf crashing everywhere around me—I did everything to survive. Singing snatches of song, remembering word games, fitful snatches of sleep. About ten hours later, the tide started to retreat and the sun to rise. Exhausted, I clambered back over the rocky escarpments and collapsed on a bed at the beach house, awaking later that day. A quick inspection revealed that I was covered in minor cuts and bruises from the rocks. I bathed and returned to Sydney on the next available train. An appointment with Dr Bob awaited, and I recounted my ordeal, dramatising my *orphan in the storm* status.

He had a much less self-indulgent take on what had occurred on my walking, walking adventure and pointed out that I had physically defined my psychological state. I was trapped midlife between two places, unable to go forward or back, faced with my own possible demise, with the sun setting and dangerous crashing waves surrounding me. Faced with this *to be or not to be* situation, I had fought with everything in my considerable arsenal *to be*. We could no longer take my disillusionment and gloomy introspection seriously; I had chosen decisively to live.

While it took quite some time for all this to settle, and several more years before I returned to full speed and confidence as a director, the incident at Pearl Beach had forced me to confront my mortality and the truth of my situation. I had spent long enough at stationary red stop signs: the lights had flicked from amber to green and there were highways and horizons ahead. I was reminded of the childhood lesson from my talking book and knew it was time to turn the page.

The Mountain and the Sea Goddess

Thwack. One blow and the greenish-yellow poison from a tropical spider splattered across the mosquito netting that shrouded the veranda bed in the Balinese pavilion where I was staying, in the hills above Ubud. Luis Buñuel, the film-maker and amateur etymologist, once observed that character was often revealed by the way we despatch insects. I will spend time juggling glasses and bits of cardboard to return a harmless stray spider to the wild but my response to the life-threatening venomous variety is instinctive, sudden and swift. There's no toying, trifling or games—just … *thwack.*

Mist rose like a slow curtain from the Agung Valley below, and terrace by terrace the lush green jigsaw of rice fields material-ised. A gold vein of the Agung River gleamed. A restless sleep of memories had passed on the veranda, and the day began with aromatic steam from a cup of ginger tea, which countered the stench from the dead spider. A rooster crowed; there were whispers, footsteps, activity from the nearby garden. I sat very still, sipping ginger in the half-sleeping half-waking dawn.

The Balinese mountain town of Ubud is a place of spirits and dance, a destination for tourists seeking more than beachside hedonism, and an artists' retreat. President Sukarno, himself descended from the Balinese, had realised in the 1960s that the West, excluded from their biblical Eden, required a paradise. There were tourist dollars in creating one. Western travellers from all corners of the globe gravitate to this island, but the Balinese themselves rarely travel anywhere. My inescapable con-clusion is that they understand something the western world, in its speed and greed, has forgotten.

I enjoy the directness of the Balinese. *What's your name? Where from? Where are you staying? Are you married?* Roughly translated as: *How do I address you? How much are you worth? Are you available?* The quick quiz can save a lot of time. Though Balinese communalism, which allows for little or no sense of privacy and which can be a confronting reality for many westerners, contains its own secret codes. It can often mean: *What's yours is mine, but what's mine isn't necessarily yours.*

My first trip to Bali came late, as a recovery measure from my *dip*. I was accompanied by painter Andrew Purvis. I think my friend Aline was hoping to kill two birds with one stone, as we both needed a little recovery; though the much younger Andrew was in noticeably better shape than my midlife self. Revived and enchanted by the place, especially Ubud, I made several return trips. My aim was to recreate the ease I felt in Ubud in my home city, an ambition possible only to partially realise, though it guided my thinking for years.

I became fascinated by Balinese history, including that of early western visitors like Walter Spies, once assistant to film-maker FW Murnau, creator of the silent vampire classic *Nosferatu*. A painter, musician and photographer, Spies encouraged and taught the artists of Ubud and co-authored the seminal *Dance and Drama in Bali*. Spies looked on the island as his personal sound stage. The addition of his choreography and smoke machines to an already ceremonial culture of gamelan, dance and chant formalised the famous Kecak Dance and opened Bali to cultural tourism. The Walter Spies Suite at the legendary old Tjampuhan Hotel, where I often stayed, is still preserved today. Antonin Artaud, the crazy French artist and spiritual theorist whose book *The Theatre and Its Double* had influenced 1960s theatrical experiments also visited and was influenced by Balinese ritual and culture. Ubud has had its share of artists, mystics and fakirs.

I was intrigued by the sights and scents of Bali, especially the island of dead, floating in Lake Bratan, home to the uncremated and their attendant ghosts and spirits. I would have many Balinese adventures, most of them revelatory. The first of these occurred soon after my first arrival on the island. Travelling at short notice, Andrew and I had booked into makeshift accommodation. We had two small pavilion rooms at a tiny motel in Peliatan, the centre of traditional Balinese dance culture. The manager, Gusti, doubled as tour guide. Taking stock of the distracted state of his recent arrivals, he began our first touring expedition by stopping at his modest village temple. Here, he explained Hindu religious philosophy.

Put simply, while Hindus worship many gods, there are centrally three: Brahma, Shiva and Vishnu. These represent the forces that must be acknowledged and kept in balance: creativity, destruction and sustenance.

All Balinese ceremonies aim at balancing life, be it through small gestures like daily offerings of flowers to elaborate funeral rituals involving fire, water and corpses in papier-mâché animals. Having explained his simple belief system, Gusti walked away and left us to our meditations. Roosters crowed. Birds sang. Otherwise, silence. Gusti returned an hour later. Nothing was said. Our tour resumed. The new, calmer mood as we travelled suggested that our real Balinese journey had begun.

The other adventure was of a different but related nature and occurred at the village of Sanur, with its discreet beach surrounded by hotels and spacious homes and huts, where Australian artist Donald Friend had once held court. I became fascinated by the story of the famous fire at the once fashionable Sukarno-era Bali Beach Hotel. The story goes that Sukarno, who believed in Balinese spirituality, ordained one suite, Room 327, be kept empty for the Sea Goddess. Swept from power in military leader Suharto's coup, Sukarno's wishes were ignored. A devastating fire subsequently destroyed the entire hotel, except for room 327, which remained intact. Local legend has it the Sea Goddess returned to claim her suite. There is now a sacred shrine to her in the new hotel.

I enquired about the legend among the locals working along the beach in Sanur. My curiosity was initially greeted with suspicion, but perseverance led me to a fisherman, a local elder, resident at the time of the fire. He was threading a net on the beach, and he listened patiently and silently to my interest before looking up and asking a simple question that stopped me in my tracks. It was one I would normally have swiftly negated, but my reply surprised both him and me.

Do you believe in magic?

Pause.

Yes.

MILLENNIUM

Delirium spread around the globe as the turn of the century approached. There were doomsday cults, predictions of Armageddon and threats of Y2K bugs that would wipe out computer systems. Instead, fireworks exploded and people danced in the streets. Sydney hosted the 2000 Olympics. The soundtrack over the harbour city was *Love Is in the Air*. But one event soon overshadowed the decade: the attack on the World Trade Center in New York City on 11 September 2001—9/11.

It was around 11 p.m. in my Potts Point apartment when I flipped the television onto the late news. After a procession of run-of-the-mill stories, there was a hiatus. *Something's just come in* ... They cut to New York and an eerie, static shot of the World Trade Center. A plane had crashed into the tallest tower around the ninety-fifth floor. *Had the plane run off course? Was it an accident?* A second plane slammed into the adjoining tower, around the eightieth floor. Flames shot up the buildings and smoke poured out. As skyscraper walls started tumbling comparisons to Pearl Harbor began, along with biblical analogies: the Tower of Babel, the walls of Jericho. I recalled my news-stand encounter over a decade ago: *That can't happen here. We've got God on our side.*

Once the third plane ripped into the Pentagon and the fourth, obviously intended for the White House or Capitol Hill, crashed, it was all over. There would be no more. It was strategic. A triptych. Finance. Defence. Political power.

The next day, fear was in the air and the world became a different place.

IN TRANSIT

I slipped an airline sleeping mask over my eyes and surrendered to dreams no longer walking walking but descending into an ancient underground tomb in luxor and meditating on worship while floating down the nile in a felucca overlaying ancient and modern hieroglyphs with warhol icons of skulls stars soup cans electric chairs and wondering what to worship as I stroll through sculpture gardens of the picasso musée recalling dinner with paloma and conversations about genet on giacometti sculpting himself into dust and oblivion as I climb the steps of strindbergs blue tower at 85 drottninggatan followed by mobs with flaming torches singing happy birthday to the playwright hiding under the piano before blood red curtains descend on king lear by bergman and the eternal storm breaks over a cracked berlin wall where everyone chants *freiheit* while a satirical hitler on the roof of the berliner ensemble shouts slogans by heiner mueller as little melisande throws her red wig down yellow stairs at the staatsoper and tuxedoed gods and goddesses crawl across industrial wasteland to get to their valhalla in the sky which is really bayreuth ...

This is your captain speaking over breakfast of a boiled egg at the taj hotel in mumbai between tables of anxious americans *honey there's a guy out there with stumps for legs and my god bashing his stumps against the window* and the memsaabs on the sofa are swapping maharani gossip about tax fiddles while I sit on steps with beggars who whisper *you get a rupee with a stump but a dead baby in swaddling clothes really sets the purses flowing* into the brothels with the young guy collecting drug money and living it up outside the best address in mumbai while we take buggy rides through backyard fires and harbourside smoke until I'm choking on loudspeakers playing brass band abba as new year chimes and skyrockets flare over our beggars banquet and sacrificial pigs are being roasted at the sing-sing on mount hagen amid painted faces and huli warriors drumming on their haunches as I walk empty streets behind a floodlit parthenon

PREVIOUS PAGES: Huli warriors, Mt Hagen Show, Niugini

past empty roman palazzi towards a tuxedoed nubian doorman his shadow reflected on cobblestones waiting for my password *just knock three times and ask for joe* then dancing up a marble staircase into red neon spelling B-A-R and the tiered tunnel of supperclub roma all in white like the inside of an aircraft with bhutto dancers and skeleton images playing on the walls while we laze squat dine on eastern delicacies and artists stroll strip surprise us ...

Cabin crew please prepare for landing at a seedy club in taipei with mickey chen whose smart eyes want to know if I prefer younger or older and I say older and we are up a flight of stairs and into a lounge of crushed velvet where elderly gangsters on the bandstand croon *ebb tide* to ageing transvestites and a plump manager offers drinks on stained formica tables where too many cigarettes have missed their mark and the karaoke segues from *la mer* into *unchained melody* and *hi lilli hi lo* with its singalong *song of love is a sad song* as I wander down to the basement with its sculpted stones that whisper to me and pass the narrow opening flanked by cells into a dark room where deformed prisoners stare back and I panic to discover the sculptures are tombstones and the voices of the dead are playing mahler nine with a hushed breath sigh wheeze roar of nature before its relentless waltz struts marches us into a shrill grimace of nightmare decay where strings disintegrate and we descend into the eerie silence at its end like all our ends as I stir awake to fog and neon as the plane taxis into **Narita Airport.**

STOPOVER TOKYO

Tokyo poor. Tokyo rich. I've done both. Tokyo in transit has its moments. As the new century dawned I dropped by Japan and, short on funds, briefly holed up in a flophouse in the Kabukicho red light district of Shinjuku. The Hotel Kent had been recommended reluctantly by friends. It lived down to expectations and somehow seemed the perfect site for my reunion with Shinjuku.

My tawdry, beloved precinct was now presided over by bureaucrats in high-rise towers to the west of the station, while Yakusa and Korean gangsters looked after low life to the east. A stroll away from Hotel Kent was the Golden Gai, where artists and musicians still congregated. The millennium changes hadn't dislodged Shinjuku's famous Piss Alley, a dead-end lane where tiny cabin bars allowed men to drown their sorrows in the company of sympathetic and often transvestite mama-sans. The main street still had space for the high-minded Kinokuniya bookstore and elegant Isetan department store. Ni-Chome, to the north, with its gay precinct, remained high on price and low on charm. It hadn't changed since the American occupation. Ni-Chome was still occupied, though a battalion of brash young American business-types had replaced the military.

Hotel Kent was named after a brand of cigarettes Albert Finney offered Audrey Hepburn in the film *Two for the Road*. Hepburn was a fetish idol in Japan, almost a cult. The drunken, late-night salarymen who had missed the last train home and tumbled into Hotel Kent, or its equivalent, with blurred vision could conjure Audrey's petite features in the sceptical faces of their bar girl companions as they negotiated cabin-sized rooms with a plastic shower recess.

Breakfast was not served, but I found good espresso coffee at a Segafredo café tucked away under nearby Shinjuku Station. Early mornings there were enlivened by office workers mixing it with survivors from the nightshift: drag queens with devastated make-up, and a procession of hookers and pimps looking the worse for wear. Even breakfast in Shinjuku came with attitude.

Yokohama Ferris Wheel

One of the other services not on offer at Hotel Kent was internet connection, and after an exhausting day and night walking, walking from ancient temples to the stunning new Prada Building in Harajuku, via drinks in unspeakable bars, I decided I needed to send a few emails. Downstairs at the front desk, the night clerk greeted me with *Mister Jim!* He'd done his English language study in Sydney and his enthusiastic announcement *I'm from Chatswood!* took me by surprise. Our Aussie solidarity enlivened his uneventful job and, after a chat, he pointed me in the direction of a building housing all-night hostess bars, assuring me that the fourth floor offered email nirvana.

After negotiating the elevator and paying my fee at the desk, I was ushered into a large room of booths, each with a computer and a swivel chair. As I settled into booth 17 and began to check correspondence, I became aware of a curious stillness around me. Swivelling around, I discovered that the internet library, as it was called, also served as cheap accommodation for salarymen who had missed the last train home. They looked like leftovers from Kawabata's *The House of Sleeping Beauties*. The corpse-like army of salarymen had fallen asleep in front of their computers, and on every single screen were frozen images of schoolgirl porn.

The Hotel Southern Tower was the accommodation for my visit the following year. Located in the third skyscraper on the right from the western exit from Shinjuku Station, it was, as a friend commented, *the Park Hyatt for poor people*. It was rigorously business-like and boasted reasonable tariff, spacious modern rooms and sweeping views of the Imperial Gardens. It had taken me three decades, but I had finally found well-placed, convenient and affordable Tokyo accommodation.

On this trip, I was accompanying an architect friend, David Haertsch, who was visiting Shanghai. While I was cool on Shanghai's instant modernity, I could see from the prevalence of hip Chinese and the influx of western young that it was a designated city of the future. However, I was more interested in the Tokyo of my past, wanting to better understand the experience of Japan and what it had meant to me. As ever, Georgina Pope was sensitive to my quest and arranged a meal for David, me and a mystery guest.

Seeichi Kawata brought back fond memories. On my earlier visit he had been a crazy young fashionista and partner of Franco-Australian friend Francois Perez. Seeichi's party-boy ways, his outrageous outfits and fabulously mangled English had always been a delight. He was master of the surprise gift, and his whole manner exuded a kind of crazy poetry. When Francois departed for India and I left for Australia, Georgina and Seeichi had kept in touch. Now, here he was, middle-aged and besuited, the mystery guest at Georgina's reunion meal. Seeichi had settled down and turned himself into a small fashion business. His English was as carefree as ever but over three courses of Italian food, it became clear that his earlier, wilder, halcyon days were much missed. Eager for the reunion to continue beyond the meal, I suggested we move on to something else. Seeichi lit up like a light bulb and spoke of a private party. He dashed off to bicycle home and collect the necessary invitation: *I'll only be a moment!*

As Georgina, David and I waved him off, I suggested that the moment could stretch to an hour, as I was sure we were talking *costume change*. Over an hour later, Seeichi reappeared as in a vision. He was on his bicycle pedalling furiously down a street of startled passers-by, in a fluoro green wig and flowing, iridescent dress.

The party was in a gallery-restaurant with under-lit glass floors full of raked desert sand and small objects. The walls were hung with miniature reproductions of famous paintings from the Louvre behind smashed glass frames, some with a small hammer attached. Techno thumped; the crowd was fashion-conscious, high-end Tokyo in full swing, including several of the most striking transvestites I had ever seen. One looked like pop princess *du jour* Bjork, with an extraordinary skirt of feathers that made her resemble a bird of paradise. In Australia, drag tends to be fun and always contains a flicker of irony or satire, but here it was less vaudeville, more performance art.

I was enjoying the company, the people viewing and the general circus, but I noticed Seeichi had assumed a dignified elder statesman role among these fashionistas and realised that he would have once been the most outrageous character in the room. After an hour or so, I sensed restlessness from my companions but, before we left, Seeichi made me promise to meet him for lunch the next day at *Spiral*, a favourite café gallery from our former times.

As we stepped out of the club into a taxi, I pondered the intensity of Seeichi's departing expression. Our nocturnal drive was accompanied by warm rain, and a sky draped with mist made the deserted Tokyo streets seem dream-like and other-worldly. Turning back, I noticed a drenched, forlorn figure in the shadows: the transvestite bird of paradise, caught without an umbrella and desperately flailing at passing taxis.

It was still raining the next day as I arrived for my lunch with Seeichi. *Spiral* hadn't changed, but, by 2005, the era had. What was once smart and new was now established and just another restaurant. Seeichi bustled in, dapper in his business suit, and we found a table. We ate and chatted about then and now. As coffee arrived, he presented me with a parcel. *Farewell gift!* Seeichi announced. I smiled. He asked me to open it. In Japan, gifts are rarely opened in the presence of the giver. So much trouble is taken with the preparation of gifts that the recipients often enjoy the packaging more than the gift itself. That wasn't to be the case on this occasion; Seeichi's was a gift for remembrance.

Even understanding his subtle sense of what I call everyday poetry, I found the contents baffling. Calico and string opened to reveal a beautiful silky cloth, which unfolded to reveal Seeichi's farewell present … crushed, sweet-scented dry leaves. Buried among the leaves was a tiny photographic portrait of him, aged around twenty-one. I look puzzled. He gently put his hand over mine and explained …

The ashes of my youth.

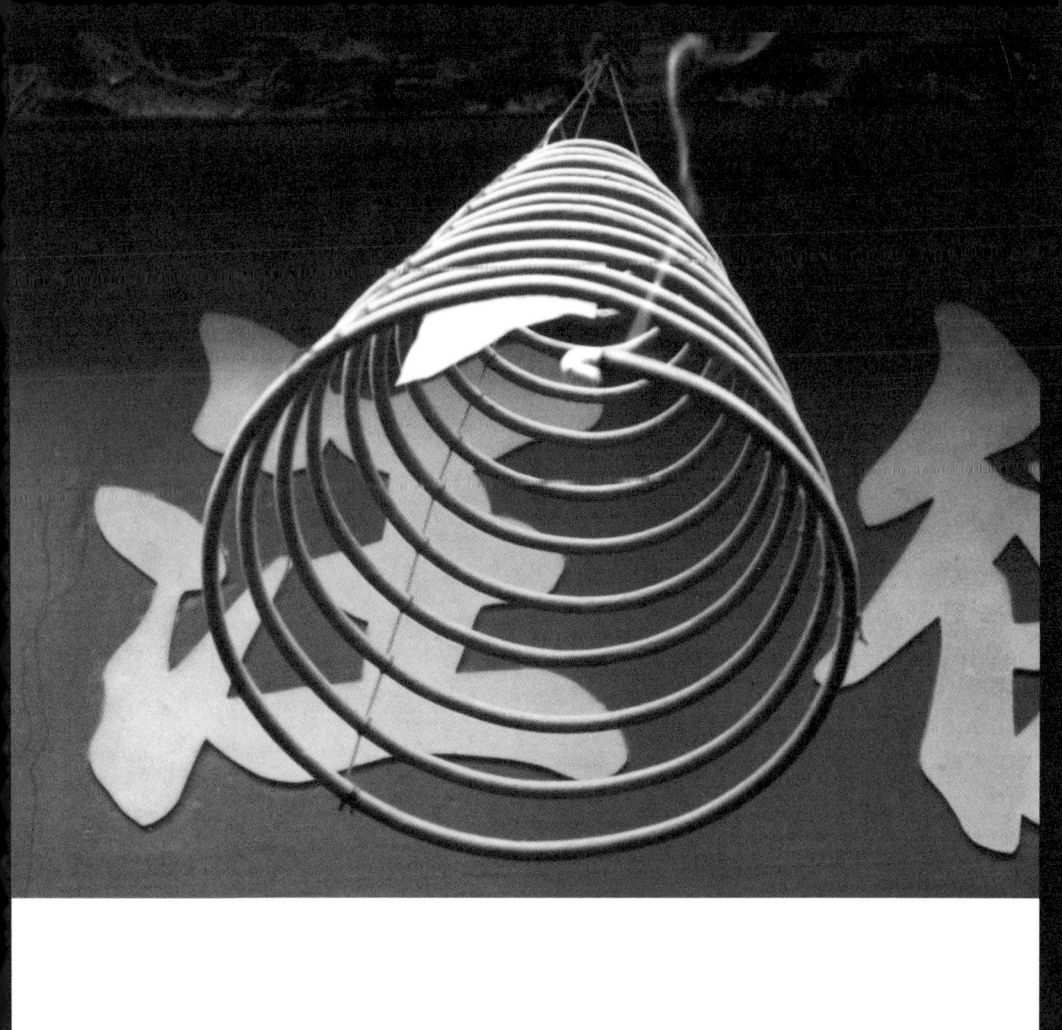

EDGE HILL

Tap-Tap-Tap.

Three knocks on the door of my house at Edge Hill.

In this peaceful suburb of Cairns, my minimalist home and rambling rainforest garden offered a retreat from theatre and the inner-city distractions that surrounded my Sydney base. I was seeking something of the restorative balm Bali had provided in the period after my *dip*. Replenished by nature, but within walking distance of a café with good espresso, I was surrounded by modernist design, floor-to-ceiling glass, polished wood floors, tropical vistas and a soundtrack of Mozart, Mahler and Messiaen. I could write and relax. I didn't initially consider cyclones, intense humidity or how the house would be maintained while I was working in Sydney, but over four years, Edge Hill was recuperative and productive.

Underlying this was a sense of waiting. For what, I didn't know; it was a sensation, not a conscious thought. Three taps on the door would offer the answer. If I'd landed in heaven, I was possibly waiting for an invitation back to hell.

My return to *the house of illusion* had been slow and fitful; there had been several new theatre productions, and my confidence, wobbly at first, developed with each one. John Bell had invited me to direct him as a cool and eloquent Prospero in *The Tempest* for the Bell Shakespeare Company. This tentative first step back into the rehearsal room produced a lively and often comic reading of a sometimes too sombre romance, one that benefited from some cross-cultural casting. Paula Arundell turned in an award-winning Ariel, all spirit and song. Rachel Maza and Tom Long as the lovers became so caught up in their roles that a baby was born and christened Ariel.

A popular Joe Orton play, *What the Butler Saw*, followed for Belvoir Street, and a less public but important student production: a Kurt Weill cabaret at NIDA. My return to cabaret roots offered a clue to what lay ahead. One of the young NIDA graduate actors, Amie McKenna, revealed such skill with the material that I mounted a special cabaret for her and producer David Hawkins. It was only a few nights in an unlikely room above a pizza parlour, but this cheeky performance opened a door that had been closed for too long. I was ready for something beyond staging classics, though I had only a vague sense of what that might be.

Tap-Tap-Tap.

It was a courier. A cheerful biker—in a mask. *Sign here, please!* The parcel was from Wendy Blacklock of Performing Lines, a small production house specialising in festival shows. What could this be? I walked through the echoing house, flicking a script by Stephen Sewell with an accompanying note, something about Brett Sheehy and interest for his 2005 Sydney Festival. The play was about a painter and his muse, obviously based on Francis Bacon and his relationship with George Dyer, a personally disastrous yet artistically rewarding affair that ended in Dyer's suicide.

Reading it, I was drawn back to London in the 1970s and Bacon's searching, seductive yet forensic gaze. The subject was dark and familiar, but its treatment was original and intriguing. I hadn't seen writing of this intelligence, quality and musicality for a long time. It was as if the painter's story had entered the realm of Christopher Marlowe, with the atheist Bacon depicted as a latterday Dr Faustus: *See, see where Christ's blood streams in the firmament.* I read the script and put it aside, then read it again, slowly this time. My email reply to Wendy quoted some well-known lyrics from an old musical, *The Bandwagon*:

A swain being slain for the love of a queen—that's entertainment!— I'll do it!

I later discovered the play had been turned down by most theatre companies, all of them alarmed by its content. Festival director Brett Sheehy sensed its potential and was determined to present it. Unlike most Australian producers, Brett possessed real artistic courage and just a hint of Harry M Miller's smile. Stephen Sewell was thrilled by my positive response. The draft I read was a two-character play centred on the intense relationship between the painter and his unlikely muse. Was Stephen interested in developing it further? He was, and we began to collaborate as writer and director. By adding a Greek chorus figure, ultimately a singer, the claustrophobic relationship opened out, resonating with Bacon's enthusiasm for Greek tragedy, especially the furies of the Oresteia. And so it became *Three Furies*. I introduced Stephen to young composer Basil Hogios, who had cabaret experience and had demonstrated instinct and imagination working on the Orton play. I was back in my element again, collaborating with writers and composers, and I couldn't have been happier.

Early meetings with Stephen in Sydney were polite if cautious, as we slowly learnt to trust each other. He was used to being constrained by directorial input but found, perhaps to his surprise, that I wanted him to push the boat out, to take the play further, and that I was especially enthusiastic about the poetic, lyrical side of his writing. This took flight as Basil added songs that mixed chants and chanteuserie. We could all sense something original slowly taking shape. The end was reached in a marathon session of to-ing and fro-ing the script, and at 2 a.m. Stephen's final version of the painter's last speech flew through cyberspace from his apartment in Bondi to Edge Hill. I was so thrilled to read it, I was almost delirious. Oblivious to everything, except what I was reading and imagining onstage, I crashed down a flight of stairs, landing on a concrete floor with a shredded foot and torn-out toenails that required ambulance assistance. Francis Bacon would surely have approved.

There is always a defining moment in any production, often an unexpected one. On *Three Furies: Scenes from the Life of Francis Bacon* it came at the final audition, in a university theatre swathed in pale canvas, which made everyone assembled for the occasion—actors, writer, designer and producers— seem like shadows.

For the painter, I wanted someone surprising, and recalled Simon Burke in John Romeril's *Jonah Jones*. I knew he had the charisma to centre the play and the musicality to enrich the language. Socrates Otto, a recent NIDA graduate who read for the painter's rough trade muse, was a fearless and imaginative young actor. Paula Arundell completed the trio, and her sultry voice and looks embodied the passion of the fury Tisiphone. In truth, it was an odd trio, previously unconnected, who miraculously combusted on that day among the swathes of canvas.

The chemistry blazed, from rehearsal room to festival after festival: Sydney, Perth, Adelaide and on to the Helpmann awards. Between festivals, when Paula became pregnant, the equally extraordinary Paul Capsis replaced her as Tisiphone. It was a cast I loved through every incarnation of Stephen's challenging play, and a production through which I rediscovered my love of theatre. Specifically, of making theatre. I realised that while I was practised at staging plays, especially tragi-comedies, what I relished most was creating new work. If what I had been waiting for was a theatre work that combined the intensity of drama and the excesses of cabaret, *Three Furies* was it.

The sheer pleasure of working on a play with songs rekindled the opera spark. A new version of Benjamin Britten's *Death in Venice* for Opera Australia followed, with Britten specialist Richard Hickox on the podium, tenor Philip Langridge as the writer Aschenbach and baritone Peter Coleman Wright as his multi-faceted alter ego.

During these productions, I entered a brief netherworld as tropical cyclone Larry swept through my Edge Hill house and my 93-year-old father's health went into decline. I had, however, been fortified against loss by the renewed creativity sparked by *Three Furies*. Endings had been balanced by new beginnings and a return to theatrical adventure.

Tap-Tap-Tap.

On the day before *Three Furies* started rehearsal, I was in the Westfield shopping complex in Bondi Junction, waiting for an elevator to the carpark with two teenagers who looked trashed from a night of drugs and dancing. As they hung off each other, barely in their clothes, the elevator doors slid open. They fell inside; I followed. Moving to the buttons, I gently enquired: *Which floor?*

The girl's eyes half-opened, and with a wicked smile she purred: *The lowest circle of hell, please.*

UNDER THE KAURI PINE

My father had an affinity with magpies. In his childhood, one had plucked out an aunt's eye. In his youth, the Western Suburbs football team he had captained wore black and white and were known as *The Magpies*. Now, in old age, he would sit and watch the birds perch on the third-floor veranda of his nursing home, which overlooked the gardens. Alongside it, but towering above, was an ancient kauri pine; the magpies used the tree as a tarmac and a home. We used to sit on the veranda and stare at the tree together on my every visit.

The stroke that had delivered him into care had come suddenly. After an earlier fall he was briefly hospitalised, and my brother and I had persuaded him to wear a beeper that would alert an ambulance in case of any accident or mishap.

I was in Cairns when the call came. The beeper alarm had been activated, and an ambulance was on the way. I fretted and paced and rang back to check if it was a false alarm; there had been several. By chance, the call was answered by my brother, who had dropped in to visit the old man. I was able to explain the situation, and Glen jumped into his car and phoned back moments later from hospital emergency. I flew to Sydney and we stood vigil together through the touch-and-go days ahead.

Months of recovery followed, initially in intensive care; later, rehab. Dad's recovery was remarkable for a man of ninety-three. After daily exercise he could walk again with the aid of a stick or frame, but the legacy of his stroke was aphasia. Dad was robbed of speech. A cruel fate for a raconteur.

After rehab, the search for care began. The terrible trudge from facility to facility. Prior experience with my mother helped, and I narrowed the choice to two options. One was modern, interior and comfortable; the other more ramshackle, but offering veranda and kauri pine. Dad heard the laughing magpies and grinned; the choice was made.

There were frequent visitors during his hospital stay; fewer during his nursing home residency. Old timers are wary of God's waiting room. There were the Molloys from Melbourne, especially his childhood friend Jack Molloy, who flew up to be with an old mate. It was Jack, also in his nineties, who told me the story of my grandfather's fight with Jack Carter in the Riverina. And there was Annabella, my mother's sister, a wonderful woman approaching her centenary. Watching Irish Dad and Scottish Annabella trade stoic smiles, I realised that, between them, they shared almost two centuries of history. The Willis brothers, Jimmy and Percy, cousins from Narrandera, were loyal and regular hands at rummy or euchre; they often let him win.

The aphasia meant Dad rarely mixed with other residents, preferring room and television and cable sports. He mostly loved the veranda and slow walks in the rambling gardens, especially on visits with my friend Aline, now accompanied by her baby, Eli. It was touching to see the communion between young and old, the tender play of hands. As neither could speak, they understood each other better than the rest of us.

There were medical ups and downs, falls, false alarms, complications. One morning, alerted by Glen to a possible emergency, I dashed to the home expecting the worst. Instead, I found Dad enjoying a hearty breakfast. Bounce back ran in the family. I asked after his condition. Dad's voice was croaky but his humour and a few choice expletives remained. He pointed to his silent throat, troublesome knees, and his stomach, which held the ulcer that would turn cancerous and take him out. He shrugged, grinned and laughed … heartily. He knew it was only a matter of time.

A strangely light atmosphere prevailed in St Vincent's hospice for the dying—not gloomy, as I had imagined. It was a chance to observe the cheerful care offered to those whose exit had been confirmed: young, old, cancer, heart, stroke, AIDS. Once the morphine was applied, it became a vigil. Glen was in Brisbane and I was at the funeral home making plans when my mobile rang. Aline, who had remained at the hospice, gave me the news. She'd stepped out to take a call. When she returned, he was gone. Glen's plane from Brisbane had just landed, so we all converged in the silent room, with the shrunken flesh and death mask. In death, as in life, he'd given us all the slip. I think he would have enjoyed that idea.

As my father's ashes were scattered across the garden at Randwick, the little ceremony brought with it ghosts of ashes past, on lakes and harbours, and concluded a difficult decade of decline, care and ultimately renewal. Dad's old bowling club mate Rainbow had given the funeral the thumbs up: *No false sentiment. He would have liked that!* The crematorium curtains had closed on Dad's coffin to the beat of the big bass drum: the end of an era.

The Randwick house held few ghosts for me. After some thought, I sold Edge Hill, moved in, renovated. The bell and drum from sideshows past were stored in the garage, awaiting arrangements for them to join other troupe memorabilia in the Stockman's Hall of Fame in Longreach, not far from where Glen had spent his time as a jackeroo, in Queensland.

There was a final visit to the nursing home with Glen to collect our father's belongings, including the scrapbooks my mother had meticulously kept and he'd pored over on a daily basis during his final year. We flicked through familiar photos of the distant father we had come to know and love only late in life—the cheeky country kid, the handsome footballer, the *who'll take a glove* troupe proprietor, the showground legend with his plaque and, finally, the proud father. It was a country face, etched with character and full of contradictions—stubborn, mischievous, gregarious, solitary.

And there was the grin.

Any sadness was banished by that grin.

Cocky as a laughing magpie in a kauri pine.

Father and sons

A PERFECT DAY

6 a.m., Friday, 2 March 2007

My eyelids flick open and take in the digital clock-radio. Classical FM is playing something welcoming, and a blaze of sunshine heralds a day full of zing. It will be crowded with walks and opera meetings, and tonight I will attend a revival of Patrick White's *The Season at Sarsaparilla* by the Sydney Theatre Company at the Drama Theatre of the Sydney Opera House.

An expedition to Clovelly Beach with Aline and her now two-year-old son, Eli, is a bright start. Aline swims laps while I play godfather and photograph Eli. Afterwards, we three start walking, walking around the coastline to the colourful fishing dinghies of Gordon's Bay, fascinating to young eyes. Back home, I make coffee while Eli sits entranced by a DVD of Mozart's *The Magic Flute*. It's interesting to contemplate the future electronic altars that might await this little man: audio walls, stereo wristbands, intravenous sound implants. Whatever the form, the hypnotic spell this 250-year-old music weaves makes it clear that Mozart will remain in the repertoire.

Mozart will be the subject of my afternoon meeting at Opera Australia with musical director Richard Hickox. Having developed a simpatico working relationship on *Death in Venice*, Richard and I are now discussing *Cosi fan Tutte*. I arrive with a list of tantalising ideas. The controversy that surrounded my youthful encounter with Mozart makes me wonder if I'll depart with my list burning a hole in my pocket. Richard and the OA team prove open and receptive. As production plans are unveiled, diplomacy turns to enthusiasm. The meeting ends with a sense that the times are right for a lively, modern take on this musically inspired sexual masquerade.

The day's interweaving threads will continue into tonight's performance of *Sarsaparilla*, the play's first outing in its author's home town since my 1976 production.

I decide to walk from the opera company offices, near Central Railway Station, to the Sydney Opera House at the other end of town. My step slows mid-city as I pass the Theatre Royal. Here, as a teenager, I had first glimpsed *Sarsaparilla* in John

Tasker's original production. I directed the play thirty years ago, on my return to Australia. Tonight I will see it through new eyes in a radical reading by the intense and visionary young director Benedict Andrews, just returned from a directing stint at Berlin's Schaubühne. Neil Armfield revived the play in Adelaide in 1984, so a tradition has developed of independently minded directors tackling this landmark work—Tasker, Sharman, Armfield, Andrews.*The Season at Sarsaparilla* is the play you discover, or it discovers you, once you've travelled and understood the resonance of its final line:

You can't shed your skin ... even if it itches like hell.

At a CD shop, not far from where I once slapped Patrick White on the back outside Edels, a guttural, bluesy version of *Hound Dog* booms. Tomorrow night is the *Mardi Gras*—another transformation from that earlier, closeted era—and there's an excited mood among the staff. A sassy, coiffed young dyke behind the counter proudly informs me that it's the original version of *Hound Dog* by *Big Mama Thornton*. I'm on my way to the baying canines of *Sarsaparilla*, so I can't resist. I slip the CD into my pocket, where *Big Mama* jiggles alongside my Mozart production notes all the way to Circular Quay.

The Opera House, Utzon's imperfect temple, appears to have joined in the general mood of expectation, its floodlit sails shimmering and reflecting on the velvety harbour. The promontory is bustling, the Opera Bar crowded, and the Drama Theatre foyer ghostly white in its assemblage.

Patrick White survivors and enthusiasts mingle with first-nighters of all shapes, ages and persuasions, each anticipating this latest incarnation of a play in which the politics of desire are played out against the baying background of dogs on heat in suburban Sarsaparilla.

The production is a revelation and a triumph, set inside and outside a revolving brick veneer house flanked by surveillance video screens, with close-ups of characters at bathroom mirrors or caught unexpectedly in private reverie. The direction and design are rhythmic, imaginative and poetic, the performances outstanding: hilarious and dramatic by turn. Patrick's *make'em laugh, make 'em cry* suburban charade is delivered in spades on this carousel. He would have loved it. The foyer bubbles with the unmistakable whiff of theatrical success. I greet novelists, biographers, veterans of the Patrick White years, and play-wrights Stephen Sewell and Tommy Murphy. Robyn Nevin, whose *gin rummy on the mosquito-proof veranda* still echoes from my earlier incarnation of this play. The outgoing artistic director wears a smile that suggests a few chickens have come home to roost on this special night.

The ensemble acting company shines, and there's a palpable feeling that we're all part of something greater than ourselves. Forty years after the play's premiere, this revival represents what many of we cultural foot soldiers have aspired to: Australian theatre as it should be and so rarely is. Our lives and culture onstage—grand, ludicrous and real—in a great poetic sweep of a play, an inspired interpretation performed by skilled actors in this cathedral of a venue. I am delighted these traditions have passed to another generation, freeing me to turn my gaze to new and different horizons.

Outside the Opera House, I study two large, illuminated posters—one announcing White's *Sarsaparilla*, the other an architectural exhibition titled *Utzon's Winning Vision*, accompanied by a photograph of the smiling Dane. The image represents the architect garlanded by angels' wings, no longer the shunned visionary. It's alchemy, and takes me back to a beach in Sanur.

Do you believe in magic?

Yes.

I sway a little from wine and excitement, thinking about the play and the illuminated Utzon and staring at the gently lapping water. In a flash, the spirits of White and Utzon appear to hover over the vast billabong that is Sydney Harbour, their soundtrack the flapping of wings, their legends still alive, guiding the past and the present into the future. Then the flapping wings dissolve like the crumpling canvas of a sideshow tent, dismantled on red earth.

As I seek a taxi, a voice echoes the last words of Patrick White's *The Tree of Man*. I had reached for this phrase to conclude my mother's eulogy at her funeral ... *In the end, there was no end.*

The harbour is still.

The night clear.

The echo outlives the voice.

ACKNOWLEDGEMENTS

Expect the unexpected is a catchphrase that has often been attached to my productions. It could also be tagged to my life and this memoir. As I knew little about publishing when I started out, I would like to thank Louise Adler and her MUP crew for initiating me into its mysteries. MUP publisher and literary editor, Elisa Berg, travelled with this book from commission to completion: I extend to Elisa my deepest thanks and gratitude. For copy editing and many a wry exchange I have to thank Bryony Cosgrove, also MUP senior editor Cinzia Cavallaro, and for the design, visual wizard Stephen Banham and associate Niels Oeltjen at Letterbox in Melbourne. In the early stages, Aaron Seeto of Gallery 4A introduced me to Olivier Krischer, who translated my photographic archive into digital source material for *Blood & Tinsel*.

Agents play an important role in organising the lives of stage and screen directors. In London, I am grateful to Michael Linnit and Rosalind Chatto, while in Sydney, I've enjoyed a long and productive involvement with HLA Management, its founder Hilary Linstead, Hilary Furlong and especially Viccy Harper; more recently, Katrina Berg, Colleen Champ, and current agents Jean Mostyn and Zilla Turner.

Friendship is hard to quantify in prose, yet simple companionship has been a mainstay through an often turbulent life and it has informed many creative endeavours, including this book. Many good friends have remained unsung in these pages and require personal acknowledgement: early colleagues and mentors, including Warwick Brady, Phillip Briggs, Ross Thompson, Kerry and Tanya Binden, Helen Rosicky, David Cameron, music teacher Warwick McEwan, critic and publisher Katherine Brisbane and her late husband Dr Phillip Parsons, David Sanderson and producer Matt Carroll. In London: producer Robert Fox, Maria Bjornsen, Julian Hope, Bill Gaskill, Harriet Cruikshank, Duncan McAskill, Nicholas Wright and David Lan, David Hare, lyricist Tim Rice, Julien Temple, long-time accomplice Sue Blane and friend in Mahler, David Meyer. In Tokyo: Hsaio Masuda, Katsunori Miyagi, Kenji,

Masa and the 21st City crew. In Rome: Robert Gallo. From the Sarsaparilla years, I would like to acknowledge and thank Elizabeth Knight, John Moyle, Inez Baraday, Bill Harding, Susan Hackett, Tim Game, Mary Vallentine, Neil Armfield, David Marr, Kerry Walker, Robert Gray and Dee, Jamie Murdoch, Patrick Nolan, David Crooks, Antony Ernst, Tony Ayres, Ann Wagstaff, Campion Decent, Luke Hardy, Michael Wilkinson, Kate and Joe Fitzpatrick, Alan Watt, Pauline Goodyer, Brian Fitzgerald, David Crooks, Alice Lau, Chris Hurrell, Jonathan Messer, Tim Wong, Terry McGrath, Anke Sternerborg, the Molloy, Dalgleish and Willis families, cousin Shirley Germain, artist Michael Ramsden and, especially, Ross Wallace and Fran Moore. I wouldn't have got by without Narong and the staff of the Royal Thai. In Cairns, I was supported by a small army of friends, including Murray Powdrell, Suellen Maunder, Michael Beresford, Richard Turner, Deborah Fisher, Andrew Prowse, Raymond Mather, Ross McIntyre, Duncan Grant, Arden Dearden and film producer Tony Buckley. Conversations with artists have left their inspiring mark in invisible ink and I wish to thank dramatist Beatrix Christian, photographer Bill Henson, writer Brian Castro, designers Ralph Myers and, especially, Chen Lu, and composer Elena Kats-Chernin.

The book was completed at Randwick and several friends were kind enough to read formative drafts, especially Aline Jacques, Tommy Murphy and Brendan Blakely. Others offered sage advice or endured much memoir chat, including architect David Haertsch, director Mark Gaal, Leanne and Caillin McKay. A few joyful writing interruptions from an attention seeking three year old suggested that young Eli Asani Jacques may one day have a memoir of his own. I'll conclude with a quote from Australian poet David Campbell:

Men and boughs break
Praise life while you walk and wake
It is only lent.

PICTURE CREDITS

The images throughout this book are from the Jim Sharman Archive, unless otherwise credited.

Every attempt has been made to locate the copyright holders for images in this book. Any person or organisation that may have been overlooked or misattributed may contact the publisher. All omissions will be rectified in any future reprints.

1
Ringside
p. 39: Courtesy Snap Photo/Austral; **pp. 56–7:** Courtesy Getty Images; **pp. 70–1:** Photograph by Jim Sharman; **p. 94:** Photograph by Jim Sharman.

2
Dancing
pp. 118–19: Courtesy Harry M Miller; **p. 130:** Photograph by Jim Sharman; **pp. 144–5:** Lee Pearce, *Pix* magazine, courtesy Jim Sharman Archive; **pp. 154–5:** Photograph by Branco Gaico; **p. 160:** Photograph by Grant Mudford; **pp. 174–5:** Photograph by Jim Sharman; **p. 188:** Courtesy Robert Stigwood; **p. 195:** Photograph by Jim Sharman; **p. 203:** Photograph by Mick Rock; **pp. 214–15:** Photograph by Mick Rock; **pp. 230–1:** Photographs by Jim Sharman; **p. 235:** Photograph by Mick Rock; **p. 241:** Photograph by Mick Rock; **p. 246:** Photograph by Robert Rosen.

3
Sarsaparilla
pp. 274–5: Photograph by Branco Gaico; **p. 281:** Photograph by William Yang; **pp. 282–3:** Photograph by Branco Gaico; **p. 284:** Photograph by Jim Sharman; **pp. 292–3:** Photograph by William Yang; **p. 300:** Photograph by Jim Sharman; **p. 302:** Poster art by Martin Sharp, courtesy Adelaide Festival of Arts; **p. 313:** Photograph by William Yang; **pp. 314–15, 322–3, 324–5 and 326–7:** Courtesy David Wilson/State Theatre Company of South Australia;

pp. 337 and 338: Photographs by Jim Sharman;
p. 347: Photograph by Jim Sharman; **pp. 362–3:** Photograph by Jim Sharman; **p. 366:** Photograph by Jim Sharman;
p. 371: Photograph by Jim Sharman; **pp. 376–7:** Photographs by Brett Hilder; **pp. 382–3:** Photograph by Jim Sharman.

Inside Jacket Images
Inside front flap
Cloud image: Courtesy Getty Images

Inside front cover
Middle: Photograph by Greg Weight; top right: Photograph by Jim Sharman; bottom right: Photograph by Grant Mudford.

Inside spine
Top: Photograph by Jim Sharman; middle left: Photograph by Mick Rock; bottom left: Courtesy Robert Stigwood; bottom right: Photograph by Mick Rock.

Inside back cover
Top row, second and third from left and far right: Photographs by Jim Sharman; middle row, left: Photograph by Robert Rosen; middle row, second from left: Photograph by Jim Sharman; middle row, far right (bleeds onto inside back flap): Photograph by William Yang; bottom row, far left: Photograph by Jim Sharman; bottom row, third from left and far right (bleeds onto inside back flap): Photographs by Jim Sharman.

Inside back flap
Top row, far left and far right: Photographs by Jim Sharman; bottom right: Photograph by Jim Sharman.

CHRONOLOGY

All productions were directed by Jim Sharman (JS) unless stated otherwise.

AP = associate producer / BL = book and lyrics / C = conductor / CD = costume design / CH = choreography / D = designer (set and costumes) / ED = editor / L = libretto or lyrics / LD = lighting design / M = music / MD = musical director / P = producer / PD = production design / PH = photography / SD = set design / SP = screenplay

1965

A TASTE OF HONEY
By Shelagh Delaney

Group Theatre production:
Cell Block Theatre

D: Ron Reid / LD: JS

Cast: Helen Morse, Helmut Bakaitis, Roberta Grant, Anthony Thurbon, Martin Harris

1966

ON STAGE OZ
By Martin Sharp, Dean Letcher, Richard Neville and Richard Walsh

Group Theatre production:
various venues

D: JS

Cast: Gaye Anderson, Jennie Cullen, John Krummel, Janie Stewart, Ross Thompson, Colin Turner

THE SPORT OF MY MAD MOTHER
By Ann Jellicoe

Group Theatre production:
Wayside Theatre

D: Ron Reid

Cast included: Janie Stewart, Charles Little, Roberta Grant, Ross Thompson, Jennie Cullen, Alan Hardy

THE MAIDS
By Jean Genet

Group Theatre production:
Wayside Theatre

D: Michael Ramsden /
M: Richard Meale

Cast: Chris Winzar (Solange), Barry Underwood (Claire), Pat Bishop (Madame)

THE GENTS
By Harold Martin

Q Theatre production:
AMP Lunchtime Theatre

D: Martin Sharp

Cast: Ben Gabriel, Don Pascoe, Doreen Warburton

THE LOVER
By Harold Pinter

Q Theatre production:
AMP Lunchtime Theatre

Cast: Ann Haddy, Max Meldrum

CHIPS WITH EVERYTHING
By Arnold Wesker

Independent Theatre production

D: Michelle

Cast included: Martin Magee, Peter Fisk, John Gregg, Dan O'Sullivan

1967

DON GIOVANNI
*By Wolfgang Amadeus Mozart (M)
and Lorenzo da Ponte (L)*

Australian Elizabethan Opera
Company: national tour

SD, LD: JS / CD: Ron Reid /
C: Thomas Mayer

Cast: Neil Warren-Smith, Ronald
MacConnaghie, Marcella Reale,
Rosemary Gordon, Maureen
Howard, Donald Shanks, Robert
Gard, John Germain, Elizabethan
Opera chorus and orchestra

THE BIRTHDAY PARTY
By Harold Pinter

St Martin's Theatre

D: Paul Kathner / LD: JS

Cast included: Martin Magee,
Sheila Florance, Peter Adams

AND SO TO BED
By JB Fagan (Book) and Vivian Ellis (L, M)

National Theatre: Perth

D: Edward Dembowski / LD: JS

Cast included: Neville Teede,
Jennifer West, Chris Winzar,
Kerry Gotto, Barry Underwood

1968

NORM AND AHMED
By Alexander Buzo

Old Tote Theatre

D: Allan Lees / LD: JS

Cast: Ron Graham,
Edwin Hodgeman

TERROR AUSTRALIS
*By Dean Letcher; devised by JS
and the company*

Jane Street Theatre

D: Ric Billinghurst / LD: JS

Cast: Helen Morse, Peter Rowley,
Jennifer West, Garry McDonald

YOU NEVER CAN TELL
By George Bernard Shaw

Old Tote Theatre

D: Yoshi Tosa / LD: JS

Cast included: Jacki Weaver, Ross
Thompson, Ron Haddrick, Doreen
Warburton, Ken Shorter, Rona
Coleman, Michael Boddy, Alan
Edwards, Dan O'Sullivan

1969

HAIR
*By James Rado, Gerome Ragni (BL)
and Galt MacDermot (M)*

Harry M Miller production: Metro
Theatre, Kings Cross, Sydney

D, LD: JS / MD, C: Patrick Flynn /
CH: Jack Manuel

Cast included: Wayne Matthews,
Berys Marsh, Keith Glass, David
Riddick, Audrey Keyes, Terry
O'Brien, Sharon Redd, Denni,
Helen Livermore, The Tribe

1970

HAIR
*By James Rado, Gerome Ragni (BL)
and Galt MacDermot (M)*

New productions in Tokyo, Japan
and Boston, USA

AS YOU LIKE IT
By William Shakespeare

Old Tote Theatre: Parade Theatre

D: Brian Thomson / LD: JS /
M: Sandra McKenzie

Cast included: Darlene Johnson
(Rosalind), Ken Shorter (Orlando),
Helen Morse (Celia), Tim Elliot
(Jacques), Garry McDonald, Terry
Bader, James Bowles, Diane Craig,
Reg Gillam, Robyn Gurney, Peter
Rowley, Serge Lazareff, Brendon
Lunney, Martin Vaughan

1971

KING LEAR
By William Shakespeare

Melbourne Theatre Company:
Russell Street Theatre

D: Richard Prins / LD: JS /
M: Ralph Tyrell

Cast included: Tim Elliott, Brian
James, Jennifer Claire, Marion
Edward, Diana Greentree, Simon
Chilvers, Helmut Bakaitis, David
Cameron, John Allen

HAIR
*By James Rado, Gerome Ragni (BL)
and Galt MacDermot (M)*

Harry M Miller production:
Bourke Street Metro, Melbourne,
followed by national tour, including
New Zealand

D: Brian Thomson / LD: JS / MD, C:
Patrick Flynn / CH: Natalie Moscoe

Cast included: Wayne Matthews,
John Waters, Berys Marsh, Paula
Maxwell, Marcia Hines, Reg
Livermore, Keith Glass, Sharon

Redd, Audrey Keyes, Tomay Fields,
Chuck McKinley, Denni, Helen
Livermore, Graham Matters,
Margaret Goldie, Ted Williams,
Creenagh St Clare, The Tribe

LASSETER
*By Reg Livermore (BL), Patrick Flynn
and Sandra McKenzie (M)*

Old Tote Theatre: Parade Theatre

D: Brian Thomson / MD,
C: Patrick Flynn, Sandra McKenzie /
CH: Keith Bain

Cast included: Reg Livermore,
Helen Morse, Drew Forsyth,
Darlene Johnson, Ken Shorter,
Melissa Jaffer, Garry McDonald,
Jennifer Claire, David Cameron,
Jean Lewis, John Hargreaves,
Anne Haddy, Ron Falk

1972

JESUS CHRIST SUPERSTAR
*By Tim Rice (L) and Andrew Lloyd
Webber (M)*

Harry M Miller production: national
concert tour followed by stage
version at Sydney's Capitol Theatre
and national tour

SD: Brian Thomson / CD: Rex
Cramphorn / MD: Patrick Flynn /
CH: Keith Bain

Cast included: Trevor White,
Michelle Fawdon (later Marcia
Hines), Jon English, Robin Ramsay,
John Paul Young, Stevie Wright, Joe
Dicker, Jon Finlayson (later Reg
Livermore)

*(There were several cast changes over an
extended run and tour.)*

SHIRLEY THOMPSON VERSUS
THE ALIENS
Film produced by Kolossal Piktures

SP: Helmut Bakaitis, JS / P: JS /
AP: Matthew Carroll / PH: David
Sanderson / PD: Brian Thomson
/ ED: Malcolm Smith / M: Ralph
Tyrell / songs: Johnny O'Keefe

Cast included: Jane Harders, John
Ivkovitch, Marion John, John
Llewellyn, Tim Elliott, June Collis,
Helmut Bakaitis, Ron Haddrick

JESUS CHRIST SUPERSTAR
*By Tim Rice (BL) and Andrew Lloyd
Webber (M)*

Robert Stigwood production:
Palace Theatre, London

SD: Brian Thomson / CD: Gabriella
Falk / LD: Jules Fisher / MD, C:
Anthony Bowles / CH: Rufus Collins

Cast included: Paul Nicholas (Jesus),
Dana Gillespie (Mary), Stephen Tate
(Judas), John Parker (Pontius Pilate),
Paul Jabarra (Herod)

*(This production played for nine years
with numerous cast changes.)*

THE TRIALS OF OZ
By Geoffrey Robertson

Friends of Van Wolf production:
Anderson Theatre, New York

D: Mark Ravitz / LD: Jules Fisher /
songs: Buzzy Linehart, Mick Jagger,
John Lennon, etc.

Cast included: Cliff de Young,
Graham Jarvis, William Roderick,
Leata Galloway, Harry Gold,
Richard Clark

1973

THE UNSEEN HAND
By Sam Shepard

Royal Court production

D: Brian Thomson /
MD: Richard Hartley

Cast: Warren Clarke, Richard
O'Brien, Christopher Malcolm,
Tony Sibbalt, Clive Endersby

THE ROCKY HORROR SHOW
By Richard O'Brien

Royal Court production, in
association with Michael White

SD: Brian Thomson / CD: Sue Blane
/ LD: Gerry Jenkinson / arranger,
MD, C: Richard Hartley

Cast included: Tim Curry, Julie
Covington (later Belinda Sinclair),
Christopher Malcolm, Richard
O'Brien, Patricia Quinn, Nell
Campbell, Paddy O'Hagan, Raynor
Bourton, Jonathan Adams

*(This production premiered at the Theatre
Upstairs of the Royal Court before
transferring and playing for seven years
and with various casts at the Chelsea
Classic and the Essoldo Theatre in the
Kings Road and finally at the Comedy
Theatre in the West End, produced by
Michael White, assisted by Robert Fox.)*

THE REMOVALISTS
By David Williamson

Royal Court production, in
association with Harry M Miller

D: Brian Thomson /
LD: Rory Dempster

Cast: Ed Devereaux, Mark McManus, Darlene Johnson, Shaun Rodger, Carol Mowlan, Brian Croucher

THE THREEPENNY OPERA
By Bertolt Brecht (BL) and Kurt Weill (M)

Old Tote Theatre:
Drama Theatre, Sydney Opera House

SD: Brian Thomson / CD: Wendy Dickson / MD: Richard Hartley

Cast included: Robin Ramsay (Macheath), Pamela Stephenson (Polly Peachum), Arthur Dignam (Streetsinger), Kate Fitzpatrick (Jenny), Colin Croft (Peachum), Gloria Dawn (Mrs Peachum), Drew Forsythe, Jane Harders

1974

THE ROCKY HORROR SHOW
By Richard O'Brien

Lou Adler presentation of the Michael White production:
Roxy Theater, Los Angeles

SD: Brian Thomson / CD: Sue Blane / LD: Chip Monk / MD: Richard Hartley

Cast included: Tim Curry, Abigail Haness, Meatloaf, Jamie Donnelly, Bruce Scott, Richard Kim Milford, Graham Jarvis

(The production transferred to the Belasco Theater for a brief Broadway season.)

THE ROCKY HORROR SHOW
By Richard O'Brien

Harry M Miller presentation of the Michael White production

SD: Brian Thomson / CD: Sue Blane / LD: John Salzer / MD: Roy Ritchie

Cast included: Reg Livermore, Jane Harders, John Paramor, Kate Fitzpatrick, Graham Matters, David Cameron, Arthur Dignam

(Max Phipps and a new cast joined the production for Melbourne and the subsequent tour.)

THE TOOTH OF CRIME
By Sam Shepard

Royal Court production

SD: Brian Thomson / CD: Sue Blane / MD: Richard Hartley

Cast included: Mike Pratt (Hoss), Diane Langton (Becky), Richard O'Brien (Crow), Christopher Malcolm, Jonathan Adams, Ken Cranham, Paul Freeman

1975

THE ROCKY HORROR PICTURE SHOW
Film produced by 20th Century Fox

Adapted from the stage musical
The Rocky Horror Show

SP: JS, Richard O'Brien / P: Michael White, Lou Adler / AP: John Goldstone / PH: Peter Suschitsky / PD: Brian Thomson / CD: Sue Blane / ED: Graham Clifford / arranger, MD, C: Richard Hartley

Cast included: Tim Curry, Susan Sarandon, Barry Bostwick, Richard O'Brien, Patricia Quinn, Nell Campbell, Jonathan Adams, Peter Hinwood, Meatloaf, Charles Gray

1976

SUMMER OF SECRETS
Film produced by Greater Union

SP: John Aitken / P: Michael
Thornhill / PH: Russell Boyd / ED:
Sara Bennett / M: Cameron Allan

Cast: Arthur Dignam, Kate
Fitzpatrick, Rufus Collins, Nell
Campbell, Andrew Sharp

THE SEASON AT SARSAPARILLA
By Patrick White

Old Tote production: Drama
Theatre, Sydney Opera House

D: Wendy Dickson / LD: Jerry Luke

Cast included: Kate Fitzpatrick, Max
Cullen, Bill Hunter, Robyn Nevin,
Peter Whitford, Michelle Fawdon,
Julianne Newbould, Andrew Sharp

1977

BIG TOYS
By Patrick White

Old Tote Theatre: Parade Theatre

SD: Brian Thomson /
CD: Victoria Alexandria

Cast: Kate Fitzpatrick, Arthur
Dignam, Max Cullen

1978

THE NIGHT THE PROWLER
Film produced by the NSW Film Corporation

SP: Patrick White, from his story of
the same title / P: Tony Buckley /
PH: David Sanderson / PD: Luciana
Arrighi / ED: Sara Bennett /
M: Cameron Allan

Cast included: Kerry Walker
(Felicity), John Frawley

(Mr Bannister), Ruth Cracknell
(Doris Bannister)

PANDORA'S CROSS
*By Dorothy Hewett, with songs by
Dorothy Hewett (L) and Ralph Tyrell (M)*

Paris Theatre production

SD: Brian Thomson / CD: Luciana
Arrighi / LD: Bill Walker /
MD: Roy Ritchie

Cast: Jennifer Claire, Robyn Nevin,
Arthur Dignam, Geraldine Turner,
John Gaden, Steve J Spears,
Neil Redfern, Julie McGregor,
John Paramor

1979

A CHEERY SOUL
By Patrick White

Paris production for the Sydney
Theatre Company

SD: Brian Thomson / CD: Anna
Senior / LD: John Hoenig /
M: Cameron Allan

Cast included: Robyn Nevin
(Miss Docker), Peter Carroll,
Pat Bishop, Maggie Kirkpatrick,
John Paramor, Annie Byron, Claire
Crowther, Deborah Kennedy,
Linden Wilkinson, Paul Chubb,
Jan Hamilton, Paul Johnstone,
Sharon Calcraft (piano)

1980

DEATH IN VENICE
*By Benjamin Britten (M) and
Myfanwy Piper (L), from a novella
by Thomas Mann*

Adelaide Festival production by the
State Opera of South Australia

SD: Brian Thomson / CD: Luciana Arrighi / LD: Rory Dempster / MD, C: Myer Fredman / CH: Ian Spink

Cast included: Robert Gard (Aschenbach), Tom McDonnell (Traveller), Ian Wilkinson (Tadzio), Roger Lemke (Hotel Porter), Basia Bonkowski (Polish Mother), Anthony Bremner (Apollo)

1981

LULU
Adapted by Louis Nowra, from Frank Wedekind

State Theatre Company of South Australia production: Playhouse; tour with Sydney Theatre Company to Drama Theatre, Sydney Opera House

SD: Brian Thomson / CD: Luciana Arrighi / LD: Nigel Levings / M: Sarah de Jong

Cast included: Judy Davis (Lulu), Malcolm Roberston (Dr Schon), Kerry Walker (Countess Geschwitz), Brandon Burke (Alwa), John Wood (Wrestler), Ralph Cotterill (Schigolch), Juliet Taylor, Robert Grubb

SHOCK TREATMENT
Film produced by 20th Century Fox

SP: JS, Richard O'Brien (L) / P: Lou Adler, Michael White / AP: John Goldstone / PH: Mike Molloy / PD: Brian Thomson / CD: Sue Blane / ED: Richard Bedford / M: Richard O'Brien, Richard Hartley

Cast included: Cliff de Young, Jessica Harper, Barry Humphries, Richard O'Brien, Patricia Quinn, Nell Campbell, Ruby Wax, Charles Gray, Darlene Johnson, Rik Mayall

1982

ADELAIDE FESTIVAL OF ARTS
Artistic director: JS / general manager: Kevin Earle / administrator: Mary Vallentine / production assistants: Rob Brookman, Penny Chapman / Festival Centre manager: John Robertson / publicity: Tony Frewin

1982 AND 1983: LIGHTHOUSE

Artistic director: JS / general manager: Mary Vallentine / associate directors: Neil Armfield, Louis Nowra / production manager: Graham Murray / writers: Patrick White, Louis Nowra, Bill Harding, Stephen Sewell, Nick Enright (translator) / composers: Alan John, Sarah de Jong / D: Sue Blane, Stephen Curtis, Geoffrey Gifford, Ken Wilby, Mary Moore / LD: Nigel Levings

The Lighthouse Ensemble: Robyn Bourne, Peter Cummings, Robert Grubb (1983), Melissa Jaffer (1982), Gillian Jones, Melita Jurisic, Alan John, Russell Kiefel, Belinda McClory (guest: *Sunrise*), Robert Menzies (1982), Stuart McCreary, Jackie Phillips, Geoffrey Rush, Juliet Taylor (guest: *Dream*), Kerry Walker, John Wood

(The Lighthouse Ensemble acted in all productions; some key roles are mentioned below.)

A MIDSUMMER NIGHT'S DREAM
By William Shakespeare

D: Sue Blane / M: Sarah de Jong /
MD: Alan John

Cast included: Geoffrey Rush
(Oberon), Gillian Jones (Titania),
John Wood (Bottom)

MOTHER COURAGE AND HER
CHILDREN
*By Bertolt Brecht, with music by
Paul Dessau*

D: Sue Blane / MD: Alan John

Cast included: Kerry Walker
(Mother Courage)

SILVER LINING
By Bill Harding

D: Stephen Curtis

Cast included: Kerry Walker (Olga),
Jacqy Phillips (Masha), Melissa Jaffer
(Irena)

ROYAL SHOW
By Louis Nowra

D: Stephen Curtis / M: Sarah
de Jong / MD: Alan John /
CH: Melissa Jaffer

BLOOD WEDDING
By Garcia Lorca

SD: Geoffrey Gifford / CD: Stephen
Curtis / M: Cameron Allan

Cast included: Gillian Jones
(Mother), Russell Kiefel (Groom),
Melita Jurisic (Bride), Stuart
McCreery (Leonardo), Geoffrey
Rush (Moon)

NETHERWOOD
By Patrick White

D: Ken Wilby / M: Alan John

Cast included: John Wood (Royce
Best), Jacqy Phillips (Alice Best),
Peter Cummins (Harry Britt),
Kerry Walker (Mog Figg), Alan John
(Dora Pilbeam), Geoffrey Rush
(Dr Eberhard)

PAL JOEY
*By John O'Hara, Lorenz Hart (L) and
Richard Rodgers (M)*

D: Stephen Curtis / MD: Alan John
/ CH: Chrissie Koltai

Cast included: Robert Grubb (Joey
Evans), Jacqy Phillips (Vera Simpson),
Melita Jurisic (Linda English), Kerry
Walker (Gladys Bump)

SUNRISE
By Louis Nowra

SD: Geoffrey Gifford / CD: Norma
Moriceau / M: Sarah de Jong

Cast included: John Wood (Clarrie
Shelton), Belinda McClory (Venice)

1984

Lighthouse productions were
performed at the Playhouse, Adelaide
Festival Centre. There was a Sydney
Festival tour of Neil Armfield's
production of *Twelfth Night* and of
JS's production of *Netherwood* to the
York and Everest theatres of Sydney's
Seymour Centre.

1985

DREAMPLAY
By August Strindberg

NIDA: Parade Theatre

SD: Tim Ferrier / CD: Ross Wallace

Cast: Graduate Year actors, including
Baz Luhrmann, Justin Monjo,

Rosalba Clemente, Helen Muggins,
Catherine McClements

THE DANCE OF DEATH

*By August Strindberg; adapted by
May Britt Akerholt and JS*

Sydney Theatre Company: Wharf
Theatre

SD: Geoffrey Gifford / CD: Ross
Wallace / LD: Nigel Levings /
M: Peter Sculthorpe's Cello Suite

Cast included: Rhys McConnochie
(Edgar), Gillian Jones (Alice),
Robin Ramsay (Kurt)

1986

VOSS

*By Richard Meale (M) and David Malouf
(L), from the novel by Patrick White*

Adelaide Festival Theatre, Sydney
Opera House, Victorian Arts Centre;
televised and released on video by
ABC Television

SD: Brian Thomson / CD: Luciana
Arrighi / LD: Nigel Levings /
MD, C: Stuart Challendor /
CH: Chrissie Koltai

Cast: Geoffrey Chard (Voss),
Marilyn Richardson (Laura
Trevelyan), Robert Eddie (Judd),
Ann Maree McDonald (Belle),
Robert Gard (Le Mesurier),
John Pringle (Palfreyman), Gregory
Tomlinson (Harry Robards)

1987

BLOOD RELATIONS

By David Malouf

SD: Tim Ferrier / CD: Ross Wallace
/ LD: Nigel Levings / M: Alan John

Cast included: John Wood (Willy),
Maggie Kirkpatrick (Hilda),

Laurence Clifford (Dinny), Paul
Goddard (Kit), Deborah Kennedy
(McClucky)

A LIE OF THE MIND

By Sam Shepard

Belvoir Street Theatre

SD: JS / CD: Tess Schofield /
LD: Nigel Levings

Cast included: Steve Bisley, Karin
Fairfax, Simon Chilvers, Cornelia
Francis, Justin Monjo

1988

THE SCREENS

By Jean Genet

NIDA Theatre

D: Angus Strathie

Cast: Graduate Year students,
including Rachel Szalay, Richard
Huggett, Deborah Unger

THE RAKE'S PROGRESS

*By Igor Stravinsky (M), WH Auden and
Chester Kallman (L)*

Opera Australia: Sydney Opera
House

SD: Tim Ferrier / CD: Ross Wallace
/ LD: Nigel Levings

Cast: Neil Rosenshein (Tom
Rakewell), Gillian Sullivan (Anne
Truelove), Geoffrey Chard (Nick
Shadow), Rosemary Gordon (Baba),
Judy Connelly (Mother Goose)

1989

THE CONQUEST OF THE
SOUTH POLE

By Manfred Kage

Belvoir Street Theatre

Cast included: Baz Luhrmann,
Stephen Rae, Justin Monjo

1990

CHESS

By Tim Rice (Bl), Benny Andersson and Bjorn Ulvaeus (M)

Theatre Royal, Sydney

SD: Brian Thomson / CD: Tess Schofield / LD: Nigel Levings / M: arranged by Alan John / MD: Michael Tyack / CH: Chrissie Koltai

Cast included: Jodie Gillies (Florence), David McLeod (Freddie), Robbie Krupski (Anatoly), Maria Mercedes (Svetlana), Laurence Clifford (Arbiter), John Wood (Molokov), David Whitney (Walter)

1991

DEATH IN VENICE

By Benjamin Britten (M) and Myfanwy Piper (L), from a novella by Thomas Mann

Restaging of the original Adelaide Festival production for Opera Australia: Sydney Opera House, Victorian Arts Centre

SD: Brian Thomson / CD: Luciana Arrighi / LD: Rory Dempster / MD, C: Myer Fredman / CH: Meryl Tankard

Cast: Robert Gard (Aschenbach), John Pringle (Traveller), Damien Smith (Tadzio), David Hobson (Hotel Porter), Basia Bonkowski (Polish Mother)

1992

SHADOW AND SPLENDOUR
By JS

Queensland Theatre Company: State Theatre of South Australia, Adelaide Festival

D: Shaun Gurton / LD: David Walters / M: Ian MacDonald

Cast included: Colin Friels, Fumi Dan, Edwin Hodgeman, Maria Mercedes

1993

THE BURNING PIANO:
A PORTRAIT OF PATRICK WHITE
By JS (two-hour documentary film for ABC Television) in collaboration with David Marr

Interviewees: David Marr, Barry Humphries, Geoffrey and Nin Dutton and various others

Readings included: Judy Davis, Geoffrey Rush, Kate Fitzpatrick, Robyn Nevin, Peter Whitford, John Krummel, Kerry Walker, Colin Friels

1994

THE WEDDING SONG
Musical by Hilary Bell (L) and Stephen Rae (M)

NIDA Company

SD: Andrew Purvis / CD: Tess Schofield / MD: Stephen Rae / CH: Stephen Page

Cast included: Craig Ilott, Genevieve Davis, Paul Capsis, Paula Arundell, Laurence Clifford, Annie Finsterer

1995

MISS JULIE AND THE STRONGER
By August Strindberg; adapted by JS (Miss Julie) and Hilary Bell (The Stronger)

State Theatre Company of South Australia: Playhouse

D: Mary Moore / LD: Karen Norris

Cast: Pamela Rabe, Robert Menzies, Jeanette Cronin

SPLENDID'S

By Jean Genet; adapted by May Brit Akerholt and JS

Belvoir Street Theatre

Director: Bogdan Koca / creative development: JS

THE EIGHTH WONDER

By Alan John (M) and Dennis Watkins (L)

Opera Australia: Sydney Opera House, ABC Television

Director: Neil Armfield / creative development: JS

1997

THE TEMPEST

By William Shakespeare

Bell Shakespeare Company: tour of Canberra, Sydney, Adelaide, Melbourne

D: Michael Wilkinson / dramaturg: Antony Ernst / LD: Mark Truebridge / M: Tyrone Landau

Cast included: John Bell, Rachel Maza, Tom Long, Paula Arundell, Tim Elliott, Kerry Walker, Peter Lamb, Lani John Tupu, Michael Turkic

1998

THE MIRAGE

By Nick Enright (BL) and Tyrone Landau (M)

STC Musical Workshop

Cast included: Josh Quong Tart, Kerry Walker, John Waters, Paula Arundell

2001

BERLIN TO BROADWAY WITH KURT WEILL

By Kurt Weill (M), Bert Brecht, Maxwell Anderson et al. (L)

NIDA Theatre

SD: Ralph Myers / CD: Alice Lau / LD: Kylie Mascord, Bernie Tan / sound design: Campbell McKilligan / MD: Michael Tyack / CH: Shaun Parker

Cast: Nicholas Berg, Nicholas Brown, Andrea McEwan, Amie McKenna, Philip Miolin, Genevieve O'Reilly, Edith Podesta, Steven Rassios

2002

KABARETT JUNCTION

Cabaret devised by JS, with music by Lou Reed, Bert Brecht / Kurt Weill, Randy Newman

MD, piano: Alan John with Amie McKenna and David Hawkins

2004

WHAT THE BUTLER SAW

By Joe Orton

Belvoir Street Theatre

SD: Brian Thomson / CD: Alice Lau / LD: Nigel Levings / M: Basil Hogios

Cast: Nicholas Eadie, Deborah Kennedy, Max Gillies, Sam Haft, Isabella Dunwill, Michael McCall

2005

THREE FURIES

Play with songs by Stephen Sewell, and music by Basil Hogios

Sydney Festival, Performing Lines, Sydney Opera House Playhouse

SD: Brian Thomson / CD: Alice Lau / LD: Damien Cooper / MD: Basil Hogios / CH: Edith Podesta

Cast: Simon Burke (Painter), Socrates Otto (Model), Paula Arundell (Tisiphone)

2006

THREE FURIES

Play with songs by Stephen Sewell, and music by Basil Hogios

Revised and revived for 2006 Perth and Adelaide festivals: Playhouse, Adelaide and Perth

Cast: Simon Burke (Painter), Socrates Otto (Model), Paul Capsis (Tisiphone)

DEATH IN VENICE

By Benjamin Britten (M) and Myfanwy Piper (L), from a novella by Thomas Mann

Revival for Opera Australia: Sydney Opera House

SD: Brian Thomson / CD: Luciana Arrighi / LD: Rory Dempster, adapted by Damien Cooper / MD, C: Richard Hickox / CH: Meryl Tankard

Cast included: Philip Langridge (Aschenbach), Peter Coleman-Wright (Traveller), Ben Nicols (Tadzio), Henry Choo (Hotel Porter), Edith Podesta (Polish Mother), Graham Pushee (Apollo)

THE MIEGUNYAH PRESS

This book was designed by Stephen Banham
with assistance by Niels Oeltjen.

Typesetting by Niels Oeltjen, Megan Ellis and Tim Mang.

The text is set in 12.5 point *Perpetua*
(Eric Gill 1928–35) with 13.5 points of leading.

The titling is set in *Klavika* (Eric Olson 2003–04).

The text is printed on 120 gsm Chinese woodfree paper.

This book was edited by Bryony Cosgrove.